Monty Don is the presenter of the BBC's *Gardener's World* and the bestselling author of a number of books.

THE ROAD TO LE THOLONET

A French Garden Journey

Monty Don

**SIMON &
SCHUSTER**

London · New York · Sydney · Toronto · New Delhi

A CBS COMPANY

First published in Great Britain by Simon & Schuster UK Ltd, 2013
This paperback edition published in 2014
A CBS COMPANY

1 3 5 7 9 10 8 6 4 2

Simon & Schuster UK Ltd
1st Floor
222 Gray's Inn Road
London WC1X 8HB

www.simonandschuster.co.uk

Simon & Schuster Australia, Sydney
Simon & Schuster India, New Delhi

A CIP catalogue record for this book
is available from the British Library

Paperback ISBN: 978-1-47111-458-8
Ebook ISBN: 978-1-47111-459-5

Typeset in the UK by M Rules
Printed and bound by CPI Group (UK) Ltd, Croydon, CR0 4YY

Dedicated to the memory
of Madame Tailleux, of Le Tholonet

CONTENTS

'Perhaps my journey to the south will bear fruit however, because the difference of the stronger light, the blue sky, that teaches one to see ... The north will certainly appear completely new to me, but I've looked so much at the things that I've become strongly attached to them, and I'll remain melancholy for a long time.'

Vincent Van Gogh, letter to Theo Van Gogh,
Friday, 6 September 1889. St-Remy de Provence.

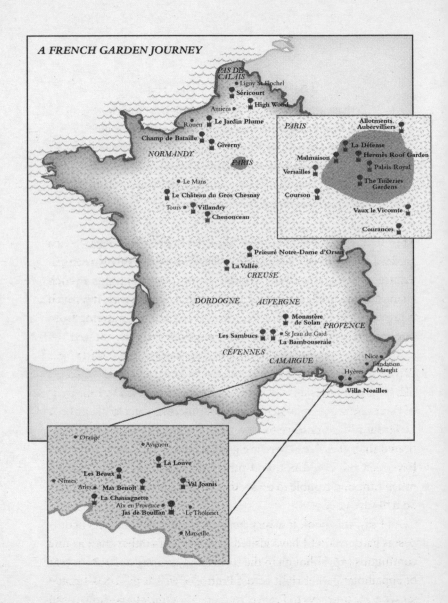

A FRENCH GARDEN JOURNEY

PAS DE CALAIS

Ligny St Flochel
Séricourt
High Wood
Amiens
Rouen
Le Jardin Plume
Champ de Bataille
Giverny

NORMANDY

PARIS

Le Mans
Le Château du Gros Chesnay
Tours
Villandry
Chenonceau

Prieuré Notre-Dame d'Orsan
La Vallée
CREUSE

DORDOGNE   AUVERGNE

Monastère de Solan
Les Sambucs   St Jean du Gard   PROVENCE
La Bambouseraie

CÉVENNES   CAMARGUE

Nice
Fondation Maeght
Hyères
Villa Noailles

PARIS

Allotments, Aubervilliers
La Défense
Malmaison   Hermès Roof Garden
Palais Royal
Versailles
The Tuileries Gardens
Courson
Vaux le Vicomte
Courances

Orange
Avignon
La Louve
Les Baux
Nîmes
Arles
Mas Benoît
Val Joanis
La Chassagnette
Aix en Provence
Jas de Bouffan   Le Tholonet
Marseille

INTRODUCTION

This book is not intended to be a comprehensive survey of French gardens. It does not claim to be a selection of the best gardens in France or even a carefully chosen group that highlights French characteristics or idiosyncrasies, horticultural or otherwise. It is much more personal and random than that. It is a ramble, hopping from one garden to another as mood, circumstance and time allowed.

The choice of some of the gardens, particularly in the south, was driven through memory and entirely personal association; some, like Giverny or Versailles, are world famous and visited by hundreds of thousands of people each year; and some, like Vaux le Vicomte or Le Jardin Plume, deserve to be much more widely visited and celebrated than they are. There are gardens that I would have liked to have seen but could not, and others that I did visit, often taking much time and trouble to do so, that were a complete waste of time. So it always goes.

As I say, this book is a very personal peregrination and encompasses gardens that I have visited over the years rather than as one continuous trip, although in the spring and summer of 2012 – a year of appalling weather right across France as well as the UK – I made six separate journeys to France, so there is a spine of real-time travel running through the narrative.

But I like meandering, both geographically and in time. I like diversions and surprises. As has been observed many times before, one of the best ways to see things is to get lost.

There are a number of good reasons for visiting gardens. Other people's gardens are often more beautiful and spacious than our own, so we get a straightforward vicarious pleasure from them without any envy to modify it. Many are loaded with historical significance and, because they have to also exist entirely in the horticultural present, bring that history directly alive in a profound and visceral way. If you are a gardener then they are inspirational, stoking ideas and practices to take back to your own back yard. And lovely gardens are surprisingly often made in lovely places, as a kind of response to the landscape, so it is easy to build a trip around them and also include beautiful scenery and food.

But they also work at a more subconscious level. Gardens are the most constant and immediate point of contact with the natural world for almost all societies. (I have visited gardens in the Amazon and Outback where this is not the case, but even in these places gardens instil a sense of ownership and possession that is otherwise impossible in the enormity of jungle, desert or river.) How people shape, tend and think about them can say as much about the society as it does the gardens.

And the French are different from us. I would sometimes say that the English and French have a love/hate relationship, at which point my French companions would smile wryly and say that they, the French, love us – it is just we, the English, who hate them. Despite a genuine warmth and admiration for our work ethic, social and cultural freedom and tolerance, they certainly see us as aggressive and often extraordinarily rude. The British have a caricature of the French being high-handed and dismissive, whereas the truth is that they are, by British standards, exceptionally polite and well-mannered. Most people treat each other with a great deal more formal respect in everyday intercourse than anyone in Britain ever does. At the same time tempers will flare much more violently before actual violence is reached. They are a people with a highly developed sense of personal and national honour which should be defended at all times.

I think that the attitude towards the footballer Zinédine Zidane illustrates this well. In Britain he is regarded as a sublime talent marred by an act of indiscipline in the World Cup final when he headbutted the Italian defender Marco Materazzi, who had insulted his family, and was sent off. France subsequently lost and, to most British eyes, Zidane had let down himself, his side and his country through a lack of self-control. In France, however, this was seen as an act of magnificent, self-destructive, very human grandeur: being better to go down losing with honour intact than win shamefully. The fact that he was an Algerian and a role model for all immigrant French citizens doubled the respect, because it showed how fully he had integrated with the very French sense of right and wrong.[1]

There are two other aspects of the French character which you see again and again through their gardens. The first is the inherent and learnt respect for, and adherence to, prescribed form. A student learning to prune will master the agreed shapes and styles before dreaming of indulging any free-form expression – and is likely never to do so. The essentials of rhythm, balance, geometric symmetry and harmony are still seen as the starting points for any garden design and not just because they make for beautiful gardens but also because they are then in harmony with the essential ingredients of an ordered, harmonious culture and society.

I often think that this expresses itself both most elegantly and irritatingly at the table. The best French meals are a performance that you have to gratefully indulge as a recipient of the wonderful food and drink that is being brought to you. Your role is to be knowing and perceptively appreciative of the depth of skill that is involved. The greater your knowledge – in other words the more

1 I am indebted to Lucy Wadham and her excellent book *The Secret Life of France* (Faber & Faber, 2009) for this comparison.

qualified you are – the greater the significance of your respect. There is an underlying solemnity in this that you never experience in other countries, such as Italy.

The second aspect of the French character that you can see beautifully conveyed through their gardens is their love of intellectual debate and concepts. Order and authority has occasionally been challenged by violent revolution as in 1789, 1870 or May 1968, but on the whole the challenges to the received order are intellectual – and often passionately and hotly disputed. Versailles, for example, the epitome of order and control, was made with endless metaphorical bosquets and walks with allusion and imagery that had a potency to almost everyone who saw them and extended far beyond their actual physical presence. Modern gardeners such as Gilles Clément receive great respect as much for the ideas behind their gardens as the gardens themselves. Gardens such as Séricourt, Le Jardin Plume, Champ de Bataille or Prieuré d'Orsan all combine the respect for the formal pattern and dance, exemplified by the work of André Le Nôtre in the seventeenth century, with a twenty-first sensibility of symbolism, concepts and even philosophising that greatly increase their appeal to their makers and any French visitors.

There are really very few instances of British gardens doing this at all satisfactorily,[2] and at times the much more down-to-earth British visitor can feel like an intellectual clodhopper. We are uncomfortable in this territory and much prefer to stick to the details of how things are done rather than why. But in fact this difference represents a divergence in the way that we have reacted to our history rather than any qualitative difference in intellectual development.

As a result of the UK's early and extensive industrialisation, the vast majority of the population had lost any direct contact with agriculture by the middle of the nineteenth century. Their only relationship with the rhythms and seasons of the soil came through

2 I suppose the best-known examples are Ian Hamilton Finlay's Little Sparta and, going much further back, the politicised landscape of Stowe.

gardens and allotments, and this is even more true today. This is why, I believe, the British, more than any other nation I have visited, are so obsessed with the process of gardening rather than the outcome. As a broad generalisation, we are more interested in the details and skills of tending plants than the way that they appear. I have worked as a gardening writer and broadcaster for over twenty-five years and gardened for twice that, and I cannot go anywhere without being asked questions about gardening: for every one query about design I get ninety-nine about specific methods and techniques. We are a remorselessly practical people who like making and doing and mind less about the thing that is made or done. Gardens are often the most obvious and accessible outlet for this.

France, on the other hand, was much later to industrialise. It remained a largely agrarian country – albeit controlled by its very few big cities – until the Second World War. The population was much more widely spread throughout the country and much, much more cut off from the centre of power, which to all intents and purposes meant Paris. Although the aristocracy owned land and beautiful estates, land ownership was also widely dispersed among ordinary people. This meant that there was – and arguably still is – a thriving *paysan* culture, which had all but disappeared in the UK by the middle of the eighteenth century.

A peasant is someone who lives off the land. Any cash crops or services are undertaken to subsidise the shortfall in self-sufficiency. Families stayed on the same piece of land for generations, marrying locally, hardly ever travelling, attached to their piece of France with an unquestioning, umbilical closeness. We have a post-industrial romantic view of this but it was more often than not crushingly hard. Historically there was a steady movement to cities, to take work in factories as it was available, but nothing on the same scale as in the UK. So when the opportunities to leave the land, become educated and take white-collar jobs increasingly arose, any reversion to the land was seen as a backward step. Working the soil, even in a garden, was something that people who could not better themselves did.

Thus the image of the tweeded gentleman or lady in twinset and pearls with dirty hands weeding in a border is very rare in France. If you can afford to pay someone to do your dirty work, then you do. This does not mean that gardens are not enjoyed and appreciated, but it does mean that there is a lack of people entering into gardening as a profession. It is not seen as an honourable trade.

So to intellectualise about gardens and to use them to play with concepts is to elevate an otherwise earthy, *paysan* activity. It makes gardening respectable and worthy of debate and discussion. As for technique, that is something you acquire by study and devotion, master, and then take the respect that is due by virtue of your qualification rather than by the work you subsequently produce. This confers a social authority that transcends the potential lowliness of the work.

All this, of course, is sweeping generalisation.

I have spent the past twenty years travelling a great deal, visiting hundreds of gardens in every continent. That period has coincided with the last great period of travel, in the 1980s and '90s, when the world was accessible in a way that it had never been before through dramatically increased availability of plane and car transport, and with an increase in wealth and the time in which to spend it. Of course this accessibility sowed the seeds of much destruction, because the influx of tourists nearly always destroys the very thing that makes people want to go there in the first place. There was also a sense of ease and flexibility that is inconceivable now in this age of terrorism.

I remember going on one trip to Italy when we took a set of saucepans for friends as part of our hand luggage, a couple of bags each, a pair of wellies and a picnic of champagne and roast chicken to eat on the plane. Yet a couple of years back I visited a food exhibition in Dundee and was given some prize-winning Scottish smoked salmon, marmalade and whisky, which was then not just confiscated but destroyed before I could board the plane to Birmingham. I can only hope that the nation slept easier in its beds as a result.

Luckily much of France is accessible via the wonderful TGV. This is so much more civilised than a plane, just as fast and cheap and clearly more environmentally sustainable. The only danger is that it can marginalise the places – and in truth that is most of France – that are not yet served by it. It is very easy to go up and down from Paris but going across the country is still complicated and slow.

Whenever I travel to new places in France I am always reminded that it is a huge country. The range of landscapes is astonishing and, although the sprawl of out-of-town hypermarkets and warehouses is seemingly unregulated and horrible, there are still vast tranches of the country that are unspoilt, sparsely populated and staggeringly beautiful. French food may no longer be the best in the world (and is certainly not as good as it was a generation ago), but can still be fabulous, especially in the markets and country restaurants. If you treat them with a modicum of politeness and respect, French people are astonishingly friendly and helpful and have maintained a rhythm and balance to life that has been all but lost in the UK.

Here, on our doorstep, we have a neighbour who carries the shared bonds of a thousand years of history and yet is different from us in an entirely enlightening and enriching way. Our connections are close and often very personal. My great-uncle was killed on the Somme in the First World War and his remains are buried there, and my father fought in France and was eventually evacuated from Dunkirk in the Second World War. Hundreds of thousands, perhaps millions of British people share the same stories. In fact we share more stories with France than with any other nation. And, on top of that, they have some of the best gardens in the world.

My first visit to France was in April 1970. I was fourteen and had never been on an aeroplane, never been outside the country. I was taken for a four-day treat by my aunt and uncle who were, by the standards of the very conventional, middle-class, Home Counties England of the time, libertarian in a way my parents could not dream of. So, as well taking me to all the obvious tourist land-marks – the Eiffel Tower, Louvre, Jeu de Paume, L'Arc de Triomphe, Sacré Coeur, rue Rivoli, Les Invalides, Nôtre Dame, a Bateau

Mouche – they let me smoke, which I did with a kind of Gallic fervour, drink – not so easy, since I had no capacity for alcohol at all – and most importantly of all, feel grown up. This was intoxicating beyond any amount of nicotine or alcohol.

I now realise that in fact what I was feeling was sexy. Paris in 1970, just eighteen months after the '68 student riots, had the perfect balance of modernity and the frisson of Edwardian naughtiness that my grandfather had told me about. It was a deeply sexy city and no subsequent trip I have made has ever matched it for excitement or intensity.

One of the things that has been lost since then was the Frenchness of Paris. Thank goodness France still has a curmudgeonly resistance to outside influences, but in 1970 it was gloriously unlike anywhere else at all and I took it all in, saucer-eyed.[3]

Pissoirs in every street, cigarette stalls where I could insouciantly buy a lovely soft packet of Gitanes, garlic, snails, berets, baguettes, cups without handles, widows in black with stockings tight under their knees, paying a moustached old lady for the privilege of using a public lavatory, hipster baths, dishes of vegetables served as a separate course, being allowed to drink wine with every single meal! And feeling, for the first time in my life, old enough to know better and young enough to try ...

But this is all too glamorous. This story does not begin here. It was, after all a very brief visit. I returned home, got kicked out of school, went wrong, got distracted – all the usual teenage stuff. Move on three-and-a-half years to a lavatory on a campsite in Aix en Provence.

3 Not the language though. I have always had a cloth ear for languages and still stumble clumsily in schoolboy French.

1

THE ROAD TO LE THOLONET

It was October 1973, I was eighteen and heading for Greece with my guitar and a friend. We had taken the train to Paris and spent the first few days at a youth hostel, where breakfast was huge bowls of *café au lait* – in itself exotic – and baguettes. By stuffing a baguette into a pocket and supplementing it with a cheap camembert that grew increasingly lively at the bottom of my rucksack, we were fed for the day.

The plan was to hitch down to Greece, camping at night and earning whatever money we needed by busking. It was an open-ended arrangement. I had worked all summer on a building site and earned enough money to buy a new guitar,[1] and I vaguely thought a winter on a Greek island would be something like Leonard Cohen writing *Beautiful Losers* on Hydra. Very vaguely.

There were two problems. The first was that I had little ability on the guitar and less with my voice. Even in an era marked by the abundance of truly dreadful buskers in every underpass and tube station, I was outstandingly, show-stoppingly awful. This evaluation

---

1 It was a brand new Epiphone FT-150 which cost £120 – six weeks' wages then and the equivalent of £1,300 in 2013 money – and had a beautiful fast action. Looking back, it was wildly expensive. You could get just as good an instrument for a third of that now.

crossed borders and the French paying public passed on by, wincing as I offered them my rendition of 'Mr Tambourine Man' and 'Streets of London'.

The second problem was that my companion was recovering from a broken leg and was encased from ankle to thigh in plaster. This made walking practically impossible and getting ourselves in and out of cars – never mind our two ridiculously over-kitted rucksacks and camping gear as well – tricky.

At one stage we got a lift with the owner of a 2CV just outside Roanne, having filtered slowly across from Bourges. It took a complicated dance of shoving, straining and squeezing to get us and our kit into the car and, just as the driver cheerily turned to see if we were comfortable, a tent pole burst through the canvas roof. He was furious, drove in silence for a few kilometres and then booted us out. We stayed by the side of that road for three days, liftless, hungry and thirsty.[2]

Eventually we leapfrogged lifts through St Étienne, Orange, Montélimar (where I can still remember how irresistibly delicious a loaf of rough rye and currant bread tasted, broken off in handfuls and eaten at seven in the morning, standing by the side of a busy road) and on down to Aix en Provence. There we found our way to a campsite so we could stay for a few days before heading to Nice, through Italy and on to a boat across to Greece.

The weather south from Orange had been a growing revelation. This was 1973. Hardly anyone went abroad. My mother had never set foot in France and my father went once, in 1939, to kill Germans and then almost get killed by them at Dunkirk. He never went back. Other than the weekend in Paris when I was fourteen, the furthest south I had been before was the Isle of Wight. Now it was autumn, yet the sun shone from a blue sky. People were tanned, wore dark

2 I remember the kindness of strangers who, on a number of occasions, not only gave me and my companion a lift but took us home, cooked us meals, went out of their way to set us on the right road. It is ironic that the most generous was a lawyer in Bourges – surely the most respectable of all the bourgeoisie.

glasses and smiled a lot. Aix was full of people my age sitting in street cafés drinking lager, *citron pressé* or real coffee. There were markets filled with vegetables I did not recognise and crêpes for sale in the street. By existing almost exclusively on bread and cheese it was possible to live for just a few francs a day.

When it got dark, it was still warm enough to sit outside nursing a beer for hours. And the daylight was brighter and there was more of it than anything I had experienced or imagined. This light entranced me. The fact that there was heat attached to it was a bonus. It was the light that lit Cézanne and Van Gogh, both artists that I was obsessed by, and I knew that Cézanne had lived and painted in Aix. Those incredible paintings that I had seen at the Courtauld Institute in London and in countless reproductions were lit by this sun, this light that now shone on me. I felt blessed.

I did not know then that I was affected by Seasonal Affective Disorder (SAD) and that the morbid, introspective gloom I sank beneath every autumn was as much to do with lack of light as anything else. No one did. SAD had not been invented. Now the southern light was raising the serotonin levels in my sun-starved brain, creating a kind of ecstasy I attributed to Cézanne. Art won over science, yet again.

After a few days of this there was a huge storm and the campsite was washed out. Our tent was a foot under water, so we gathered our sleeping bags and took shelter in the only dry building, which was the wash house. For forty-eight hours we hunkered down with half a dozen other people, wedged between the sinks and loos. It was all very jolly: with the rain beating down outside, this was camping as I knew it, and, carefree young things that we were, we had guitars, local wine at 4 francs a bottle (about 30 pence), a little hash, bread and lovely French cheese. We thought that this was living. There were no phones, no world outside that flooded campsite and its white-tiled wash house. The Yom Kippur War was raging, Watergate was building up a head of steam in America and the oil crisis was about to start a cycle of inflation and strikes that would bring down a series of governments in Europe, but none of this reached us at all.

Sharing our shelter from the storm was an American hitching through Europe accompanied by an entirely silent girlfriend who slept with him in his sleeping bag beneath the washbasins. It was a tight fit. He had done a degree at Brown University and spoke enthusiastically of student life. Up to that point I had no intention of ever being a student. I hated school and left vowing never to return to academia in any form, wanting to be free of all institutions. This desire was considerably helped by my exam results, which were so bad that no one would have me anyway. But listening to him I realised that there was a student world that involved self-motivated learning and a meeting of true minds. The fact that he was hitching with a girlfriend, albeit one who seemed never to employ her voice, and I was sharing my journey with an old school friend who was half-wrapped in plaster of Paris and not turning out to be much of a friend at all, showed the obvious benefits of student life.

I decided not to continue on to Greece. The truth was I never really believed in it. I had never met anyone who had been there and Leonard Cohen had left Hydra ages ago. But I knew I badly wanted more of the Provençal light and more time in Aix.

I had seen a language school in rue Gaston de Saporta, in the centre of the town, and, on a whim, went in and tried to sign up to do a course. It was completely booked and in any event there were fees. I had no money and absolutely no prospect of earning any, despite lugging my guitar around. But I decided to go back home, get a job – which back then was effortlessly easy – and retake my English A level at night school. That summer I had managed not just to do badly in the exam but to fail it completely. Not even an O grade. I knew that writing answers to questions I thought much more interesting than the ones actually asked had not helped but I also knew that this result was a travesty. The great awakening in that storm-battered washroom in Aix was that the world would not suddenly realise that I had been shamefully misjudged: I had to go and prove that to the world. Then with honour regained and the money saved from the job I would come back and spend a year in Aix, learn fluent French and paint like Cézanne.

So, up to a point, that is what I did, labouring on a building site through the winter, hod-carrying and digging footings by hand all day and resitting English A level at Farnborough tech in the evening. It was hard physical work. There were few machines, no health and safety restrictions and constant graft, often in foul weather. I would go straight to college from this work, slathered in mud and cement with a copy of *Brave New World* or *Dubliners* wedged into my donkey jacket pocket. My fellow workmen teased me for my airs and graces and fellow students steered well clear. But it paid 59 pence an hour which was enough to pay rent, petrol for my motorbike and a couple of new paperbacks each Saturday, as well as saving £10 a week. Best bitter was 13 pence a pint and half an ounce of Old Holborn and a packet of Rizlas about the same. Other than light, I wanted for little.

I got into the habit of rising at five thirty and reading for a couple of hours before going to work. It felt like time I was stealing from the remorseless mundaneness of Home Counties England. Quietly, before anyone was awake, I was slowly earning my passport out. That year I worked my way through the works of D.H. and T.E. Lawrence, James Joyce, Virginia Woolf, Aldous Huxley, E.M. Forster, George Orwell, Thomas Mann, Jean-Paul Sartre, André Gide and others. I was a sponge, leading a double life, soaking up a world that had ended before the war and was both removed and foreign yet accessible in the same way as France was from the Home Counties.

So the exam was taken, earning that grade I had previously assumed was mine by right, money was saved and in October 1974 I set off on the night train from Victoria for Aix en Provence. I was lugging an absurdly heavy suitcase that contained a Dundee cake and a jar of marmalade amongst the new corduroys, water-purifying tablets and immersion heater that clipped over the rim of a cup.

Apparently my father had exactly the same two items in his kitbag when he set off with the BEF in 1939.

My grandfather, who had worked in Paris before the First World War, told me never to trust the word of a Frenchman unless it was written down. Ever. I had never previously had any kind of personal conversation with my father, although he did once teach me how to kill a sentry soundlessly with his commando dagger. Now, he took me to one side, muttered and shuffled a bit and said in too loud a voice, If you do any fucking, wear a johnny. It was hard to know which of us was more embarrassed.

I spent the crossing being quietly sick over the railings. We arrived at Gare du Nord at dawn and I hauled my suitcase on to the metro across town to Gare de Lyon. The train that was to take me on down to Marseille was due to leave from there at ten that night. I have no idea why I did not take a day train. Perhaps it was felt that the journey needed breaking. I do remember that I sent my suitcase ahead on a separate goods train. I suspect one could not do that now. I also remember my shock that the ticket to Aix cost 200 francs, which was about a week's wages. But the upshot was that I had a long day in Paris with £100 in travellers' cheques,[3] to pay for my board and lodging until I had set up a bank account in Aix (which took weeks), and 30 francs (about £2.50) in cash. I was footloose, young and fancy-free in Paris, the most seductive city on the planet, with a wodge of money in my pocket, yet I felt anxious and alone. It rained all day. I had no waterproof. I walked for hours, revisiting the Jeu de Paume to look at the Impressionist paintings but feeling ill at ease and not connecting with them or anything else, not knowing how to use the empty day at all, but aware I was wasting it. Here, free at last, setting out on the adventure I had longed for, I was tired, hungry and feeling very alone.

I remember going back to the Gare de Lyon in the afternoon and double-checking that it was the right station. Checked I still had the

3 There were no credit cards back then, and cheques drawn on a British bank had no validity abroad.

luggage ticket. Checked I still had the train ticket. At the time I felt unsophisticated and hopeless but I now know that this is the underlying state of anyone who ever takes a bus, plane or train anywhere. All travel is riven with the anxiety of being taken to the wrong place.

Boarding the train as early as possible, I found my couchette, chose a top bunk and settled in. For fully an hour I had the compartment to myself but then, just as the train was about to take off, five North African men hustled on and took the other berths. In Aix I had been told stories of how Algerian men invariably availed themselves of pretty young boys at any opportunity: apparently anyone in the Algerian quarter of the town after dark was fair game. Girls would do at a pinch but boys were preferred. Sharing a space the size of a modest cupboard with five swarthy men who clearly had deliberately chosen this couchette – and me – for a night of debauchery, I felt alarmingly young and pretty. I lay there, spending the second night in my clothes, clutching my virginity and scarcely daring to breathe.

However, they quietly and politely turned to sleep and, eventually, so did I, waking at seven and slipping out into the corridor to find the train stopped at Arles and sunshine streaming in through the corridor window. The train headed south to Marseille and I remember the surge of exhilaration at the orange tiles of the roofs beneath the absolute blue of the sky, the cypresses and olive trees, all as exotic as anything I could then conceive.

I changed at Marseille and took a little train to Aix, hauling my case from the station, stopping at every corner to change hands until I found my digs at rue Cardinale in the seventeenth-century part of the town south of Cours Mirabeau, next to the thirteenth-century church of St Jean de Malte.

The landlady was ninety – so old enough to remember Cézanne but too old to hold on to those or any other memories – and the house had that darkness and smell that I learnt to associate with French town houses that had not sold their souls to the twentieth century. Electricity was used under sufferance. The stairs were terracotta polished by footfall and a silent maid. The furniture in my room was heavy and dark, with a four-poster bed and a jug and basin for washing. Breakfast was brought to my room at eight by the mute maid and a six-course dinner was served in the dining room every evening. This was shared with the other lodgers: a Swedish bodybuilder, two Americans studying French and, disturbingly, someone I had been at school with five years earlier. It was civilised, comfortable and hopelessly unsuitable.

After a week I moved to the country at Les Bonfillons, between St Marc Jaumegarde and Vauvenargues, where Picasso briefly lived and is buried. I bought a Mobylette for 1,000 francs. A thousand any-thing seemed a lot, although in fact it amounted to about £90, brand new and on the road. I walked into a shop, pointed at the one I wanted, filled in a form, paid the money and rode it away. The sim-plicity of it was beautiful.

Mobylettes – a 49cc moped with pedals so you could save fuel going downhill or on the flat – were absurd but ubiquitous back then, more common than bicycles. There was an elderly man in a beret with a couple of baguettes strapped across the back of his Mobylette on every street and country road. Most people used them for journeys of a few kilometres, but I went everywhere on mine, planning a trip each weekend that would take me, very slowly, to the Lubéron, l'Étang de Berre, the coast – as far as the two-stroke engine would go on a tank of fuel. It was not sexy or romantic or glamorous in any conceivable way, but it was freedom and that, there, then, was bliss.

I joined a rugby club and played a few games on the baked pitches of Marseille and Toulon. Then, at a home match in Aix, I got kicked in the eye and found myself lying in Aix hospital next to a farmer whose friend (*mon vieux copain*) had shot him in the eye when they were out hunting thrushes. It was an accident, he said. Could have happened to anybody. His wife, denied of suitable ingredients for her pâté, spent the night cuddled up next to him in bed. I was deeply embarrassed but impressed. They offered me a nip of marc from a flask and I can taste that clean, slightly musky mainline of alcohol in my mouth now.

My own right eye was lost in the taut black swelling that made the right side of my face the outline of a rugby ball. I asked why the other eye was black and was told that I had fractured my skull but they had every hope of saving my eye. Having had no notion that there was the possibility of losing it, this was a little alarming. I went for a pee and slipped on the large, slightly viscous, pool of blood on the lavatory floor. I was just nineteen, and terrified and thrilled in equal measure.

I did not tell my parents about the eye. There was nothing they could do and I guessed that they would expect me to take that sort of thing in my stride. The standard means of communication was an aerogram, which took about four days to reach its destination.[4] Making a phone call would have meant going to the post office at the bottom of the Cours Mirabeau and queuing for ages to book a call before waiting up to half an hour for the connection to be made; you were then directed to a booth where the phone would be ringing – without any guarantee of it ever being answered.[5]

When it was established that my damaged eye had vision I was discharged with a large patch and rode home one-eyed on my Mobylette. After a week I could raise the lid a millimetre or two to expose a satisfyingly bloody mess that nevertheless looked back at the mirror. Sight saved. A few weeks after that I went back to have the haematoma cut out. They injected local anaesthetic into the eye to numb it. I flinched. 'Come on, Mr Rugby Man,' said the nurse with a mocking but incredibly sexy smile. 'Be brave.' The scalpel descended on my eye and cut into the lid like a fingernail scoring the

4 I never understood why it took so long. The aero bit of the journey lasted no more than a couple of hours and a letter posted from any British airport would reach its destination in Britain the next morning. Somehow crossing the Channel made all foreign distances equal.

5 If answering machines existed in 1974, few households had one and of course mobile phones were the stuff of science fiction.

flesh. I didn't feel at all brave. They stitched me up, told me I was off games for six months until my skull healed and that the intense headaches were only to be expected and that I was lucky. Another millimetre and the eye would have been removed.

I moved into the centre of Aix and rented a second-floor flat in rue Portalis that I shared with the Swedish bodybuilder called Stefan who ran a complicated stable of three or four Scandinavian girl-friends, one of whom was usually leaving in tears, only to reappear seemingly unconcerned a few days later. Aix was full of students renting flats in lovely eighteenth-century buildings. We didn't know they were particularly lovely beyond the fact that we liked them, but for most of us they were probably the most stylish, charming places in which we would ever spend time.

Rue Portalis opens out into Place des Prêcheurs, which had flower stalls every morning and a big market every Tuesday, Thursday and Saturday when there would be stalls of just huge tomatoes, puckered and ribbed like pumpkins, piles of strange sundried tomatoes look-ing like rounds of shrivelled toast, ten different types of olive on dishes, and great vats of oil and little wizened old ladies in black with bundles of herbs from the hillside which they sold in twists of news-paper, oranges and lemons stacked head high and aubergines with skin as glossy and black as a guardsman's toecaps, mounds of peaches and nectarines and apricots, little bundles of courgettes the size of sausages still with flowers bursting from their ends like flames, charcuteries of every imaginable variation set out in baskets with pieces to taste on little wooden plates, onions that were not just golden but bright red, and onions long and slim, and garlic – huge swags of pink garlic gloriously exposing itself. There were crêpe makers and sweet sellers, walls of nougat and strange Algerian sweets, and the cafés around the square filled with leather-skinned men smoking yellow cigarettes and drinking wine and pastis at eight in the morning. I never lost my wonder that such a world existed and that all I had to do was stumble from my door and take a few steps down the road to immerse myself in it.

I had been brought up in the shadow of food shortages and rationing. My parents wasted nothing and there was a culture of eating what you were given and being thankful for it. Foreign food of any kind was rare and only valued if it was the bastardised French haute cuisine that still masquerades as good food in Britain today. Pasta was only known as a novelty dish, boiled to a pulp and served floating in grey watery mince. It was called, without any hint of shame, let alone irony, spaghetti Bolognese. On the whole the food was seasonal and fresh, but it was plain and repetitive and came bundled with guilt and repression. No one was overweight and few had diet-related illnesses, but hardly anyone expressed any sensual delight in what they ate. The English regarded meals like sex: you did it mostly indoors, in private, showed good manners and restraint, didn't take too long about it and were sure to say thank you.

So to come to a place where abundance and colour and fragrance and texture washed and swirled so openly was completely liberating. Everybody looked for and demanded the best food and not to relish it in every glorious manifestation was to turn your back on life itself.

I found that I had to buy very little if I waited until midday, when the stalls packed up and anything that would not last until the next market day was left behind. Mounds and piles of fruit and vegetables were quickly scavenged by students like myself. Once a week we could afford to eat in the restaurant on the corner of the street. For 10 francs (about 90 pence) you could have the set three-course meal, and another 3 francs bought a large carafe of the house wine.

2

JAS DE BOUFFAN

I have always tried to visit the homes of writers and artists who influence me, believing that seeing where a man ate his breakfast or the wicker chair beneath the tree that remains is a key of sorts to their work, and back in January 1975 I did try and visit Jas de Bouffan,[1] Cézanne's family home for forty years.

In fact I never got beyond pressing my nose against the big iron gates and glimpsing the house at the end of a long avenue of bare-boned plane trees. The house was on the edge of the unfashionable western side of town and a new autoroute had just been built running right by it – and presumably through its former fields.[2] On a grey, cold winter's day it was bleak, noisy and as far from my idealisation of Cézanne as could be conceived. It started to rain. I got back on my Mobylette and returned to town.

---

1 The word *jas* is only found in Provence and seems approximate to the Welsh *hafod* or summer grazing place.
2 When Cézanne's father – who had made money as a hatter and banker – bought the house in 1859 it was a rundown but quite large farm, which remained a working farm throughout Cézanne's life, the large house surrounded by its fields. The family always kept their town house and at first only used Jas de Bouffan as a summer home. They moved there in the 1860s and it remained Cézanne's principal home until it was sold after his mother's death in 1899.

Thirty-seven years later I came back and went through the same heavy gates. As I went in, a man who had clearly enjoyed much refreshment stopped me and asked what I was about. I told him. Then, he said, you will like to come and see the Cézanne I have in my apartment in town. Really, I said, a real Cézanne? But of course, he said. A lost painting but fully authenticated. Done when he was a young man. An immature work to be sure but it could be mine for a mere 50,000 euros. I politely declined the offer and went in but he followed me inside, clutching at my sleeve. Strong words were exchanged. He tottered off, cursing me.

The area is still bleakly dominated by roads and blocks of flats but the trees, now in the full leaf of midsummer's day, were cool and dark, the shadows latticing the grass. Boughs that had been pollarded some fifty to a hundred years ago canted in, striking recognisable poses. It is fanciful to think of Cézanne being influenced by their linear lean but perhaps in his day they were polled back to mere stumps on a trunk.

The house, set fully a hundred metres from the road, is an elegant ochre cube with pale eau-de-Nil shutters. The garden is not up to much. Good trees, areas of scratchy grass, the pond, almost unchanged, the water as green as the leaves that shade it. But no sense of it being tended or designed, no flower beds or structure as such, just the grass cut now and then.

But that is the point. Cézanne, for all his comfortable bourgeois home and domestic padding, is the painter of transcendence. The most ordinary things become suffused with light and life, and it is this that makes his work sublime. There is the game to be played of checking the 'real' garden against his paintings and finding almost everything in its place, as though there is an alchemy of archaeology and sacred relics. So the stone block is still at the end of the pool, the trees are larger but there is no reason to presume that they are not the same ones, and the house has scarcely altered in any way. But there was nothing that could not be found in a hundred other places at any given moment, just as there were a thousand bowls of apples or arrangements of cloth that could have been painted when he was at work.

The house is at that point of abandonment that does not feel like dereliction and yet would have builders and architects shaking their heads and sucking their teeth whilst they added noughts to their estimates. It is due for a major repair and restoration and is closed to the public but I was shown round.

There was no electricity and it was dusk, so the only light slanted in the half-opened shutters, cutting a beam through the darkness into a large central hall, steep stairs and wrought-iron bannister. A sedan chair sat on the corner of the first landing. Up through the core of the house was another tiny staircase for servants, with slit-like doors on to each floor.

Like so many large French houses, it was used by the extended family in a series of apartments with a communal kitchen and large living rooms. At the top of the house were the servants' quarters, which were tiny, plain rooms with fireplaces and unexpected partitions. Off one room was a space that was barely more than a closet, big enough only for a bed. The walls and ceiling were decorated with elaborate moulding, quite unlike the rest of the top floor. This, according to my guide, was built so that the original owner of the house could come and claim *droit de seigneur* with the maid of his choice. As long as it all stayed up here, in the servants' part of the house, it was acceptably outside marital territory.

Cézanne painted murals in the salon, and in 1907, after Cézanne's death, Louis Granel, the man who had bought the house from the family in 1899, suggested that he detach them and donate them to the nation, although he had already been offered more than 100,000 francs for them. The nation, in the shape of a Monsieur Bénédite, came and inspected the murals and, on consideration, decided that it did not want them. Monsieur Bénédite thought Cézanne's work of little value: he had already rejected three of five paintings offered to the nation in 1896 by the estate of Gustave Caillebotte. The murals were subsequently detached and sold in 1912.

The floors throughout are tiled and the patina of polish and age has made them almost plum coloured, glimmering in the dark. With the flaking limewash and the wasted light falling like rags and my caught-breath reverence, it made the empty building pulse with intensity.

At the top of the house was Cézanne's studio, with a window cut into the eaves to give northern light. This was quite an invasive thing to do to this impressive, four-square building. The fact that Cézanne's father was prepared to deface the frontage of the house in this way, along with the allowance that he paid him, adds up to strong and practical support by a father for a son who sold nothing before he was thirty-five and was locally thought of as a simple-minded dauber. Even in 1974 I recall people expressing amazement that Cézanne's work had taken in so many people. This, of course, was coupled with intense pride that he was Aixois.[3]

Cézanne lived at Jas de Bouffan until 1899. He only left it then because the sale was forced by his two sisters after the death of his mother, so they could extract their share of the inheritance.

This means that the vast majority of his work that was not painted outside *sur le motif* was painted in this surprisingly small attic room. Cézanne's catalogue runs to some 954 paintings, 645 watercolours and 1,400 drawings. Given time spent in Paris, given his love of painting outside and given that I am guessing randomly, it is not unreasonable to suppose that he produced hundreds of separate works within these four walls. It is my experience that buildings and landscapes act as batteries, taking the charge from significant acts, good and ill, and holding a trace of them, sometimes with overwhelming and palpable intensity. But there was absolutely nothing in that room at all. It was empty of everything that had ever happened there. All the ghosts have gone.

3 Aix was incredibly insular in the nineteenth century. The population remained constant between 1807 and 1920. Until 1877 the only road to Marseille was through desolate hills and the railways did not reach it until 1870. Even today it is a branch line and you have to go to Marseille and change to get a main line connection. That Cézanne was seen as a great painter by the rest of the world did not alter his local reputation as an embarrassing failure who was a shilling short of a pound.

The house is closed until the repair work is done. It will become something between a Cézanne theme park and a beautifully cared-for homage to one of the greatest painters the world has known. Maybe it will bring the ghost of Cézanne back but, with the motor-way and the grim housing and the unravelling of heritage and art and national pride, I doubt it. I think on my visit I saw a glimpse back a hundred years just as it was slipping away for ever.

On the other side of Aix is a corrective to too much melancholy about *temps perdu*. After Jas de Bouffan was sold Cézanne moved into an upper floor of a house in rue Boulegon in Aix, making a studio in the attic there. But he was now rich and could afford better. In 1901 he bought a plot of land, an olive grove[4] just north of the town, and built himself a studio. For the last four years of his life he lived in his rue Boulegon apartment, rising at four and walking every day to his studio where he lit the stove and read. At five, milk was delivered and he made coffee before starting work. He broke for lunch at eleven and then worked outside if possible till evening.

The studio has been beautifully maintained and looked after and is left as though Cézanne had just walked out of the room. In his day the steep road that is now constantly threaded with traffic was a dusty track but behind the gate it seems to be genuinely unspoilt. The garden has regrown after the devastation of the Great Frost in 1956, when the original eighty olives on the plot were all killed. If it were in the UK it would have had a committee developing Action Plans to restore it as nearly as possible to its 1906 state, in tune with the inte-rior of the studio. As it is French, and Provençal French in particular, it has just been allowed to grow, almost untouched. I like it for that. And in any event, the garden is a sideshow, a setting for the studio.

In March the trees were scrawny, and scruffily unkempt. But when I went back in mid-summer they had become cool, sleek

---

4 Cézanne apparently adored olives and the oil from Aix was considered to be partic-ularly good. I remember being told in the early 1970s, when it was still a fresh wound, about the terrible frost of '56 that destroyed whole hillsides of ancient, venerable trees and transformed the landscape around Aix.

havens against the sun, casting a delicious green shade. It also smelt good. Pine, sand, sun, stone, cistus, thyme mingled to make that particularly oily, musky, southern fragrance.

Inside is a stage set, carefully propped to look as though the artist has just left the room, but it works. The walls are painted a shade of grey that intensifies the oranges and blues of the carpet and fruit and on a dresser are apples, a jug, three skulls, stools and chairs, the ornate stove that warmed him and his morning milk. His coat, smock and beret hang on a hook. In the corner is a door no more than fifty centimetres wide but fully three-and-half metres tall – a slot built in to slide out huge canvases.

You struggle to avoid becoming a pilgrim in these places but it is futile. To poke and peer with the relaxed curiosity of familiarity seems sacrilegious. This is an inner sanctum. Although reverence does not get you any closer to the work, it is inevitable and in its own way richly enjoyable. But to step inside the work and allow it to get further inside you, you need to go *sur le motif* and take the road to Le Tholonet.

3

LE THOLONET

Despite the cheapness of living I found was running out of money. So I got a job. Not a proper job and not a job that paid me in money but it was a job that hugely enriched me.

A cousin of a friend of an acquaintance I was briefly introduced to had written a name and phone number on a scrap of paper. If you are in Aix you must look this woman up, he said. She is terrific.

So I went to the post office and called the number. Madame Tailleaux answered and, after a sentence or two of my inadequate French, asked me, in a cut-glass English accent, if I wanted to come to lunch.

That would be lovely.

Stay there then, she said. See you in an hour. And she rang off.

Madame Tailleaux – I never called her anything else or knew her first name – duly arrived in her Renault, stopped in the middle of the road, asked a couple of other youngish men if they were Monty, finally located me and swept me off to lunch at her house, La Bertranne in Le Tholonet.

A pattern emerged. I would go to Le Tholonet a few days a week and work in her garden, and in return she would make me lunch (a proper French two-hour lunch), introduce me to local people and act as a guide, mentor and friend. She would also expect me to accompany her on jaunts, often without notice. The Renault would stop in rue Portalis and she would call up to the window for me to come down because we were going to Gardanne to buy some tiles, or to come quickly (it would be eleven in the morning) because Poublier who lived two fields away from La Bertranne had a bouillabaisse ready. She wanted a companion and liked young people and I fitted the bill.

She seemed very old to me but was no more than sixty – just a few years older than I am now. She was half-American, half-French, had been brought up in pre-war England and married a French painter. Her house had various lodgers, waifs and strays and friends of different nationalities who were treated as a cross between children and members of a commune. Whilst the basic lingua franca of the household was French, she rarely completed a sentence in the same language that she began it and often jumped from French to English to German to Italian as she talked, seemingly unaware of doing so.

Her husband's studio was still fully set up at La Bertranne although he had not lived there for years. It had a full-size replica of Picasso's *Guernica* on one wall. Only recently I learnt from her son Carlo that she had been sent to a concentration camp in the war for helping the Resistance and Jewish escapees. She hated injustice and authority in equal measure, treating both with an aristocratic, imperious fury, and was scared of nothing.

Thirty years ago I drove to Le Tholonet with Sarah, vaguely hoping that she might still be there so Sarah could meet her. With the arrogance of youth, I assumed that because my life had changed so much and ten years seemed so significantly long to me, everyone else's life would be utterly different too. We drove down the road to Le Tholonet, talking about her, when she appeared, walking out of the woods. I stopped the car. She looked a little older but almost exactly the same. I got out. Madame Tailleaux?

Ah, Monty, she said without breaking beat, how nice to see you. Will you come to lunch?

So we did. The house was empty, a bit shabby but unchanged. Lunch, as ever, was delicious. She gave us a huge plate made by the potter across the fields. We still use it for oranges, glowing against the indigo glaze. Then we left and I never saw her again.

But I thought of her a great deal and realised that what I loved was her fearlessness and complete lack of philistinism as well as the connection to the artists and writers of the 1920s, '30s and '40s that I had discovered for myself as inspiring but remote figures. She had been, both through the stories and accounts of her life before and during the war, always thrown away, no more than asides really, the living key to a world otherwise unobtainable to me and her influence spread far beyond the actual time we spent together or the things that we did. So last summer I travelled back along the road to Le Tholonet to see if I could find La Bertranne. I had no plan. I just wanted to go down that road again.

The route from Aix was fringed with villas for perhaps a kilometre and then quickly left town and cut and twisted into the hillside through pines and oaks growing amongst pink boulders. There were blue shadows, hollyhocks in the long grass and a meadow dotted with thousands of white spiders. Forty years ago I had noticed a little marble plaque tucked into a stone wall, commemorating six people 'Fusillés par les Nazis le 17 Août 1944', presumably right here, at this bend in the road, far enough away from the town to be out of earshot and with a bank high enough to absorb bullets. It was still exactly the same. Sad, only half-noticed, shameful. A plastic water bottle was stuffed with a florist's lily and hydrangea. Someone's father, grandfather – perhaps even husband – was still mourned at the edge of this lovely road.

And then against that clear blue sky, with a lick of pine branch framing its contours, Mont Sainte-Victoire was rising and growing before me. Unlike most mountains, which have a monumental presence, Mont Sainte-Victoire always seems, as Cézanne so brilliantly portrayed, to be still in the process of becoming, as though its heaving geology is just momentarily stilled and the iconic shape is a temporary assumption. It is tentative and usually slightly faded, almost gauzy in some lights. That is why Cézanne painted it again and again.[1]

To know the mountain and the paintings a little better, forty years ago I climbed to the Croix de Provence at the top. There is a track all the way up, steep and at times needing all hands as well as feet but, like so many of the wonderful Grandes Randonées right across France, clearly marked with red and white stripes painted on the rock, helpful without being bossy and at times daring you on without unnecessary and unwelcome consideration for your health or safety in the process. The Alps could be seen in the east, their snow surreal in the hot, resinous light. They were the first snowy peaks I had seen. As the afternoon light angled down from the west towards them they turned golden and then pink. I stayed watching, transfixed, until the light slid down and the peaks sank back into shade, and then stumbled down the mountain in the dusk.

I had assumed that a full generation later La Bertranne would have been bought by a German banker and replete with swimming pool, gym and sleek fast car outside. When I found it, the shutters were a different colour and it looked freshly painted. Half tempted to turn back and not risk the disillusionment, I went up the long track, encouraged to find it as bumpy as I recalled, and parked by the house. The banging and sawing from builders seemed to confirm my suspicions and I was turning to leave when a voice said, Monty! A figure appeared in the doorway with Madame Tailleaux's deeply sunken eyes and high cheekbones. It was her face but carried by a man, probably in his sixties. This was Carlo, her son, whom I had not met but had heard much of. It turned out that he had come across me on telly in England, where he had lived for a while, and had also heard something of me from his mother. Madame Tailleaux

---

1 He painted more than forty oil versions of the mountain as well as numerous watercolours.

had only died a few years previously, well into her nineties. He was moving back and repairing the house.

We sat on the terrace and drank a glass of wine and talked of those years long ago that we had not shared at all but had, in another sense, shared quite profoundly. I was, Carlo said, in many ways a replacement for him. A biddable version of the impossible, uncontrollable son. It was a strange role for me, who had always been the black sheep of my own family, to become the safer substitute for someone whose adulthood was so much freer and more interesting than the versions that I grew up with at home. He said that the garden had meant a lot to her and my helping her keep it in some order would have mattered. He wanted to live here, didn't know if it would work out, but wanted to try. He wanted to make it beautiful again in her memory.

I left, bouncing slowly down the track to the road, between the barley fields infiltrated with fennel and Sainte-Victoire looming out of the shadows in the east. I felt at peace. It was not so much a case of seeing old friends as of seeing and laying the ghosts of my old self, and settling that piece of my past easily into my present.

4

VILLA NOAILLES

There is a no-man's-land quality to the coastal strip of Provence. I have never found any identity there that I can recognise. This is not so strange when you think that it has been primarily a holiday resort for the past century. I remember taking a coach trip from Aix to Nice, staying in the youth hostel there and then going to see the Fondation Maeght at St Paul de Vence. It was the first time I had seen sculptures integrated into landscape and a garden built around sculpture as an integral component. It was and remains an extraordinary experience. I walked on the beach in the dark and it felt as though the sea was a reluctant visitor, that Nice had drawn up its lines there because that was where the land stopped rather than where the sea started.

In the 1980s Sarah and I spent one Christmas in a borrowed villa in the woods above St Paul. We drove down from London in a brand new car, Grace Jones singing all the way, emerging from the freezing fog of the north into southern light like crawling out of a tunnel. We had vague directions for finding the house and it was getting dark as we bounced down a rough track. Big gates opened with one of the bunch of keys we had been given and the house sat just inside. It was completely dark and, fumbling, none of the keys worked. There seemed to be no other houses nearby. Either this was completely the wrong place or all the plans had gone askew and the house was not available after all.

We drove on down the track to see if there were any neighbours we could ask and came to a large house with lights above the front door. I knocked. Nothing. Walked round trying to see in the windows but the shutters were closed. For some reason I tried one of the keys in the door, and it opened easily. There was a note welcoming us in the hallway. It turned out that the first building was the gatehouse and this – the right villa – was equipped with swimming pool, tennis court, gym and a fridge stocked with champagne and the best local produce.

For twenty-four hours the luxury was a novelty and we played with it like a toy, trying everything out. But that soon waned and Nice on Christmas Day was a soulless, grim place. I have not spent Christmas away from home since. But we did have a couple of good meals at the Colombe d'Or in St Paul de Vence, where the walls are decorated with paintings and drawings by Picasso, Matisse, Braque, Chagall and others who paid for their meals with art. It was famous and expensive but somehow accessible back then.

And we found some beautiful pots for our garden. We had seen lovely olive oil jars and wanted to buy one for our hosts as a present. We were talking to an English ex-pat couple and asked if they knew the best place to buy them. He, seventyish, thin, nut brown, in shorts in December, said, 'Certainly. Bat on down to Antibes and turn right to Biot. You'll see a field full of pots on your left. They are the best in Provence.' So we duly batted on down the coast road and found a field with thousands of pots in rows – some as big as ready-mix cement lorries and others you could hold in one hand. We bought one for the huge sum of £100 and then, just as we were leaving, saw another, nicer one, so did the obvious thing and bought that too, just fitting them in the back of the car. We kept the nicest and left the other in the garden,[1] although I rather suspect they did not like it.

The Musée Picasso at the Château Grimaldi in Antibes, which Picasso used as a studio for three months between September and November in 1946, is wonderful. At least it was in 1984 when we visited it after buying our pots in Biot. Picasso came to Antibes after the war with his new lover, Françoise Gilot, who was some forty years younger than him. As payment for the studio space Picasso left all the work that he did there – twenty-three paintings and over forty drawings, most featuring Françoise Gilot – on condition that it should remain in situ. To visit is to step inside an extraordinary slice of restless, astonishingly confident creativity.

Picasso had met Françoise Gilot a few years earlier in 1943, in a restaurant in occupied Paris, when he and Dora Maar were dining with Marie-Laure, Vicomtesse de Noailles. As Françoise Gilot later wrote, Marie-Laure had a 'long, narrow, somewhat decadent-looking face, framed by an ornate coiffure that reminded me of Rigaud's portrait of Louis XIV in the Louvre'.[2]

Marie-Laure de Noailles was the great-great-great-granddaughter of the Marquis de Sade and had married Charles de Noailles in 1923 when she was twenty. Charles de Noailles was a vicomte with a vast fortune and the pair proceeded to spend large amounts of it patronising modern artists in various media. They helped finance the films of Man Ray and Luis Buñuel, the paintings of Salvador Dalí and Balthus, the sculpture of Brancusi and Miró, among others. The couple also commissioned a Cubist garden by the Armenian

1 This pot took pride of place in our London garden but was broken in the great storm of October 1987. We carefully mended it and it came with us to Herefordshire but was smashed when one of our cats rubbed against it. We kept the pieces and took it to a local potter who specialised in large garden terracotta pots. After a few weeks we rang him to see how it was going. Impossible, he said. It can't be done. It is technically impossible to make a pot this large with clay this thin. To scale it was thinner than an eggshell. He made a copy as well as he could, and we still have this, but it is a hefty, clodhopping thing compared to the original, which we found was between 3–400 years old. We still have the shards, which we cannot bear to throw away.
2 *Life with Picasso*, Françoise Gilot and Carlton Lake (Nelson, 1964).

designer Gabriel Guevrekian. The garden was made as part of the villa that they had built just after their marriage. Overlooking the small town of Hyères, this was a holiday home where they held artistic court.

Guevrekian was an architect who eventually made three gardens, each one an artistic statement, deliberately using the principles and ideas of Cubism. There was no intention of making it natural or relating it in any way to the surrounding environment. Charles de Noailles was a serious gardener and botanist but this particular triangular wedge of ground was intended to serve only two functions: to be looked at from above as a static work of art and to be occupied as a space for parties. It seems to have served both purposes admirably during the period in the 1920s and '30s when the de Noailles used Hyères most intensely.

I visited early in the morning, after a coffee at the bar opposite Hyères railway station, when the shadows from the surrounding pines were filling the sharp prow of the garden with shade. It was intended that the first sight of it would be from above, looking down through the big openings in the curtain wall, but the modern visitor skirts the edge, seeing too much too soon. It seems too small, too dingy to justify the excursion, especially one that meant setting the alarm for five thirty.

But go up to the raised level of the house and look down and the garden works. It is powerful. It sits well with itself. The hard triangular bow and chequerboard squares break and reshape any hint of natural lines, challenging preconceptions of how a garden 'ought' to be, yet it remains as accessible and inviting as any lawn flanked with herbaceous borders.

Go down into it and it teases you, inviting you forward and yet not really having a forward to go to. The only paths are zigzagged at an angle up the wall. Every clear step is blocked by a planted square, with the resulting diagonals all on different levels. But movement is not the point. Take up a position and it feels comfortable. Apparently it was the favoured place for cocktails, the lack of routes encouraging an easy mingle. The soft ochre of the back wall is warm with its play of shadows, and the slightly aggressive corners and angles, all elbows and knees from above, become playful.

A lot of playing was done at Villa Noailles, both in public and private. It was elaborately, formally decadent. I met the present head gardener, Pierre Quillier, whose grandfather had been butler for the de Noailles during that interwar period. Pierre told me that his grandfather had forty-eight staff under him, all of them always in freshly laundered white uniforms, and that he constantly moved between their houses in Paris, Fontainebleau and Hyères. What struck me as most extraordinary about this was that the de Noailles were so young when they had these enormous, elaborate households. Younger than when Sarah and I drove down to St Paul feeling terribly grown up precisely because we were not terribly grown up.

The villa at Hyères was always filled with artists, politicians, writers and actors. It was a summer-long house party. Whoever the guests were, young and old, unknown or world famous, all had their clothes taken away when they arrived. In return they were given simple white tunics so everyone was dressed the same. The idea was to remove the barriers set up by class, wealth or creed. No cars were allowed, so visitors were dropped off and then remained within the walls of the villa, in this strange, privileged state of artistic equality.

For about ten years it became the centre for French artistic modernity and the patronage of the de Noailles was almost essential for any artist to get on. I asked Pierre if his grandfather ever talked of any of the guests. Apparently Salvador Dalí was a favourite and he was always hungry. Pierre's grandfather found him in the kitchen on a number of occasions, stuffing food into his mouth.

5

VAL JOANIS

Back in the 1970s I remember setting off on my Mobylette to Manosque, heading north up to the Provençal hinterland. My journal says, 'There was one particular stretch from Jouques to St Paul lez Durance which had tiny lawn-sized fields each bounded by a thick drystone wall out of which grew pale blue flowers. Almond trees lined the road which twisted and climbed through the mountain. Behind me lay the silhouetted shapes of St Victoire, La Chaîne de la Ste-Baume and the mountains by Marseille. White houses with earth-coloured tiles merged into the hillside. I did not see a soul save a shepherd two valleys away.' Lovely as it still is, it has inevitably changed for the worse, at least for the visitor looking for the frisson of the romantic. Not too many shepherds left, I suspect.

That, minimal as it was, was the extent of my voyaging into the Lubéron and Haute Provence. Hardly a glimpse. I regret that, as it is incredibly beautiful and still to some extent free from the overcrowded commercialism that taints the Riviera and the southern strip of Provence. It has attracted an eclectic mix, from Samuel Beckett, hiding from the Germans in Roussillon (and writing *Watt*) after his Resistance activities in Paris in the Second World War, and Albert Camus, buried at Lourmarin, to the Marquis de Sade's castle in Lacoste. However, in the past forty years it has become the trendy place for wealthy Europeans to retire or take holiday homes, and there is a sleekness and order that only money can buy. Villages such as Ménerbes, Lacoste, Gordes and Bonnieux have become famous for attracting the famous. They are still lovely and essentially unspoilt. But there is a kind of self-knowing quality to them that was not there forty years ago. The innocence has been sold to tourists like us.

Take the Roman road north out of Aix towards the Alps and instead of going east towards Manosque, carry on to Pertuis. A few kilometres west, before you reach Villelaure, are the vineyards of Val Joanis. A long track takes you through 185 hectares of them, sweeping round to a courtyard where a square of large white stones is studded with a grid of vines. It is interesting what changes perception. The previous five minutes have been spent driving through hundreds of hectares of vineyards which come right up to the walls of house and garden. Yet because these vines in the courtyard are set in stone not earth, are in a square grid not rows and are surrounded by tarmac, they become an installation. Viticulture as art. It sets the tone.

Vines have been grown in this region since Roman times and Val Joanis has been a vineyard since at least 1575 when Jean de Joanis, secretary to Louis III of Naples, built his house there. But the garden, at least the garden open to the public, is new. There has been a herb garden here since the current house was built a couple of hundred years ago, growing herbs both for culinary purposes and as medicine – most specifically to fend of the plague that was always lurking around Marseille.[1] It was in effect a potager, but a distinctly herby one. The present garden was made in the late 1980s, both as an

1 Plague came in and out of the port at Marseille and led those that could afford it to have country houses inland, up in the hills where they could be safe. These houses ranged from simple whitewashed *cabanons* to the estates like Val Joanis and this dual existence of the fetid but prosperous city and the extreme simplicity of the country home that could be reached on foot in a day was a feature of eighteenth- and nineteenth-century Provence and the Var.

elaborate accessory to a rich person's estate and as a showpiece for visitors.

I visited Val Joanis in early March and again in mid-summer, by which time it had been bought by the Roozen family from Holland, who made their fortune with orange juice and chose to spend it on grape juice. The point is that the garden is an extravagance rather than a working potager. Apart from anything else the family is rarely there. There is no one to eat the vegetables or fruit. But it looks magnificent and the concept – and France is the land where concepts count – is fine and clear. The link between the ranging hectares of vines and the intensely manicured potager is umbilical.

The vines are the outward manifestation of the cultural depths of *terroir*,[2] pruning, variety, climate and the sensual sophistication that any wine-making, wine-drinking society nurtures. Sprawling across millions of hectares, they have a kind of insouciance and careless ease that barely hints at any of these things. Talk to a winemaker and every item, every aspect is accounted for as a lifetime's study. A potager takes it all and distils and condenses it into a domestic space.

At Val Joanis the training and pruning of fruit – which is such an integral part of the process of caring for the vines – is elaborated to an extraordinary degree. Every variation and permutation of espalier, cordon and fan is on display. The vegetables are grown lovingly and with skill, with twenty-five varieties of tomato, aubergine, pepper, chard and artichoke all flourishing in the extreme heat, though a combination of extreme watering and extreme tending means that the garden can supply the full battery of the vegetable garden arsenal. Herbs, even if plague is not now quite such a threat, are still important, with inula, sage, vervaine, tansy and thyme that would all have been part of the earliest medicinal herb garden, and

2 *Terroir* is one of those concepts that is easier understood with the hand and heart than the brain. It essentially means the nature of both the soil – which directly influences what will grow and thrive – and the definition of the landscape itself, the geology and geography that influences climate, weather and above all human perception of the world. All this is bound up in the precise identification of produce and people's relationship with both its production and consumption.

fennel, basil, tarragon and all the usual culinary herbs present too. But the fruit, in all its precise and ornate glory, is what takes this above and beyond an exceptionally well-maintained allotment.

When I first visited Val Joanis in spring the gardeners were hard at work finishing the winter pruning. The head gardener was operating secateurs with a battery pack on his back. I know what that kind of equipment costs. The battery alone will set you back as much as a dozen of the best secateurs that money can buy. Expensive kit. It tells me that the role of pruner and the importance of the job demand recognition with overtly expensive, top-of-the-range gear.[3] Pruning matters terribly in France and is a language that many understand. It confirms the rightness of order and method and is an agreeable display of skills that have to be learnt and mastered. The British have access to exactly the same information but bypass them, mostly regarding pruning as at best a means to quite a different end and at worst a display of horticultural pedantry. In France, the pruning is part of the process that makes the product. A wine could not possibly taste so well if produced chaotically.

When I returned at the end of June, with the temperature rising above forty degrees and the cicadas roaring, the garden was made almost monochrome by the intensity of light and shade. The pruned bones were hidden by foliage and for all its fecundity the garden had lost some magic. It was like a fine-set face made puffy and bloated with years of ease. In March it was busy and working, whereas by the end of June everything was for show. Food grown for display never convinces. There must be need or pleasure, preferably both, to bring it fully to life.

But this is quibbling at the edges. It is a beautiful, impressive garden. The oaks and hornbeams, pruned to columns, cones and

---

3 Or he borrowed it from the teams that prune the vines. I have seen huddled teams of pruners, muffled absurdly against the cold of mid-winter Herefordshire, following a crawling tractor down rows of apple trees, pruners operated hydraulically by the tractor's PTO, remorselessly cutting back acre after acre of unwanted growth. Apparently fingers are often snipped by mistake. I have cut the top off one of my own fingers with secateurs. It hurts.

blocks, had a gravitas and solidity that was easy to overlook in spring. The lavender was almost hyper-real and extravagant, as though all northern-European lavender was merely a ghost of the real thing. Perovskia stood in rows like pale mauve bodyguards flanking espalier apples and pears and hollyhocks watching over the courgettes. It was as though the cottage garden had been reshuffled and the jumbled mix of flower and fruit and herbs lined up and straightened and set properly square.

You cannot visit a vineyard and pass judgements on its garden without at least trying its wine. I tried quite hard. The 2007 is a joy. Sitting beneath a pollarded plane in the courtyard, its black interior almost completely hollowed out, I thumped the trunk to hear its drumtone and a large indignant owl flew out.

After leaving Val Joanis I stayed the night in a modest hotel in Lourmarin. It was reasonably priced and both convenient and secluded. When travelling a lot, especially when filming, I stumble from hotel to hotel with a kind of resigned world-weariness. Part of me would love a beautiful room, fabulous view and luxury in every possible form. But another large part just wants it all to work and not be too noisy. Cleanliness, enough space to put my suitcase on the floor and still be able to move, a comfy bed, hot and cold running water and a flushing loo fulfil most needs.

My room in this establishment had deep red walls. The pictures on the wall hovered on the line between bad-taste eroticism and coy porn. I opened a drawer and revealed a range of dildoes in various sizes. In another were a set of handcuffs and a leather mask. It transpired that this was a swingers' hotel and monthly gatherings were staged for couples from all over the country. I had been given the best room. Hence, I gathered, all the special extras.

6

LA LOUVE

I took the road from Lourmarin up into the hills through some of the loveliest countryside in Europe, slowing for a large wild boar that stood in the road, looked lazily at me and excreted thoughtfully before tipytoeing off in that high-heeled way even the fiercest pigs have. It led to the village of Bonnieux, whose houses tier down over the valley, across from the billows and mounds of blue distant hills. There is a kind of inevitability in these southern French villages with their cafés and boulangeries and dogs and elderly shoppers. They have worked out how they want to live and seen it through. To the northern visitor, seeing what they most want to see and glossing over the summer drought, difficulty in communication and all the inevitable restrictions of remote provincial life, it is tantalisingly, ravishingly ideal. The reason for going there was to visit one of the most perfect gardens in the whole of France and certainly the garden that most exactly captures the spirit of Provence. This garden is called La Louve.

I walked down a steep side street to a front door opening straight on to the road, knocked and walked into a hallway floored with gravel. That first touch – and crunchy sound – is the signal to pay attention. Something is happening here. It is unlike any other experience and already interesting and good.

It gets better. The garden is as complete and coherent as a garden could possibly be. It has the sureness of a perfect melody: you sing along, knowing exactly which note to hit, even though you are simultaneously surprised with the uniqueness of it all.

I have a standard routine when writing about a garden that I have visited. Whilst I am there I fire off photographs without any thought as to pictorial quality or lasting value. I am simply making notes alongside the scribbles in my notebook. The pictures are downloaded and the notes transcribed. It is all stored and sometimes hardly looked at for weeks or even months. During this time the memories mature and if, as often happens, I am visiting a dozen gardens in as many days, they meld and merge with just the clear defining characteristics remaining. When it comes to writing, I put all the pictures up on a screen and edit them down. I have two large screens on my desk and the idea is that one has the pictures and the other the words. Memory, research, photographs and notes are all plundered to try and distil the essence of the experience on to the page.

But with La Louve I found editing the pictures almost impossible. I usually quickly get it down to a hundred and then reduce that to fifty. The whole process is a good way to reacquaint oneself with the place and takes a leisurely ten minutes or so. With La Louve every image was stunning and seemed integral to the spirit of the place. Nothing at all was extraneous or conflicting. Of course it also means that one could choose any image almost at random and immediately have the garden complete and singular before you.

This is incredibly rare. I paid three visits to La Louve over the course of three months and each time found more to see and more to admire. Yet it is small, the planting contains little of horticultural, let alone botanical, interest, there is a very muted palette, hardly any flowers, and it was created and planted with almost wilful ignorance and neglect of basic horticultural wisdom. Thank God.

The garden was made between 1986 and 1996 by Nicole de Vesian, a fabric designer who, after retiring from working with Hermès, moved to the Lubéron to make a garden. She knew nothing at all about gardening but an awful lot about colour, shape, texture and style and had the wit to realise that the constituents of a good garden always owe more to good design than horticulture. So far so unremarkable. But Nicole de Vesian deliberately applied two other vital tenets to her garden. The first was to radically restrict her palette. No gaudy colours. She wanted her garden to be like an old tapestry so everything is muted, toned down, faded, washed out and weathered. Browns, sepias, greys, blues and greens. Stone, wood, earth. Not a blade of grass. Under a grey northern sky, that could easily slip from stylish to dreary, but under the brilliant Provençal light it is tonally rich and soothing. It also needs a very dry climate. Rain in this part of Provence is a refreshing treat. Weeks and weeks on end are guaranteed to be bone dry.

The restriction is also applied to plants. There is no attempt at horticultural bravado. There is nothing in the garden that might not be readily found in a hundred local gardens, nothing that is not comfortably at home. This is a deliberate and clever choice. Nicole composed her garden predominantly from plants that were either indigenous to the area, like lavender, rosemary, myrtle and teucrium, or ones that have made themselves at home over millennia, like euphorbia, cypress, box and bay.

The second piece of simple genius she applied was to respond directly to the shapes of the landscape. She set her little garden, clustered about with other houses and gardens, in the context of the furthest horizon and everything that lay between. The views are an integral part of the garden. This adds grandeur and scale to what is a very intimate, private space. The shrubs are clipped to reflect the curves of the hills and trees pruned to frame them. Garden designers often talk about 'borrowed landscape' (meaning a view) and usually imply pulling them into the garden as a bonus. Nicole de Vesian did almost the opposite, opening out her garden so that it becomes part of all that is around it without in any way being diminished.

It is extremely intimate. There are seats everywhere, although always in ones and twos. It is a garden for talk and contemplation, not big parties. The paths are narrow, clearly made as materials accumulated, and delightfully wonky. Every exit and entrance is just wide enough to pass through, brushing the scented foliage as you do so. There is nothing haphazard about this. It was all as precisely and meticulously made as the most ordered minimalist house or garden. Apparently Nicole chose the individual stones for each wall and kept a beady eye on them as they were made, often asking for courses to be rebuilt to suit her aesthetic standards. She did not plan the garden but assembled it, making it up as she went along, trusting her eye above all else. The thing she hated most was uniformity and you see this in every tiny detail, almost to the twigs on the ground. Every aspect is a still life, every plank of wood, stone, bush, step or branch tailored to be unlike its neighbour and yet working perfectly in harmony with it.

This could be exhausting. That it is not is tribute to the skill in creating and maintaining the garden where things seem to be incident and accident rather than over-meticulous performance.

There are few pots and there were none in Nicole's time. She apparently hated them, along with geraniums, red, yellow and orange. I always give a quiet three cheers for this type of quirkiness even if it clashes directly with my own preferences. The more opinionated, individual and provoking a garden can be, the more interesting and stimulating it usually is.

There are three levels. The first, reached through the house, is gravelled, with a table and chairs, stone troughs, walls and balls. The seemingly random stonework is all held exactly in place by precise wedges and fillets – a sign that for all the easy informality an exact eye is at work. Tightly clipped shrubs of box, myrtle and rosemary jostle in the space beneath the shade of tall pines. This is a place to sit and read and eat and talk, where the house and garden flow to and fro between each other.

The second level is reached by very steep, very narrow steps and has a stone pool built against the corner of limestone rock that supports the walls of the road and the house, so that both seem to grow from deep underground. The water is crystalline and throws spangles of light and shadows of plants against the stone. Entrances and paths are made so narrow that if, like me, you are broadish of shoulder and beam, you have to squeeze through.[1]

The garden hems itself about you, aromatic, rustling, tactile, and then releases into new, open space. It is an old trick this, perfected on a monumental scale by Luis Barragán in his gardens in Mexico, compressing space right down in order that it can be expanded out again when previously there was either too much or too little room for that to work. But it is beautifully done with the simplest of means in La Louve and that simplicity is in itself inspirational. The paths are made of bits and pieces of stone, tile and cobbles, carefully selected stone by stone, like the walls, and equally carefully positioned in relationship to each other but laid simply on or in the earth so there is not a hint of slickness but oodles of style.

More steps lead down to the largest part of this small garden where hundreds of lavender plants are set in dry dusty soil, each plant a glaucous mound and the same size but clipped alternately. There is the nod towards a crop and the lavender fields of the village as well as the formality of seventeenth-century French gardens. Yet it is very simple and easy on the eye. Very sophisticated. Very elegant. Terribly French.

There is a rhythm and flow to everything, contained and positioned by the cut-off flat tops to the cypresses, stone walls, balustrade, table tops and steps. Almost all the vertical lines are curved, leaning or drawn with a meandering hand, whereas most horizontals are clean cut both in shape and direction, straight lines following the walls, steps, edge of the stone pool and the flat terraced levels like decks of a ship. On this very steep site, with most of the garden always either above or below you, it creates balance and harmony.

Nicole de Vesian loved gardens but was not a 'good' gardener in any conventional sense. There was apparently no soil preparation, no thought of making compost and plants were plonked in – usually much too close together – wherever she thought they might look best, without any regard to conventional wisdom on where or how the plant might thrive. There have been some problems as a result of this but surprisingly few. I have long thought we mollycoddle garden plants too much. They are tougher than we tend to give them credit for. The right plant in the right place is what matters, not the plant correctly grown regardless of how it relates to everything around it.

After ten years Nicole sold up to make a new garden – at the age of eighty – nearby.[2] La Louve was bought by Judith Pilsbury, an American art dealer based in Paris, both as a southern second home and as a self-conscious work of art. From the outset she decided to curate the garden rather than make it her own in any way.

I asked Judith why she considered Nicole's garden a work of art and what differentiates a beautiful, original garden from an artwork. Her answer was that although she treated it as art, it probably was not made as anything other than a garden. Nicole dressed, ate, designed fabrics – and gardens – with the same fastidious care and superb attention to detail. She could not help but be artistic. In that spirit some people make art from everything they touch, however functional it is or how prosaic in lesser hands. In general a work of art probably has to declare itself early on. It is not something to be anointed after the event. Art has to be a deliberate act.

This seemed fairly contradictory but she added that art in a garden is the province of childhood. We love the gardens of our early years and inevitably they are gardens that we are intimate with. All the best gardens have a strong influence of memory and innocence. They are our Eden. Everything after this aspires to that. But for certain, she said, botany has nothing to do with art and horticulture very little. Despite the oft-used cliché, you cannot 'paint with flowers' but you can definitely sculpt with plants: the one thing

2 She had a heart attack and died before beginning the new garden.

that Judith said she had learnt from La Louve is to clip and clip often.

Accepting a garden exactly as it happened to be when you first saw it would normally be a recipe for the kind of paralysis that you can see in some historic gardens in the UK, but La Louve seems to live and breathe independently of its owners. This might be a testament to the way that it transcends horticulture to become a work of art, but I guess that this is also because it still feels in a state of becoming rather than a finished work, and it is still relatively young. Most gardens hit their mature stride at about twelve years old and can comfortably hold that for another twenty years before any radical reassessment is needed.

Judith Pilsbury's timing was spot on. She sold it in 2012, having enjoyed La Louve in its flying prime. Whether the new owners can continue to curate it as Nicole de Vesian's garden remains to be seen. Perhaps it will be completely changed. Perhaps it will become something even more beautiful or spectacular. But it is hard to conceive how La Louve could be improved or fit so exactly into the spirit of the place. If it is to change, I am glad that I saw it when I did.

From La Louve I took a taxi to Avignon's beautiful sleek upturned hull of a train station, had time for a coffee and caught the TGV right to the terminal at Charles de Gaulle airport. I was there inside three hours. It is perhaps the best travel experience to be had in Europe, and a very suitable way to end the visit to one of the best gardens I have ever seen.

7

MAS BENOÎT

At the western end of the Lubéron mountain range the land
becomes richer and is filled with thousands of orchards, all immaculately pruned, no doubt for maximum productivity but with a
flourish, like a dancer adding a twirl. I drove through at the end of
March when the blossom was out and it was an extraordinary thing,
field after narrow field of rows of sculpted trees posing in their
pretty flowering dresses.

I paid a visit to the outdoor sculpture studio of Marc Nucera at
Noves. Marc trained, in the way that the French would find completely natural and necessary, as a tree pruner, working in orchards.
He then applied these skills to decorative pruning and topiary,
taking the sliding curve from hedge trimming to topiary to land art
in an easy stride. His mentor was the garden designer and land artist
Alain David Idoux, who in turn was encouraged by Nicole de Vesian
at La Louve. Marc continues working in topiary but also increasingly
in wood and stone, financing his art by maintaining and overseeing
various gardens for clients. That easy interplay between sculpture
and horticulture would be more awkward and self-conscious in
Britain. Ian Hamilton Finlay pulled it off at Little Sparta but on the

whole we like our gardening 'experts' to be unsullied by anything as flaky as art.

Sculptors' studios are always glamorous and exciting, littered with work half done, unsold or awaiting collection, the rawness of half-worked material hunkered and clustered in groups often better than an isolated, finished work. Marc's studio covered a hectare, filled with work, often using trees that had died or fallen and were going to be turned into firewood. I use a chainsaw a great deal myself so am respectful of other people's work. I know the process, know how the eye and muscles have to work. But there has been one huge problem for anyone wielding a chainsaw with creative intentions in the past thirty years, and that is the work of the sculptor David Nash. He outshines almost anyone else working in the same medium, so that much that is otherwise admirable seems a poor imitation of his work. He has carved a hole through which almost everything else passes. Also, chainsaw sculpture often looks surprisingly thin and inadequate outside. Nash's work, which I admire beyond that of almost any other living artist, looks best within the white walls of a gallery. I once spent a day walking in the Forest of Dean Sculpture Trail and came across a carefully arranged mound of charred and pointed stumps in a clearing in the woods. It looked as much like the remnants of a bonfire as a piece of profound art and its impact was diffused and lost in the context of the trees around it. More sub-David Nash I thought. Just doesn't measure up to the real thing. It turned out, of course, to be a piece by the great man.

I followed Marc on his motorbike, one soft-shoed foot trailing alarmingly just centimetres from the road, for half an hour south towards the Alpilles and a village called Eygalières. It is a region of farms converted into villas by wealthy eurobusinessmen, swimming pools replacing ponds and irrigated lawns herb-strewn meadows. He showed me a house called Mas Benoît where his sculptural topiary is much in evidence. He is amazingly good at it and the combination of the highly stylised, Japanese-influenced tightly clipped trees and shrubs and the loose, parched landscape works well. I later found out that Mas Benoît is very much part of the itinerary for all the tasteful garden tours that progress around Europe, usually led by a highly knowledgeable guide and often taken by people whose own gardens either do or could feature in such a tour, rather like nineteenth-century tours of cathedrals, but specialising in gardens that people would otherwise not have access to.

I was shown the huge spiral marked with olives and a thick, low stone wall, and the doughnuts of lavender clipped around the bases of the gnarled old trees in the farm's olive grove, and the concept behind these things was explained at some length – although neither my French nor my concentration was good enough to remember quite what that concept was. But all that good taste and conceptual art did not amount to a good garden. Whereas La Louve was intimate, self-confident and felt as though the hand of its maker was everywhere, Mas Benoît – and I imagine so many other of these expensively laid-out and maintained gardens attached to the villas around it – felt installed and hollow. The skill, honesty and integrity are all there, the palette sophisticated and the plants work ecologically and environmentally with their surroundings. In short it has all the elements that well-informed, resourceful people draw upon when making ambitious modern gardens. But somehow the simple process of making a garden that exists for no other purpose than to please had got lost.

Of course I felt churlish even thinking these thoughts. Marc was utterly charming, went to great trouble and there is not a shred of cynicism in any of this work. And I loved some of the details of the topiary, such as the box that began clipped to form the backrest of a stone seat, then became bare stems before bursting out in loose, untrammelled foliage. This garden was my first brush with the French inclination to conceptualise and philosophise about the very practical. The idea of Mas Benoît was clearly the most interesting thing to everyone concerned and all the physical elements of the garden existed primarily to service those ideas. It seemed a long way from the instinctive, barely articulate intensity of Cézanne or Van Gogh that had drawn me to this region thirty years before.

A few kilometres west was Saint-Rémy, where Van Gogh stayed at the Saint Paul asylum in his madness, and beyond that Arles and the flat wetlands of the Camargue. I guiltily thanked Marc for all the trouble he had gone to, wished him well with his work and went west.

8

LES BEAUX

Encrusted on a promontory above the plain of the Alpilles is Les Beaux, whose position gave it military control of the area for millennia, with prehistoric occupation and a medieval population of over 3,000. This now numbers in the twenties. The castle was razed twice, in 1483 and again in the 1630s on the order of Cardinal Richelieu. What is left is a fossilisation of limestone and ruin, the ghosts of ramparts welded to geology. But it is beautiful and tourists do exactly as I did: wind up the hill, park and gawp and take pictures, stay a little and leave. Some stay and eat and get married – an elaborate wedding party was being prepared amongst the ruins when I was there – but the view is the thing.

From the battlements you look back over orchards and olive groves hedged by black cypresses to the Alpilles and across the Crau to Mont Sainte-Victoire like a lumpy liner on the horizon. Further south the marshy rice fields east of Arles peter out to the stony, dry, dead flat stretch across to Marseille. From this height all gardens are merged and invisible, the landscape defined by agriculture.

This is one of the oldest human landscapes in France, the flat-lands of the Crau and the Rhône delta fanning up and away in all directions from the sea, with ancient drove roads moving vast flocks

of cattle, sheep and goats away from the grass-shrivelled drought of
the stony plain to the pastures of the Alps, Nice, the Cévennes and
Cantal. Look down from Les Beaux one, two thousand years ago and
it would have seemed much the same.

A tour arrived, a gaggle of the elderly all in beige blousons and
bad shoes, so I slipped away. Not because I despised them but
because they were what I could, and probably will, so nearly be.

9

ARLES

My dear sister, I believe that at present we must paint nature's rich and magnificent aspects; we need good cheer and happiness, hope and love.

The uglier, older, meaner, iller, poorer I get, the more I wish to take my revenge by doing brilliant colour, well arranged, resplendent.[1]

On my way down to Aix in autumn 1973 the train pulled in at Arles. That was pretty exciting, given that the only thing I knew about Arles was that it was where Van Gogh had exploded in fifteen months of artistic genius. This same railway line, the old PLM (the Paris-Lyon-Méditerranée railway that was replaced by the TGV), was the one that he, and Gaugin, took when travelling to the town, and his house at Place Lamartine – the famous Yellow House – was just a short walk, almost in sight, from the station where I was waking to southern light. But that really does not count as 'visiting' Arles.

My visit proper was in March 1975. We went to the amphitheatre where the bullfights are held and had a picnic against the walled ruins of the theatre. I was with my brother and two American

1 Vincent Van Gogh, letter from Arles to his sister Willemien Van Gogh, Friday, 14 September 1889.

friends, Guy and Abbie. My brother had been involved in a bad car smash and we were on a recuperative trip, and I was gathering and sorting the stuff I had hurriedly left in Aix a couple of months before. Guy and Abbie had their little daughter in a pushchair. They both wore red sweaters. I have no memory of that visit at all and only know that it happened because I have a picture taken by my brother. I have never seen or heard from Guy or Abbie since then and remember only that he was a lawyer from San Francisco who gave up his job to study French for a year and that I liked them both very much. Their daughter must be nearly forty now.

In fact, when I recently visited Arles in March I did so entirely under the impression that it was the first time I had been there and remained under that illusion until just before my next visit in mid-summer, when I found the picture. The date is on the back of the photo: Wednesday, 26 March 1975. How many other places have I been to about which I can recall nothing at all? How many of the places I want to visit are triggered by memory rather than desire?

Thirty-seven years later to the day, I arrived in Arles in the dark, a modern traveller with no sense of place or direction. There was a road, buildings, lights. Just the 'where' of movement in time, but not place, that airports and chains of hotels inhabit. The hotel did its best to shatter that sense of anonymity by giving me a room across a yard and up a long flight of outdoor steps. It was small, damp and haunted. I never found out who the ghost was or looked like but I swear there was someone else in that room that night.

The next morning I was supposed to leave early but went in search of the hospital, Hôtel-Dieu, where Van Gogh was taken after severing his ear at the end of December 1888.[2] It remained the main hospital in Arles right up to the mid-1970s and did not cease to be a medical institution till the mid-1980s. It is now a Cultural Centre.

Arles is one of those towns that swallows your footsteps and it is astonishingly easy to get lost. Clutching a postcard of Van Gogh's painting *The Courtyard of the Hospital at Arles* and stopping to scrutinise the map every few streets, I found it eventually. The courtyard looked almost unchanged. Same paint, same layout, almost the same planting.[3] But my grandfather was alive when Van Gogh painted it and I remember him much better than I recall Guy or

2 Van Gogh cut off his ear (or perhaps part of it) on 23 December 1888. Despite severing an artery and losing a lot of blood, he delivered the severed flesh to the nearby brothel, then went back to the Yellow House and fell into a deep sleep. On 24 December he was taken to the Hôtel-Dieu but allowed back to the Yellow House at the beginning of January. After his release in the middle of February, his neighbours gathered a petition saying that his drinking was out of hand and 'His instability frightens all the inhabitants of that quarter, and above all the women and children.' He had become the local loony, the man raging at himself whose eye you assiduously do not catch. As a result he was locked up in a cell in the Hôtel-Dieu.

3 In a letter to his sister Willemien, written at the end of April 1889, when he was in hospital for care of his mental health, Van Gogh wrote, 'In front of these galleries an ancient garden with a pond in the middle and 8 beds of flowers, forget-me-nots, Christmas roses, anemones, buttercups, wallflowers, daisies etc. And beneath the gallery, orange trees and oleanders. So it is a painting chock full of flowers and spring-time greenery. However, three black, sad tree trunks cross it like snakes, and in the foreground four large sad, dark box bushes.'

Abbie.[4] I am not sure which was made more real by the comparison – the hospital courtyard or the painting.

Van Gogh plundered and filleted Arles for the twentieth century,
reducing every scene and street to a location or a simulacrum of the
'real' painting (almost invariably known through a reproduction). It
is extraordinary when you consider that he was only there for fifteen
months. He completed almost a work a day in that time, almost all
of which were painted locally – within walking distance – from life.
It was an artistic *blitzkrieg*, almost impossible to imagine or absorb,
and in many ways it is better to go to Arles pushing Van Gogh from
one's mind or, better still, blissfully unaware of his existence or
influence.[5]

Arles is dominated by the Rhône and the Rhône, at least to a
British eye accustomed to a big river being measured by the Thames
or Severn, is enormous, a great swathe of water cutting through the
landscape, and the huge container ships add a hard industrial edge
that makes Arles completely different to the holiday retreats of eastern Provence or even the land the other side of the Alpilles that is so
comfortably and conveniently served by the TGV. Ironically, until
the railway came, rivers were generally the quickest, safest, most
comfortable and reliable way to travel around France and sailing
down the Rhône from Lyon to Avignon was the acknowledged ideal
way to enter Provence.[6]

4 There may be a tiny link: my grandfather's family were in the jute trade in Dundee
which, at the end of the nineteenth century, was the centre of a huge international business. In autumn 1888 Van Gogh and Gaugin bought a 20-metre roll of jute to paint on
because it was cheap. It is too fanciful to think that this jute might have come from
Dundee but there is just the slenderest of historical straws to clutch at.
5 Not me. I remember going to the huge Van Gogh exhibition at the Hayward Gallery
in London in January 1969, when I was thirteen, and having to run from the gallery
because I found the intensity of his work impossibly overwhelming. I was scarcely
able to speak for hours afterwards.
6 The arrival of the railway in the 1850s completely destroyed the importance of the
vast fair that was held every July at Beaucaire, across the river from Tarascon and
halfway between Arles and Avignon. For centuries this had been one of the most
important international trading fairs in France, with the river bringing people from all
over the Mediterranean, but by the end of the nineteenth century it was a shadow of
itself, serving entertainment rather than commerce.

When I returned to Arles in mid-summer, I rejected both rail and river, flying to Marseille and travelling from there by car. I stayed at the majestically named Grand Hôtel Nord-Pinus, right in the centre of town in the Place du Forum.[7] This is the hotel where matadors have traditionally stayed before the bullfights in the amphitheatre and it reminded me of Cuba, locked in the style and charm of a 1950s film. The rooms are high and big with huge mirrors that the matadors dress in front of like nervous bridegrooms before walking the few hundred metres to the Roman amphitheatre to kill or be killed in their dance with the black bulls of the Camargue.

It was a Saturday, so after breakfast of fresh apricots and good bread in the square I walked down to the boulevard des Lices. This is where the bulls are released during the Easter féria and Féria du Riz in autumn,[8] and on Saturdays there is a huge market that lines either side of the road. White vans, bumper to bumper, form a corridor for the crowd to amble down, protecting the stalls. Almost anything is sold here, from every kind of fruit and vegetable to LPs, bowls in brilliant primary glazes and flick knives. I very nearly bought a flick knife myself but decided against it because I thought it might be difficult to explain away if I whipped it from my pocket and exploded out the blade to take a cutting on telly. The stallholder then showed me an alternative by inviting me to simulate an attack and waving a knife whose blade opened smartly using just one hand. The great virtue of this, he said, was that the other hand could block an attacker – like so. I assured him in bad French that I wanted

7 A corner of it, on rue de la Palais and Place du Forum, can be seen in Van Gogh's painting *The Café Terrace on the Place du Forum, Arles, at Night* which he painted in September 1888. The café is now called Café Van Gogh and has pools of tourists taking pictures of each other in front of it.

8 The *course camarguaise* is the localised version of the Spanish *corrida*. It traditionally involved cowboys, riding the local white horses, who brought the bulls into town with the intention of taking the scores of animals through the streets and back out to the meadows in one unbroken herd, whilst local youths tried to separate off individual bulls. In the ampitheatre the bulls are the stars, rather than the matadors, and the aim of the 'fighters' (*raseteurs*) is to remove a red ribbon, a pair of tassels or a piece of string from the bull's horns, using a special hook. In theory no one gets killed and great honour to all – including the bull – is accrued.

something to cut twine rather than throats. In the end I bought a lock-knife with a juniper wood handle, to add to the dozens I already have but keep on losing. In fact, I have already lost the juniper-handled one. It will probably turn up in the compost heap.

Great metal dishes of paella and oily meaty stews brewed and bubbled and there were stalls with ceramic bowls of honey from every individual plant of the region. French food is as good as any in the world with its wine, cheese, olives, herbs, hams, sausages, terrines and tomatoes, but the truth is that so little of this open generosity reaches restaurants. For some reason most restaurants in France have lost that link between the market and the dish that used to be umbilical thirty or forty years ago and which can still be found in every town and village in Italy.

The night before – tired after a long day's filming and certainly not as tolerant as I could or should have been – I had ordered a dish of monkfish with a pea purée at a restaurant in the square. The fish arrived cold and covered in a frothy sputum of uncertain provenance and the purée was a floury mix of peas and broad beans. I ate a little but left most of it. When she collected the plates the waitress asked what was wrong. I told her. After five minutes she returned with the manager to berate me for my lack of taste and to tell me that everyone else who had eaten that particular dish had enjoyed it, so therefore my criticisms were unfounded.

This is not an untypical response to criticism of anything served in French restaurants, particularly as you get more expensive and self-regarding. It is a curious mixture of cultural cringe and arrogance based, I think, on the working assumption that there is a correct way to prepare and enjoy food of all kinds. If you do not know what that way is or if you fail to exercise that knowledge, then you are not in a position to cast judgement. That all feeds back into the incredible deference the French have for authority, training, rank and status. A chef would not be a chef if he had not reached that position by being good. Therefore all chefs, by virtue of their status, are good. Therefore their food is good. The only point to debate is which one is the best. Whereas in reality a lot of French meals, especially expensive ones, are dreadful.

But you could bypass restaurants anyway by starting at one end of the market and nibble and taste and come out the other having eaten your fill for the day, as well as buying shoes, jewellery, 'exotic' underwear, a bunch of gazanias and bad furniture.

A gypsy band with scuffed shoes, stained shirts and drunken grins on seamed faces was loudly and drunkenly blowing its discordant tunes, haranguing the crowd with trumpet and trombone. The bass drum was broken and stuffed with a cushion and patched up with gaffer tape. Until the 1930s and the arrival of the gramophone and radio all music would have been like this – local bands playing half-well at weddings and dances or on street corners. The sound followed me round the town all morning and I could still hear it in the afternoon as I lay in the dark of my room and tried to snooze.

Arles is full of tourists, of course. Thousands of them, walking around either lost or in a guided gaggle. There is an appalling white train that pushes through the narrow streets, loaded with trippers. Even the Americans look embarrassed. But somehow Arles survives this humiliation. It is so beautiful and the Roman remains so prevalent and the town so unspoiled and so adept at incorporating the very old and the new[9] and the slightly faded without constantly trying to patch and replace, that it shrugs all this nonsense off like an unfortunate piece of clothing. The silly train and the badly dressed tourists pay for it all. The French coolly tolerate them whilst managing to keep hold of their souls. It is a smart trick.

Having found it harder and harder to get good food in France, I did have a superb lunch at Chez Caro, in a side street off the Place du Forum, while I sat watching the waiters from the Hôtel Nord-Pinus carrying trays of dishes from the kitchen at the back of the building down the side street to the tables in the square like medieval pages.

Sitting in the sun, drinking my third glass of lovely Domaine du

9 . . . up to a point: the railway and canal cut straight through the Roman necropolis.

Pas de l'Escalette (hence the snooze) with teams of swifts chasing through the sky above the Place du Forum, I thought about the cultures of grass as opposed to the cultures of soil and stone. Northern Europe uses grass to fill all the spaces: there is a green backdrop to life, as noticeable by its absence as its presence. But the south does not have that at all. Stone and earth blend. We northerners tend to think of the south as being fiery and bright and hot, but in truth it is a faded, soft place, which is what Nicole de Vesian got so exactly right at La Louve. But try and replicate that under a cold grey sky and you have unrelieved drabness – which is why you need the green.

10

LA CHASSAGNETTE

About twenty minutes south of Arles, as you go through the flat marshlands of the Camargue with their deeply ditched fields of rice, white horses[1] and black bulls, fenced by rushes attached to riven fencing posts, you come to the restaurant La Chassagnette in the hamlet of Le Sambuc. This was the first wholly organic restaurant in France to be awarded a Michelin star and it sources the vast majority of its fruit, vegetables and herbs from its own two-hectare vegetable garden.

The restaurant itself is predictably sleek and stylish in that pared-down rural style that the more expensive holiday resorts specialise in. That is fine and good. The food is not cheap here. Diners come from far and wide and want the whole experience. It feels like a special place. For those eating outside – and most, it seems, do – the tables are painted a lovely shade of glaucous blue fading to green that you see on shutters in Arles and are sheltered under a canopy of vines. If that is not protection enough, there are big woven baskets to

---

1 In fact the tough little white horses of the Camargue are born brown and only develop a white coat after they are two years old. They are one of the oldest breeds in the world and are completely at home in the wetlands of the region, with exceptionally broad hooves for their size.

dip into, filled with hats to shade both diners and dinner. You can stroll round the garden before eating and there is a generous mix of flowers, vegetables and herbs in the area nearest to the restaurant: all handsome and all, I was assured, planted and used in earnest, including a wide range of the flowers. But step through a gap in the hedge and the garden gets down to business. For the gardener, this is when it becomes really interesting.

Restaurants are fiercely pressurised places and to set out to be essentially self-sufficient creates a kind of stress that gardens, commercial or private, rarely have to deal with. It goes without saying that the kitchen expects not just enough quantity of a wide range of ingredients but the very best quality – measured by any standards anywhere.

The man responsible for this, Claude Pernix, seems remarkably relaxed about it and has a ready grin, and is keen, as all gardeners are with each other, to discuss the details of particular crops. His work has been made easier by the enlightened approach of the head chef, Armand Arnal, who, as well as having superb talent, has the confidence to be relaxed about that which he cannot control.

Every Thursday, he and Claude go through the crops that will be at their best for the coming week and Armand builds his menu around them, rather than treating the garden as a wholesaler and hunting for ingredients for the dishes he wishes to make. Both men see themselves as working together to make the most of what is at its best, with the kitchen at the service of the produce as much as the garden serves the kitchen. Although one might think that this was the essence of all good food, it is surprisingly rare and goes against the dreadful trend of chefs using the kitchen to display the range of their talents rather than the quality of the food.

At La Chassagnette gardener and cook really know what they are about and will, for example, use three different tomatoes in one dish to harness the particular qualities of each variety, marinading a piece of fish in a very fresh sauce made from the juices of 'Black Russian', served with another variety chopped raw and a third roasted and by the same token choosing the varieties that they grow for their ability to perform in that particular clay soil and harsh climate. The chef has to have a deep and intimate understanding of how all the ingredients grow at every stage of the year. Perhaps the grower has to have the same level of knowledge about how it is to be prepared and eaten to create the perfect food.

The cliché of the male gardener plonking a basket of prize-winning produce on the kitchen table and then leaving the female cook to prepare it has as little to do with good food as the vainglorious chef seeking applause for his handiwork using unseasonal mass-produced ingredients from the other side of the world. There has to be synthesis.

The willingness to marry what the plant, grower and chef all do best is completely in tune with the organic ideal, which is to interfere as little as possible so as to produce the healthiest, tastiest ingredients. That means having a deep understanding of how things grow in that particular place, rather than a generalised knowledge – often alarmingly limited – that is applied regardless of circumstance. In other words, there has to be a watchful modesty about the whole process. You harness and steer rather than bully crops to perform.

So Claude is constantly fine-tuning his methods and techniques. He was very keen to show me the way that he made raised beds from the heavy soil and then covered them with a few centimetres of river sand. A root crop would be sown in drills into this and a salad crop oversown above it. This has a number of advantages. The salad leaves are cut before the root crops developed, and without harming them in any way, and then, when ready, the roots can be pulled clean from the sand. Finally the sand is worked into the soil and gradually it lightens.

He had fine-tuned onion and garlic production too, sowing them in ridges to improve baking in the sun and to avoid fungal problems by sitting in heavy damp soil.

I saw much of the sowing when I visited in March and then tasted the harvest when I went back a few months later on midsummer's day. By then the tomatoes were being harvested – and they grow 1,000 through to November. There were some astonishingly large beefsteak varieties, their meaty flesh bulging beneath the thinnest of skins which would be easily damaged in the rough and tumble of mass production, as well as being hard to transport, but their taste was beyond anything I had experienced before, with a soaring intensity and yet a clarity that was not overwhelming. In fact, once savoured I wanted to go straight back for more. Which I did.

The mid-summer garden was surprisingly weedy by house-proud garden standards, but I have noticed that the French often tolerate weeds in a way that the British do not, especially in gardens that are proudly 'bio' or organic, as though it gives them a kind of rough, unshaven veracity. There is also the fact that this is a working plot, not made to be admired for its upkeep but measured solely by its produce.

In the restaurant there was a blackboard with '*Le Bonheur est dans le potager*' artfully scrawled, along with a little sketch of a bunch of flowers, but the tomatoes, each lumpily individual, that were bringing such *bonheur* to the diners were transported in plastic crates and the only writing in the potting shed was on a wall of square slates hanging on nails, with plant names scrawled on to them. Very stylish but remorselessly practical.

Although I tasted the produce of the field in the field, by the time it had been through the machinations of the kitchen it had assumed a price way beyond my reach. So I set off to find lunch elsewhere.

For all the unspoilt romanticism of the Camargue, with its particular and strange mixture of animals, birds and crops, it can appear a bleak, windswept, salt-soaked place with malaria and that sense of land only just clinging to itself. You can take the car ferry across the Rhône at Salin de Giraud, which takes you back towards Marseille and Salon de Provence or carry on looping back north towards Arles into the Parc naturel régional de Camargue. The waters of L'étang de Vaccarès appear on your left and the flat monotony becomes fascination, with flocks of flamingoes, hen harriers and black kites, and sea lavender growing by the side of the road. Continue on north, and there is a little restaurant called La Telline on your right, looking like a private house. It is small, simple and unpretentious and serves the best food I have eaten in France for years. On the mantlepiece a collection of old irons and eight radios balance on top of each other on a sideboard. And two wooden ducks. It has the character, food and service of forty years ago, which is to say the soul and straightforward connection with place that makes for the best of all food.

The restaurant takes its name from the clams gathered from the étang and a plate of them, small, pebble-like, each one a mere morsel, with a glass of cold rosé, is a lovely way to start a meal. Then local beef or eels cooked on the open fire in the dining room with the area's fabulous wild rice and perhaps a glass of Côtes du Rhône, and finally little meringues, another Arlesian speciality, served with your coffee. Then ideally a snooze, or at the very least someone else to drive.

11

NÎMES

On one occasion I flew from Birmingham to Marseille and noted that the ticket was really quite expensive – over £100 – given the harassed and begrudging nature of all modern cheap travel. However, despite the sense of being herded out at the destination like an unwelcome hitchhiker, there is the inevitable relief and pleasure of setting foot on French soil. On this particular trip I then took a taxi to Nîmes, a journey that takes about an hour to cover the eighty-odd kilometres. It cost over 200 francs. Other than stopping the vehicle and getting out to hitch the rest of the way there is nothing to be done, and a kind of hysterical inevitability kicks in as the meter scales new heights.

In fact all travel has historically been either very expensive or hideously uncomfortable and often both. The diligences[1] were an ordeal where passengers were packed in like sardines and alternately freezing cold or insufferably hot. French roads were famously

1 Diligences were the standard large stage coaches of the nineteenth century that worked the roads of France. They had two internal compartments and a third on top protected by a leather curtain. They were big lumbering things, taking the best part of four days of extreme discomfort to go from Lyons to Paris.

bad, save for the immediate area around Paris, and trains ran well between major cities but did not make a truly national network until the 1880s. If you had sufficient money there was a golden age between the end of the nineteenth and the last quarter of the twentieth centuries, and by the 1970s we were all getting wealthier to the point that the student could dip a toe into what had become an actively pleasurable experience. I recall that even the cheapest flight would serve a meal with any drink you chose as a matter of course.

It has always been the case that it is much easier and quicker to travel up and down France than across it, but French trains are very good and cheap and the TGV is a marvel. Once you are commuter distance away from Paris the *péages* are empty and very fast but their very ease filters the experience of France entirely down to the inside of your hermetic car. But any of this is better than taking a taxi.

That particular trip was rounded off by arriving as it got dark at one of the modern pods that are the hotel equivalent of cheap flights. It houses, waters and washes you but in a niggardly fashion – as though seeing how little they can get away with providing. Nevertheless it was right in the centre of town, with the amazingly intact Roman arena across the square from the Boulevard de la Libération. I had spent a night in Nîmes thirty years before but saw little beyond tantalising glimpses of perfect Roman remains integrated with great style into the town, like a sleeker, more sophisticated Arles. I wanted to explore more.

Tired, waiting to meet companions who rang me to say that they had eaten on the train from Paris, and having a very early start the next day, I dined at the hotel. You know what you are letting yourself in for when you make that decision. It is an act of submission. Still, I saw that the menu had sardines and figured that this was France and we were not far from the Mediterranean so ordered them as my first course with a steak to follow. Minutes later the waiter arrived and placed a plate in front of me. On it were an opened tin of sardines, a piece of toast and a few salad leaves. I was caught between complaining and applauding. It was triumphantly anti-cuisine, like ordering a casssoulet and being served a tin of baked beans with a spoon in it.

I left before dawn the next day, as the coaches drew up in the empty square and started loading hundreds of suitcases belonging to the trippers being shunted on to the next stage. I never saw anything more of Nîmes. Next time.

12

MONASTÈRE DE SOLAN

I left Nîmes early to go north to visit a nunnery. Not just any common or garden nunnery either, but a Greek Orthodox one,[1] tucked away in remote countryside about seventeen kilometres north of Uzès and twenty-four kilometres west of Orange. It is entirely self-sufficient and the nuns are vegan, which makes the quality and quantity of their harvest more than a pastime. It matters.

Not only was there the frank curiosity, after a lifetime of visiting gardeners, of the first visit to gardening nuns, but also the slightly more elevated motive of seeing a working monastic garden as an insight into one of the prime historical sources of the potager. The monastic tradition of not just being self-sufficient in all that they ate but also trading profitably and sometimes aggressively seemed to be alive and well at Monastère de Solan.

We parked by a very modern, rather beautiful winery, all honey-coloured limestone blocks and redolent of efficiency, money and style. It seemed at odds with what I had been told about the order of nuns, who were largely silent, incredibly hard-working and devout.

1 This part of Languedoc has a long tradition of religious unorthodoxy. Uzès had one of the first Jewish communities in France and was strongly Protestant during the religious persecutions of the fifteenth and sixteenth centuries.

I learnt later that the stone for the building was local, from the Pont du Gard quarry at Vers, just fifty kilometres away, and was half the price of concrete, which was the only viable alternative material that would provide sufficient insulation to achieve the coolness that the winery needed. In other words as well as being efficient and stylish, it was also cheap.

The same stone has been used for all the buildings that have accrued piecemeal over the past 800 years, which added an architectural harmony to the slightly unsettling combination of focussed and frankly busy contemplation. All the nuns – dressed in black from their tightly wrapped headpieces to their stout boots or shoes – moved briskly. None spoke. In fact because this was a day when visitors were entertained speech was permitted, but in lives dominated by silence and plainsong, the habit of chatter had long been lost.

The mother superior, who had been at the monastery since its current foundation twenty years ago and turned out to be an astonishingly young-looking Cypriot who spoke very good English, showed me their vegetable garden. I am not sure what I expected to see exactly, possibly some continuation of the cloistered range of buildings, probably rather ornate and structured, with bowers, masses of herbs and enclosed from the world. It was none of these things.

We walked down a dusty path to an open field of a hectare or so devoted simply to the production of as many vegetables as possible. It was enticingly scruffy without in any way being shoddy. What is done is done well but what is not necessary is not done at all. There were large heaps of compost and dung covered with black polythene and irrigation pipes running the length of rows of seedlings. The water for plants and nuns alike all comes from their own borehole. A low electric fence ran round one section. To keep off the *sangliers*, I was told. Such a nuisance! Everything about this looked and felt like a place of work.

There was the full range of crops that anyone might grow in that climate – tomatoes, great rows of cucumbers, aubergines, peppers, beans, onions, garlic, carrots, potatoes – and also vast swathes of squashes. I asked why they grew so many. After all, a pumpkin plant takes up a great deal of space for relatively small return compared to the intensity of a root crop or rows of dwarf beans. Mother Superior smiled sweetly and politely explained that they grew and stored well. When your well-being if not your existence depends upon it, then that combination of qualities becomes the primary consideration when choosing what to grow.

A line of ten black-clad figures crouched close together, some in broad-brimmed rush sunhats, all cowled, hand weeding carrots. It was a scene that would have looked exactly the same 800 years ago. The nuns do all the manual work, from tilling the ground to weeding to harvesting to preparing and cooking the food to washing the dishes. The fruits of their labours.

A row of apricot trees hung heavy with bright orange fruits and a cat slinked amongst the weeders, rubbing the occasional favoured shank. A bell tolled. It was six o'clock. The nuns gathered their buckets of weeds and hurried from the field. Mother Superior asked if I would join them for dinner. I said that I would love to. When did they dine? Now, she said. Come with me.

Dinner was in the refectory and taken in complete silence save for a reading – rather a loud reading – from a volume of theological history. There were four long tables with nuns and a couple of visitors already seated at them. I was shown to a seat at the end of one and Mother Superior went up to the head table where she joined the Patriarch with his long white beard and the hair on his large heavy head scraped back under a tall flat-topped hat. He was the first male I had seen and rather shocking. I immediately thought of the inverse of a bee colony, with the nuns as drones and workers rushing around feeding the king bee sitting solemnly at the centre. He said grace in a deep voice and then everyone set to with real gusto. The food, which was set before each place in metal bowls and eaten off metal plates, was perfectly good – a potato cake, mangetout peas, a kind of courgette terrine (those squashes), salad and apple purée – but plain.[2] The apricot chutney by my plate was welcome. If you have to eat only what you produce then the chances are it will be repetitive and bland, so any kind of condiment or relish will become as important as the ingredients it is enhancing.

After about fifteen minutes the patriarch rung a little bell and the nuns immediately stopped eating and bowed their heads. The reading, thank heavens, stopped. More grace was said and everyone left rather quickly. The whole affair took no more than twenty minutes.

By the time I got outside everyone was back at work. Mother Superior told me that they spend about five hours every day in

2 Cooking, like every other household work, is done on a rota. I asked the mother superior if some nuns were better cooks than others. She smiled and said carefully that sometimes she was glad that the rota allowed a few weeks to pass before certain sisters returned to the kitchen . . .

services, with much of that time spent singing. This is the only music that they have access to. On top of this, and as well as growing and preparing all their own food and doing the housework, they run a winery, make jams, vinegars, preserves, oils and ice creams and then sell it in an incredibly well-run, sleek shop and at the market in Uzès. Lunch is at ten, dinner at six and for the rest of the time they either work, sing or pray. They are busy people.

I was given a guided tour of the winery, of which they are rightly proud. It is a beautifully designed, environmentally efficient, minimalist building that is as cool as a cave within the pitted honey limestone of its walls. Fresh oak barrels glowed tawny in the dark and made the air rich with that coopery tannin fragrance. An electric forklift ran on the rubber floors, moving the palettes of cased wine high on to storage racks. Any hint that this was a sideline or even some kind of indulgence is dispelled instantly. This is a good wine produced that is treated exactly as a very modern commercial winery would.

Much of the fruit is made into jams or jellied blocks like marmelo and contributes to the thirteen different flavours of vinegar that they sell. Herbs are dried and added to soap and vinegar as well as sold in packets. It is a business aimed at surviving and must be how most medieval monastic houses were run. Outside prayer, which was the framework of their days, there was work of the most practical kind.

But the nuns' lives are full of contradictions. The relentless rigour of hard work combined with a blithe happiness that they palpably carried. All the nuns laughed and smiled a great deal. They never used phones, radio, TV, internet, newspapers or musical instruments, yet had twenty-first-century efficiency and systems in their commerce. They denied themselves much but their shop is as full of material temptation as the best delicatessen or National Trust outlet.

Perhaps this is true of all sects or cults, where the insiders have an especially carefree air because they have let responsibility for this world go and placed it in the hands of the cult leader – in this case a combination of the Patriarch, Jesus and God. What they did have that dispelled any of my cynicism was great dignity and respect for the outside world. They always had visitors staying and taught a great deal. In all theirs seemed a deeply attractive life.

13

CÉVENNES

I walked across the Cévennes in November 1981. A friend was writing a book of walks in France[1] and I tagged along for a couple of them. We followed the route of Robert Louis Stevenson, who wrote an account of his walk in 1878 called *Travels with a Donkey in the Cévennes*. This is a grand title for a painfully slow journey that still only took him twelve days, but like all the best stories, it was a disaster from start to finish. His donkey, which he named Modestine, was lazy, on heat and completely uninterested in accompanying Stevenson anywhere, let alone trudging through the empty wastes of the Cévennes.[2]

Unencumbered with a donkey[3] but carrying full camping kit (I still have the tent I bought specially for the trip), we walked thirty to fifty kilometres a day, wearing, I seem to recall, stout brogues rather

1 *Long Walks in France*, Adam Nicolson, photographs by Charlie Waite (Weidenfeld & Nicolson, 1983). Adam was younger than my children are now when he wrote this book and it still stands up as wise, incredibly well informed and beautifully written. Charlie's pictures are amazing too.
2 Stevenson did not really reach the Cévennes until halfway through his journey, at La Bastide-Puylaurent, starting at Le Monastier in the Haute Loire.
3 Although lacking a donkey, we were joined for a couple of days by a beautiful hound. We could not find an owner and the police were entirely uninterested. In the end we called a taxi at Le Bleymard to take him back to Chasseradès and hopefully to his rightful home and owner.

than modern hiking gear, and staying in hotels if open (not many were) but otherwise pitching our tents by streams.

I remember the Cévennes being astonishingly empty of people and animals, a countryside seemingly abandoned, although there were villages and wisps of smoke rising from farmsteads. We certainly never saw another walker in the seven days it took us. Historically this area was always inhabited in a very scattered fashion, with hundreds of hamlets of perhaps just a dozen people, each one the centre of a tiny world circumscribed by half a day's walk in any direction. One of the extraordinary things about France well into the nineteenth century seems to have been the difficulty of counting the population because people were so hard to find.[4]

It was cold and pretty bleak, although we were young and enjoyed each other's company, so it was fun, and the empty vastness of France compared to the pretty clutter of Britain is always stimulating and exciting. Walking through any landscape, feeling its stones and slips beneath your feet and the meaning of gradient in your weary legs, tells you so much more than any map or scrutiny from a car window can ever do. Walk a hundred kilometres and you know something of that land. Drive through it and you merely know where it is.

Mont Lozère was the first ski resort of any kind I had ever seen, and the chair lifts and chalets stood like industrial ruins in the cold granite landscape. The first snowfall would smooth away and hide it all, but for the moment it seemed at once derelict and unfinished. At 2,000 metres the air was thin and the walking noticeably harder.

South of Mont Lozère the landscape showed signs of regeneration, with farms clearly being done up as holiday homes. Thirty years later this is the norm and the Cévennes has become a

---

4 Stevenson described it as 'one of the most beggarly countries in the world ... like the worst of the Scottish Highlands only worse.' But then he was lovesick (the walk was partly an effort to take his mind off the departure to America of the object of his passion) and lumbered with a sexed-up donkey. These things incline one to a splenetic view of the world.

fashionable, even trendy, place for Parisian and Lyonnais lawyers and smart professionals to have their second homes. It seems better that than the dereliction which would have meant losing houses and holdings altogether.

This area south of Mt Lozère was the home of the Camisards and the perceived stronghold of Protestant resistance to the Catholic hegemony in the sixteenth and seventeenth centuries. Louis XIV systematically set about wiping them out[5] and in doing

5 In 1685 Louis revoked the Edict of Nantes (1598) which had allowed Protestants to observe their religious practices peacefully. A quarter of a million Protestants left France at the end of the seventeenth century, with Huguenots settling in Spitalfields in London at that time, but the Cévennes had been a fiercely loyal Protestant stronghold and so was a focus for both support and repression. By 1700, sixty Camisards (so-called because of the dark peasant smock or *camisa* worn in the Cévennes) had been executed and more than 300 sent to the galleys. In 1702, the Abbé du Chayla, one of the chief persecutors of the Protestants, was murdered at Pont de Montvert at the base of Mont Lozère, triggering riots that involved burning Catholic churches and murdering their priests. For a year the Cévennes was uncontrollable and independent but in the winter of 1703/4, using the new roads, nearly 500 villages were burnt and their inhabitants massacred. The rebellion continued for another seven years with continued brutal repression but was finally crushed in 1710. It has not been forgotten by the twenty-first-century Cevennois.

so had to build some of the best roads in the kingdom because the population was so dispersed throughout the mountainous terrain. These roads, built at the end of the seventeenth and beginning of the eighteenth centuries, were routed along the mountain spines and specifically designed for his troops – in particular the artillery – to get into the region and then rain shells and gunfire down on to the Protestant villages below until the troops were able to go down and kill the inhabitants without resistance.

Robert Louis Stevenson made a detour that almost doubled back on itself from Pont de Montvert to Florac, which we did not do, continuing straight to Cassagnas. Florac had been one of the frontier towns of Catholic/Protestant clashes, but by the late 1870s Stevenson found the two branches of Christianity living side by side in the town, 'in mutual toleration and mild amity'.

Stevenson does not mention the mulberry trees that are found all over the Cévennes. Perhaps in winter, without their leaves (although they are one of the last trees to shed their leaves in autumn), they were not significantly conspicuous. However, the mulberry was one of the key commercial features of life in the region for much of the nineteenth century, and they can still be found everywhere in the Cévennes and across the Rhône valley into Provence. This is *Morus alba*, the white mulberry, whose foliage is the food of the silkworm, *Bombyx mori*.

Silk, which came from China, was enormously valued, not least because it was enormously expensive, and towns like Lucca in Italy built civic fortunes on its trade and latterly its production. James I tried to establish a silk industry in Britain at the beginning of the seventeenth century[6] and Henri IV planted mulberries at the Tuileries at around the same time, specifically to provide fodder for

6 Buckingham Palace, then Buckingham House, was planted with one of the first of Britain's mulberry groves specifically for breeding and rearing silk worms. But the wrong kind of mulberry trees were planted – *Morus nigra* rather than *M. alba* – and the business failed.

French silkworms.[7] Planting of mulberries continued throughout the eighteenth century and French sericulture reach its peak in the first half of the nineteenth century, with a huge trade.

The mulberries were pollarded to produce fresh young growth with tender leaves, which were cut and taken into the farmhouses where the worms were reared, often in the attics or kitchens as they were the warmest places. Initially the worms ate sparingly but as they grew their appetites became ravenous and vast quantities of leaves had to be gathered, with coarser ones from older growth used as the worms grew larger. This meant managing the trees so that there was a big enough supply of new growth. Unwanted leaves were used to feed goats. The worms ate constantly, with a sound like heavy rain filling the valleys. When they had spun their cocoons they were taken to towns like Anduze for the silk to be gathered and processed. This business brought prosperity to the region but meant that farms became neglected in favour of this cash crop.

However all this came to a crashing end at the beginning of the 1840s, when a silkworm sickness began to spread and cripple production. In 1865 Louis Pasteur was asked to help and he went to Alès, just north of Anduze, where he eventually discovered a microbe that was spreading through the moth and its eggs. A cure was found by 1870 but it was too late. Cheap silk was now being brought in from the East via the newly opened Suez Canal. The silk-weaving industry was still going strong but production had gone global and the need for a huge supply of mulberry leaves no longer existed. The mulberries were allowed to grow out (which is why so many have broomstick heads on a clean trunk, after years of pollarding) and the peasants returned to their neglected and degraded farms.

7 Le Brun, the painter who worked on Vaux le Vicomte and Versailles, was put in charge of all artwork relating to the silk industry and French silk fabrics became fashion leaders in Europe in the eighteenth century which in turn meant that silk weaving in France was considered the finest outside China. By the end of the eighteenth century the French silk industry, centred around Lyon, had overtaken the Italian one which had brought such colossal wealth to Lucca.

Like Robert Louis Stevenson in 1878, back in 1981 we finished our walk in St Jean du Gard, clearly leaving the Cévennes and moving into softer, better-heeled country. Now, thirty years later, I wanted to head back into the Cévennes again, albeit the very southern edge of it, to visit a garden that exemplifies the new breed of farmers and smallholders that have taken to the area since I made that walk so many years ago. But first I went to a garden just a short distance away that I had been meaning to visit for a very long time.

14

LA BAMBOUSERAIE

La Bambouseriae is about fifteen minutes east of St Jean du Gard, and not far from the little town of Anduze (very touristy in summer). I visited in early spring when the cherries and magnolias were just in flower but otherwise everything was still quite bare. This is harsh country and gets harsher as you go up into the mountains. Winter is very cold and summer blisteringly hot and spring was yet to decide which way it would turn.

La Bambouseraie is now a large established garden visited by tens of thousands of people every year, but as with so many great gardens, it was the work of one individual fixated by an idea. All extraordinary gardens begin life as a dream that is just as real for the dreamer as any reality. The garden then follows in its wake. The dreamer in this instance was a man called Eugène Mazel. He was a merchant who made a fortune importing spices from the Far East and in 1855 bought an estate just outside Anduze. He was looking specifically for land suitable for growing the plants that he had become obsessed by in the East, most of which were almost unknown in France at that time. He already had a garden in Saint-Jean-Cap-Ferrat and he moved the plants from there to Anduze, with its ideal microclimate, to form the basis of his collection.

The site had no water supply so in 1864 he built a canal, both over ground and in conduits underground, to bring water the three kilometres from the river Gardon, so he could make the existing lakes and water works as well as providing a reliable source of irrigation, before rechannelling the overflow back to the river. It took two years to construct and the cost was enormous but it meant that he could grow the bamboos that needed a moist, warm climate in this erratic, fundamentally inhospitable place. At its peak his new garden employed forty full-time gardeners but in 1890 he went bust and the park was impounded by the bank. Twenty years later they sold it to Gaston Nègre, who saved the collection. One of Nègre's descendants still runs the garden.

I knew this story and had seen many pictures of the garden. I have also seen bamboos growing in places like the West Indies and Thailand, where they have a scale and rhythm that is magnificent. I expected a horticultural distillation of those qualities allied to the idiosyncrasy of obsession which is such an essential component of any good garden. But if these things are there, they could not be found on the day I visited.

You arrive via car park, shop and undistinguished entrance. This is not in itself a criticism – all the complications of public access and parking have to be fitted around and after the creation of any garden is long laid out. But it both dampens the experience and builds up expectations. It had better be good. Good it is, but with the nagging and eventually overwhelming sense that it is not good enough. The truth is that the bamboo is lovely but everything else is pretty hideous. Given that it is, after all, a self-professed bamboo garden with an overwhelming ratio of bamboo to all the other plants put together, one might think that the good outweighed the bad, but a garden cannot work like that. There has to be a harmony and sense of unity that can survive bits you like less than others, and this is ruined unless the whole thing more or less works together.

Individual bamboo canes have a slightly arthritic, swollenjointedness that adds substance to the silkiness of their lines and texture and I like them very much indeed. Add to that the various colours that bamboo will grow in – black, bright yellow and all shades of ochre, rich green, a dusky, smoky purple – and the way that it can be little more than upright fingers of grass or great tree trunks the thickness of a (slimmish) waist, and you have a plant with real elegance and beauty. But bamboo looks good primarily because of the gaps between the canes, especially if they can be kept trimmed and clean of wispy side growth and the floor mulched with its own foliage. The rhythm of these canes growing tall and straight, five, ten metres tall, repeated a dozen, a score, a hundred times, is beautiful, and then when you have some slanting diagonally, adding movement and energy, the whole thing comes alive.

Now La Bambouseraie has all this in spades. The bamboos are terrific. But the setting, with the fake Dragon Valley, is kitsch and out of kilter with their simple elegance. You half expect it to be called Bamboo World, with a train to take you round sections of bamboo from each different region of the globe. The whole idea of the place is a kind of colonisation, absorbing these very foreign plants in a very French space and doing so in a colossal way, so that instead of these foreign cultural influences making France more diverse they are absorbed and made French.

It always feels churlish to criticise something that is obviously a sustained labour of love and gives so many people such pleasure. Tens of thousands of families visit and clearly have a good time. The cherries were all in flower at the end of March when I was there and they were exquisite. There was a huge avenue of magnificent *Sequoia sempervirens* (D. Don), the coast redwood introduced to the West by my forebear a couple of hundred years ago. That gave me a little glow of dynastic pride. There was a simply enormous *Magnolia grandiflora*, the biggest I have ever seen. To anyone who loves plants these things are exciting. But none of this supplies the heart that every garden must have. Plants alone do not make a garden. There has to be more. After looking forward to seeing it for so long, it was a great disappointment.

Just as I was beginning to really dislike the place, I turned a corner and my growing grumpiness and rather lofty disapproval melted away. A rectangle of bamboo stems, perhaps three metres by six, had been gilded so that, looking into the mass of green upright canes, there was a clean-edged gold rectangle shining from the striated shadows. It was completely, breathtakingly beautiful, both in concept and execution.[1]

La Bambouseraie sponsors a pair of artists each year to come and work in the garden, giving them a grant, inspiration and exhibition space. It is a noble scheme that immeasurably improves the garden both in practice and concept. Time and again in France I came

1 Gold leaf proper takes great skill to apply, using a fine brush and the grease from one's nose to lift and place the sheets that are thinner than the finest coat of paint. It has a nasty habit of curling and folding up into itself and reducing to nothing. The artist, Cécile Andrieu, would have used false gold leaf, which is easier but still needs skill and great patience to apply smoothly and evenly. It would have taken a long time and immense care.

across this easy relationship between everyday horticulture and the principles and ideals of high art. This did not make the gardening any better and did not mean that the art is any good – at Séricourt in the Pas de Calais the garden was filled with an exhibition of dreadful sculpture – but the relationship and the intention elevates everything. And in this case made the journey to La Bambouseraie wholly worthwhile.

15

LES SAMBUCS

As the crow flies,[1] it is just twenty-five or so kilometres from St Jean du Gard to the little hamlet of Le Villaret, but the incredibly twisty mountain road will take a dramatic but stomach-churning hour and it is much easier to go south via Ganges and then back up into the hills again.

At the height of summer, I was on my way back to visit a small garden, or perhaps a garden in a smallholding, called Les Sambucs. I had been introduced to it in spring when, although the almond blossom was spectacularly out, the hillsides were still leafless and stripped. It was now full-leafed and sweltering and the black blazes of last year's fire damage had become a warning more than a reminder.

Les Sambucs was made and run in the spirit of the *soixante-huitards* who gravitated to the Cévennes in the 1970s and '80s to live a reasonably alternative life unencumbered by too much Parisian bureaucracy. If it was an unforgiving place to eke out a living, at least there were plenty of empty houses that could be rented cheaply.

1 In the Cévennes, which has some of the best birdlife in the whole of France, especially of raptors, the bird could be a golden eagle, griffon vulture or, at night, a Eurasian eagle owl. Despite the continuing penchant for shooting songbirds for sport or pâté, France has a fabulously diverse and rich ornithology.

Uncomplicated maths will tell you that anyone remotely involved in the '68 riots would have to be in their early sixties by now. As Cevennois they have paid their dues and if they can make that life pay their rent and wages, then they know as much as anyone about how to manage the soil, climate and austerity.

Nicholas Bruckin had an English father but was brought up in France. He is a bear of a man, a burly Viking with hands like spades and a twinkle in his eye. He and his wife Agnes have ten hectares where they have chestnut woodland, grow vegetables and have made a garden. They run a restaurant and B & B but above all they live off and in the place. Theirs is the peasant tradition in the most honourable manner. To be clear: a peasant is one who lives off the land. There will be cash crops to purchase what cannot be grown but the goal of work is survival, not profit. In practice one of the most available cash crops was the time and labour of the individuals, who would often be forced to work for others to raise money. Many small British farmers work full time as lorry drivers, teachers or digger drivers simply to finance their real lives running their patches of land. Peasant culture in Britain died in the eighteenth century, if not the seventeenth, as industrialisation meant that people's labour could earn them far more than their work on the land. But with it went the connection to place that comes with daily contact and graft and is expressed in the hands and aching muscles and passed on in the blood.

The house that they live in formerly belonged to Agnes's grandmother. Where the garden now is, below the road into the village that curves around a little valley, the grandmother kept her chickens. It was rough, rocky land and from it they have made a garden that is filled with fantasy. Above the road is forest, mainly of chestnut afflicted with disease. The chestnuts used to be an important crop but now no one bothers to collect them and the chestnut coppices are not cut. Looking later at the map, I saw that this mountainous woodland stretched unbroken for miles and miles and miles. Again and again one is reminded that France is so big and wild compared to Britain. Where the hens scratched, at the edge of this wildwood with the elders (*Sambucus*) that give the place its name casting an easy shade, you sit and eat the food prepared in a tiny kitchen across the garden. I like the way that the admission fee to the garden covers the meal. Lunch in the garden and the garden in the lunch, all one.

They are a complementary couple. Whereas Agnes serves food daintily laced with flowers and is responsible for most of the planting and the loose, whimsical tone of the garden, Nicholas hews the stony soil (It is good, these stones, he says, because it keeps the heat) and brings up barrowload after barrowload of boulders from the river when it has been in flood, with which he has constructed a range of paths, seats, buildings, walls, pools, waterways, fountains and follies in the garden all with that river-washed smoothness, like giant pebbles.

Nicholas used to keep goats and cattle but now just grows vegetables and eats meat and milk from his neighbours. They do it better, he says. When I visited in March little was growing. It had been a tough winter, very dry and very cold. They had had no rain since November and the temperature got down to minus eighteen. On my second visit it was over forty degrees and the heat bounced back off the rocks like an opened oven door.

The vegetables are grown away from the garden, further down the road. The land looks rough, weed-filled, stony and dusty but Nicholas beams. I tentatively ask about the weeds. They are good, he says. He is glad to see them. He leaves each piece of ground fallow for a year after taking the harvest from it, be it strawberries, potatoes, tomatoes, onions, and lets the weeds grow. This covers the soil and the roots add organic matter. When it gets really hot much of it shrivels up. He will then plough it all in as green manure. It looks scruffy but it works. He is working with his here and now and not following a preconceived idea of how things ought to be done. This is unusual. But perhaps the slavish following of horticultural form and etiquette is a luxury given only to those who do not need to make things work as much as they need to be seen to be doing the right thing.

In spring the air was clean and clear and almost sparkled. The bones of the garden, marked out by Nicholas's stonework, was charming and eccentric. *Hobbit* fans will love it. In summer the heavy shade of the garden was delicious but hid much, and the planting had become full and too indiscriminate for my taste. Too much of nothing. It is too hot to sit in the sun during the summer months and, according to Nicholas, too noisy at night. The frogs he said, that are attracted by the water that he has so laboriously channelled and routed around the garden are so very noisy. Incredible. But then in August it mercifully stops. Why was that? Because, Nicholas patiently explained, the snakes eat them.

It is, as you might expect, all 'bio'. He uses practically no machines, preferring his battered wheelbarrow and a hefty mattock. There is no greenhouse or polytunnel and they hardly store or preserve anything. This is not down to lack of opportunity, skill or effort but simply a desire to eat what is in season. Many of us trumpet the trinity of organic, local and seasonal but hardly anyone lives it out as purely as Nicholas and Agnes. Whilst I admired it tremendously I said that this must be rather limiting in winter. In winter, Nicholas said, we eat a lot of soup – a lot of leek and potato and pumpkin soup – and meat. We hardly eat any meat in summer because the vegetables are so good. In winter we eat sausages from the pigs of our friends and try and put on weight. Then in summer I am out here early, by five, before it gets too hot and get slim again. He smiled. He smiles a lot and radiates a kind of gentle, easy contentment worked from this stony land.

There is a kind of sub-hippy, rural society that manages to live the life born of '68 far more successfully than in the UK. Perhaps it is just the weather. Scorching heat and bitter cold pull people together whereas grey, falling skies and rain dilute and wash it away. It is also a pre-industrial way of life. Before industry demanded fixed hours and clocking on and off with prescribed holidays, people worked around the immediate demands of the seasons and the work in hand. Whole families of craftsmen would put in eighteen-hour days to get an order out, but then happily take two or three days off. In winter, when the days were short and the weather often made the ground unworkable, the only real work was feeding the animals. People slept a lot, sat around, told stories, mended things. Until the coming of electricity, gas and coal, as well as transportation to deliver these things, light and heat in remote mountainous regions were expensive and severely limited. Bed was the cheapest and most comfortable place to be. Even in places with a benign climate and within easier reach of towns, the rural world closed down for months at a time in winter and travellers commented on this time and again when visiting France right up to the First World War.

Of course where you have an economy based upon the pursuit of cash and profit, this is a form of economic and social suicide.[2] But a peasant society is founded upon a desire to keep on keeping on.

This does not always mean a mixed, self-sufficient set-up. The whole basis of *terroir* and provenance is that some areas, sometimes very local indeed, are better than any other for producing just one product, so everyone focuses on that. In much of the world – and in northern France – this has come to mean vast agribusinesses swamping the landscape with large-scale monoculture with disastrous financial, environmental, sociological and ecological effect. But all over France and especially as you go further south, there are examples of people producing specialist products from wine to *foie gras* in a very small way.

This area of the southern Cévennes is known for its onions. I visited a grower – who I only knew as Bruno – just nearby in the village of St André de Majencoules. He was a fifth-generation onion grower.

2 The cash crop of silk cocoons that was so important to many peasants right across the Cévennes and Provence was not a winter activity. It would have been ideal if it had been, but it depended upon the fresh growth of the mulberry trees, which did not begin until March and was finished by mid-summer. However, the women of the area went to work in the silk-weaving factories and, according to Nicholas, all had eye problems. The arrival of nylon – especially nylon stockings – finally killed the silk industry.

The terraces of his small farm, with their white stone retaining walls with steps and quoined revetments tended as carefully as the crops, grew nothing else at all and he said had not done so for over a hundred years. Just these onions, year after year. The best and sweetest white onions in France. The unspoken implication of course was therefore they were the best in the world. This was far from a happy hippy set-up. All weeds were chemically removed, it was extreme, long-term monoculture (other than a few goats, which he fed on mulberry leaves and made cheese from their milk). But he was following a groove that was deeply worn in the landscape by his forebears who had lived in the same house and farmed the same land and who also always planted on the fifteenth of May and harvested on the fifteenth of August.

Bruno had no desire to expand his production or to intensify it. This is what his land and family does. The church, standing seven terraces up on the steep hillside, was where he married and where he, like his father and grandfather before him, would be buried. Its clock chimed his hours. His job was to look after the continuation of that and everything that defined him was bound in the actual dimensions and shape of his land, just as he was defined by his height and appearance.

The overwhelming impetus of the *paysan* culture is tied to a particular piece of land that will produce just enough to enable you and your family to do it again next year. It was this anti-capitalism that was one of the attractions for the *soixante-huitards* and the Cévennes was – and is – one of the places in which it is most possible to live that life.

There was also the long history of rebellion. The Camisards were an 'alternative' society defending their faith. They were regarded as heroes brutally crushed by an overpowering state. It became so brutal and involved such a large display of force because it was so hard to find them. The Cévennes has long been a hiding place. Likewise in the Second World War. There is a common notion that the Cévennes was the centre of Resistance activity, but Nicholas quickly corrected me. The Cévennes was a place to hide rather than fight, he said. The Germans hardly ever came in here. For the most part life went on as normal.

All morning, while I was being shown around Nicholas's garden and land, I could hear what at first I thought were exceptionally throaty, inventive blackbirds singing in the bushes and trees. In fact they sounded more like nightingales, which I knew was unlikely as nightingales sing at night. I asked Nicholas what they were. *Rossignols*, he said. They are very common here. Very noisy.

And so they were, one every hundred metres or so, competing and challenging the broad daylight with descanting, swooping, thrilling song. But I never saw one. They were all hidden.

16

DORDOGNE

I have only had the misfortune to visit Bergerac airport once. Getting there involved one of those farcical taxi journeys during which the meter revolves faster than the wheels. When I got up in the morning at my hotel in Vezac no one – literally no one – seemed to be around. It was as though the hotel had been abandoned in the night. I made myself some coffee, wandered around, poked about and packed. The pre-booked taxi duly arrived mid-morning. Still not a soul stirred. Odd. And predictably the fare came to every penny of the cash that I had gathered, predictably more than the plane ticket, more than the hotel bill, more than a weekend for two in Prague with breakfast thrown in. The nice taxi driver – who had spoken loudly to her children on the phone for most of the journey – accepted the barrowload of notes with the formal grace that every French trader displays.

The airport itself is a low-slung, mean affair and it was crammed with badly dressed people, all looking a bit too red, speaking with loud English accents. Perhaps there are two types of traveller. Those that hear their native tongue in a familiar brogue and immediately think warmly of home or those who hear the same with a sinking heart.

This was the first time I had ever been to the Dordogne and although I knew that it was a favoured ex-pat spot for the British, I had not realised quite what that meant. If you are spending time trying to immerse yourself in a country, to blend in enough to notice that which is unwittingly revealed, to walk into Bergerac airport is to have your cover suddenly blown. You are revealed for what you always have been: another horrible middle-class Brit, talking too loudly and taking up too much space.

I tried to check in but was told that the plane I was booked on was delayed for nine hours. The taxi had cleaned me out to my last euro and my baggage – a big suitcase – could not be checked in or left at the airport, so I could not even go for a walk. Then I noticed passengers boarding a flight to Bristol. Was there room on that flight? There was a seat but it would be no use to me because my ticket was non-transferable. How much would it cost to buy another ticket? There was some tapping on the keyboard. Less than the taxi fare from the hotel. Fine. I'll have it. Then my credit card was rejected. The last call for the flight was being made. So I rang home. No answer. I rang mobiles. Nothing. Finally, as a very long shot, I rang a friend in Glasgow, who was out shopping with her children, got her to pay for it over the phone and rushed to join the end of the boarding queue. No one has ever been happier to get on a Ryanair flight.

I just had time to call the driver who was due to collect me at Birmingham and ask him to come down the motorway to Bristol. He arrived at the moment I strolled to the front door of the terminal having leisurely collected my suitcase and I was home before the original flight had been scheduled to take off. If the taxi hadn't cost so much and had left me some cash I would almost certainly have gone into Bergerac town, had some lunch and caught the delayed flight. So that night, as I dined at home, I raised a glass to the extortionate fares of French taxis.

I had not really planned to go to that part of France at all. There are wonderful gardens in the region – most famously Eyrignac and

Marqueyssac – but I was running out of time and culling possible garden visits with ruthless zeal. The truth is that most gardens will keep for another day. Better to visit what you can in a reasonable state of mind rather than scurrying around marking your horticultural card like a train spotter without really taking anything in. But I did have a day to spare so got a lift from Limoges to Vézac, mainly to see asparagus growing.

Now you can see asparagus grown almost anywhere in France but I had been assured that this was very, very good asparagus and that the grower, Thierry Boyer and his family, were very, very nice people. And I had to go to Bergerac anyway.

The Boyer family are an interesting story of adaptability. The family farm in the village of Vialard had grown tobacco[1] for years. The most singular image of France from my youth was the cigarette. Whereas the British smoked with the slightly truculent relief from their labours of the working man or in the nervous, snatched, sulky manner of the office worker, the French made smoking insolent, clever, creative and sexy. Artists smoked, intellectuals smoked, musicians smoked and everyone who ever stood at a bar and ordered a vin rouge or pastis always smoked. It was patriotic to smoke. After all, they had invented the word ('the little cigar') and smoked as though they and only they truly owned the cigarette. Somehow the French were able to have an unfiltered cigarette hang from the lip, attached only by the dampness of the paper, and talk and smoke whilst remaining wreathed in sophistication. When I tried, the cigarette either fell out of my mouth or became slobbered and started to disintegrate, and invariably smoke rose directly into my eyes so I blinked and sneezed in an entirely uncool, unGallic manner. When I was a teenager just the words Disque Bleu, Caporal, Gauloises, Gitanes were exotic, smoking taken to a level that guaranteed sophistication and above all more and better sex

1 Tobacco was introduced to France in 1559 by the French ambassador to Portugal, Jean Nicot, from whom the Latin name *Nicotiana* is derived. He sent plants to Catherine de Medici who was to make her garden at Chenonceaux a year or two later.

(although in my own case substituting 'any' for more and better would have shown a huge improvement). I still love the smell of Gauloises and would smoke a packet of Disque Bleu a day if there were not more imaginative ways of killing myself. The point was that they were uniquely, unmistakably French.

They were made by La Société Nationale d'Exploitation Indus- trielle des Tabacs et Allumettes (SEITA), which was a state-owned monopoly and all French-grown tobacco would go to French-made cigarettes, so in a very direct, practical sense, smoking was a patri- otic act. Some brands, like the Gitanes Maïs with yellow papers made from maize (grown in France of course), seemed never to travel outside France and only be smoked by workers – not least because they were very cheap. To smoke them oneself would have been an affectation too far.[2] But then, at a time when all cigarettes were cheap, French cigarettes had less tax than British ones, so were especially cheap. They conferred instant moody sophistication on the smoker (or at any rate on the carefully nurtured self-image of this teenage smoker) and although I knew I would not be able to buy cigarettes at the Duty Free on the return from my first trip to Paris when I was fourteen, I bought a dozen packets from half as many tabacs, absurdly covering my steps, and eked them out across excruciating parties and lonely walks in the Hampshire country- side.

Perhaps these walks were wreathed in tobacco from Thierry's father's farm, although by the time I started he was beginning to stop, or at least cut back, on his tobacco production, realising that relying on a single crop was likely to lead to trouble in a world that saw increasing imports and that the patriotic loyalty to all things French was waning. Thierry took this process further and stopped growing tobacco altogether in 1998, concentrating on the rich, very free-draining alluvial soil, on growing vegetables, amongst which

2 This did not stop thousands of middle-class boys handrolling their cigarettes in the trail of the British worker, but perhaps the knowing nod towards rolling a joint added to the cachet of skinning up in front of one's peers.

his asparagus is prized as being as good as it gets. Everything is sold in the shop to which another thirty-odd fellow members of the farming cooperative contribute, almost all specialising in very local products, ranging from the specialities of the Périgord Noir region – walnuts, truffles, duck and *foie gras* – to every shade of vegetable, fruit and meat as well as local wine, oil and herbs. Certainly when I visited it was thriving. I had assumed that most customers were from the 3 million people that descend on the area every year to take their holiday but Thierry assured me that this is not the case. There is a seasonal boost to trade but the vast majority of customers are local people looking for the best and most fresh fruit and veg. Supermarkets, even French supermarkets, cannot supply that.

One could see this as just another farm shop that serves its immediate vicinity, rather like the corner shops or delicatessens do in towns, but the big difference is that the customers cut right across the social scale. Exactly the same cross section that use supermarkets shop there. It is only and all about the food. The local provenance, knowing not just where but who it comes from, matters a lot. The sense of *pays* and *terroir* is never far below the surface. But although the prices are competitive there is no problem for anyone, whatever their circumstances, with paying more for better quality. Certainly outside the larger suburbs, the French have yet to succumb to the cheating lie that is 'cheap' processed food.

The asparagus that Thierry grows is the white kind, *asperge blanche*, as opposed to the almost ubiquitous green asparagus that I and most other vegetable gardeners cultivate in the UK. This is the same species, *Asparagus officinalis*, but whereas in Britain (and in Provence) the shoots are harvested after they have emerged from the ground, sunlight stimulating chlorophyll and turning them green, white asparagus is harvested the minute there is any sign of growth, so that the edible stem is a white, blanched shoot. The flavour is perhaps milder and the stems more tender. Whatever the pros or cons, much of European asparagus production is subterranean.

I went with Thierry, past the walnut orchards and the honied cliffs above the river, and the clouds of poplar seed floating in the evening light like flecks and wisps of cotton, to the current field (the crop is grown on a four-year rotation) a few kilometres away in Carsac Aillac on the banks of the Dordogne. The field was divided into rilled strips by widely spaced high ridges. Other than a few weeds, there was no growth to be seen.

Thierry, a man with the ruddy tan and weathered eyes in an impossibly young face of those that spend most waking hours out-side working and the swollen and dirt-engrained hands of a gardener,[3] handed me the cutting tool which is a metre-long haft of metal with a well-worn wooden handle at one end and a shallow-scooped blade at the other. You might reasonably assume it was a chisel for work at a lathe. Walking down the first ridge he pointed to a nipple breaking the surface of the fine, silty soil, barely more than a warty bobble. Sliding the blade into the side of the ridge, he located the stem, severed it and lifted enough to pull it cleanly free, reveal-ing fifteen centimetres of tapering, fat white asparagus. I had a go. Finding the stem rather than blindly stabbing at the soil was harder than it looked. Every morning at dawn in the season – April to July – Thierry is in the field cutting each spear by hand. Hence his hands. Hence being rather good at it.

I had a cup of tea with him and his family in the kitchen and the father came in, one withered hand clutching dandelion leaves and wild chicory, a kerchief raffishly looped around his neck. For the rabbits, he explained before insisting on kissing 'all the girls', from his three-year-old granddaughter to the visitor nearer his age. Tea? he said. Wouldn't you rather have beer? Brandy, perhaps? No? Well, it was beer for him. Across the yard the cars still brought shoppers, passing others with large bags and baskets full. Life seemed good,

<hr>

3 Anyone who has spent a lifetime working on the land has huge hands swollen with use, taut beneath the skin. But the rising generation of arable farmers have hands that move from the steering wheel of a computer-controlled tractor to the trackpad of their laptop and their fingers rarely show signs of hard labour.

the family working together, the land productive, the community sharing its spoil. It depended upon all the family working harder and longer than most people would consider reasonable, but this seemed to be the best that such a life might offer. And, from the outside, it seemed to offer as much as most of us dream of.

17

AUVERGNE

In May 1982 I joined my friend Adam for another walk, this time through the Auvergne, going north from Murat to Volvic, just outside Clermont-Ferrand. This, in the Massif Central, is the core of France. It does not – to me at any rate – have the defining characteristics of many other regions to distinguish it from anywhere else, but it is symbolically untouched and unthreatened by any question of identity, be it from surrounding nations or within France itself. This is important because France had a fragile sense of self until relatively recently.

Napoléon did much to centralise and unify the country and remove diversity – for good and ill – but France still remained a country with hundreds, even thousands of very localised dialects well into the nineteenth century, with loyalties that were profoundly stronger to a local rather than national identity. Occitan was still the dominant language in the south. Cézanne spoke Provençal to his friends and family in exactly the same way that Welsh speakers use their language today, which is to say completely bilingual but with Provençal, not French, as his first language. This was also true in the Basque country, in Alsace and Brittany. Between these linguistic extremes were endless variations of dialect and patois.

In Britain we are used to our regional accents and treasure them as an important mark of identity. But dialects are increasingly rare. I remember thirty years ago sitting in the back of a van with half a dozen local farmers on the North York Moors. When they spoke to me it was with a broad Yorkshire accent that meant I clutched a little at some words. But when they spoke to each other I only understood one word in three because they used the local dialect with completely different words. It had to be learnt rather than deciphered. However one of the characteristics of dialects, as opposed to languages, is that they are only shared verbally and very rarely have any written record. This is how they remain local, because to know a dialect well enough to use it easily you have to hear and talk it constantly. The nearest that most of us come to that in twenty-first-century Britain is jargon, which usually starts out as a shorthand between people who find that conventional language is not equipped for easy discourse on a particular subject but quickly becomes an identifying lingo, and to know the jargon is to become part of a like-minded group.

Reading about the seventeenth and eighteenth centuries, it is astonishing how little Paris knew or communicated with the regions – and this included anywhere more than about two or three days' travel from the centre of the city. Travel was often the key to this. Until the middle of the nineteenth century, getting around France was hard for anyone with money and power, let alone the poor, and many *paysans* never travelled further than a day's walk from their birthplace during their entire lives. Like spoke unto like, and anyone more than fifty kilometres away was unlike. A survey was done in 1880 that showed only one fifth of the country (less than 8 million people) used French as its first language. In 1863, a quarter of all army recruits only spoke patois.[1] By the end of the nineteenth century, after concerted efforts to centralise French as the common

1 The etymology of the word patois is from Old French and means 'incomprehensible – rough speech'. So it was much more than a Geordie and Scouser conversing with their distinctive accents and more like the equivalent of Jamaican Creole or pidgin English.

language, there were still more than fifty major dialects and hundreds of sub-dialects that had been identified, plus others still unknown.

All this explains some of the French obsession with correctness and etiquette. The right way to do something is, by definition, the universally agreed way to do it, whether 'it' is the way to address a shopkeeper or the word for shop. It also explains the Académie française, whose main role is to purify and tie down the French language. And it helps explain the official attitude to immigrants. Rather than seeing diversity extending the range and notion of what it is to be French – which is pretty much the British position over the centuries – the French are remarkably tolerant of anyone as long as they fully buy into the existing, established idea of what it is to be French.[2]

In May 1982 I knew nothing of this. I was off for a jaunt in lovely spring weather. Like the Cévennes, the countryside has always been poor and harsh and people migrated away whenever they could although, typically, still thinking of themselves as Auvergnats. On the Quai de la Mégisserie in Paris, just by the Pont Neuf across to the sharp end of Île de la Cité, I met the Bru et Fils family of florists and seed sellers, whose grandfather came from the Auvergne in the 1930s looking for work. He had no skills other than those of a countryman, so he sowed seeds and sold plants and their seeds to Parisians. He began with a stall that became a shop and was a success, although nowadays Parisians do not buy many seeds but still buy plants, although increasingly only those in flower, neither caring for nor really understanding the simple horticultural advantage of buying a perennial when not in flower to allow it to establish its roots, and therefore produce more and better flowers in due course. They want

2 The riots in the *banlieues* of Paris by a disaffected, largely immigrant, population were doubly disturbing for modern French society because they were so un-French, directed against the idea of France itself and largely without intellectual content. It is often pointed out that the French will tolerate any race, colour and creed as long as people completely assimilate with the French way of life. But if immigrant groups ask for respect for their differences, that is a much more difficult thing to deal with.

their flowers to be displayed on the stall exactly as they will be in their pot or window box.

I asked Philippe Bru, who was born and raised in Paris just as his father had been, where he went on holiday, and he said, Back home. I asked where that was. The Auvergne, of course, he said.

I remember thinking how interesting it was that he, whose only connection to the Auvergne was third hand, thought of the Auvergne as home, and also that he referred to it as 'the Auvergne' rather than a particular village or town. But then my father, born and bred in England, as were both his parents, thought of himself as 100 per cent Scottish.

I can remember very little of my walk with Adam (and cannot find any pictures, although Charlie Waite took superb ones of the area), other than it was a good week. We had a system that worked perfectly. We would rise early and Charlie would drive us to where we had finished the day before, before going himself to photograph that previous section with notes of what might make a good picture. Then, at an agreed map reference and time, he would pick us up and we would all go to the next stopping point for that night. It meant we carried only minimal kit, slept in a bed and ate each evening at a table. On the other hand it was a tough walk and there were no phones, no possible way of contacting Charlie other than being at the agreed map reference at the agreed time. But it worked.

Little things remain in mind. Arriving in a village starving, everything closed and empty save for one unshaven, heavily moustached man in a café eyeing us as if we were vagabonds. There was nothing to eat. But then he said that perhaps he had something and came back fifteen minutes later with perfect omelettes that he had cooked, bread and Cantal cheese, which is said to be one of the oldest in the world. Heaven. Stopping to swim in an icy pool whose black depths suddenly seemed terrifyingly fathomless and drying myself on my shirt which I then wore claggy and cold until sun and sweat made all things even. The thigh-burning steepness of the walk from Super Besse along to Le Mont-Dore, and wading through knee-high snow up the ridge of Puy Mary and drinking the most delicious Orangina I have ever tasted after glissading down. I occasionally try and recapture that magical ice-cool sweetness that flooded my exhausted and parched body and always fail, barely connecting the artificial, over-sweet fizz with that exotic treat. Walking to Volvic and past the bottling plant for the water which was unknown to me – in fact bottled water was still only the province of the swishiest London bars and restaurants and treated as a very sophisticated drink – and seeing the water pouring from the hillside and tasting it from a fountain. It is now the bottled water I prefer and every single time I taste that volcanic edge, I recall that day.

There is an innocence in this, a sense of a pure past that is now unreclaimable and, I suspect, increasingly hunts you down with the ache of loss as the years pass, but which is for me irrevocably associated with that corner of France.

18

LA VALLÉE

Drive to Gilles Clément's garden in the Creuse and all the world is green. I came from the north – in fact directly from visiting the gardens at Villandry, and in the case of both garden and countryside, entered another world. Whereas Villandry sits easily in the rich, productive land of the Loire and comfortably absorbs every kind of tourist , holiday-maker and spreading measures of affluence, this is not trendy France. Few successful Parisians or ex-pats choose to make their homes, second or otherwise, here. It is not glamorous. But because it has not been titivated for metropolitan tastes, the Creuse feels like the real deal. The countryside is gentle, rolling and tipping and only really good for grass. But it is good grass and makes good cattle. This is the country of Limousin and Charolais cattle and they dominate the fields, lounging with placid muscularity, slowly becoming beef.

Gilles Clément is one of France's leading landscape designers and intellectuals who writes and talks about the nature of gardens and landscape. His own philosophy of garden design arose from a childhood incident when he was poisoned and spent two days in a coma as a result of pesticides entering his bloodstream via an open cut when he was spraying his father's roses. By that age he was already a

keen entomologist and botanist, and he became committed to working with the land in a way that did not impose or curtail the lives of
other occupants. This is what gets bracketed under 'sustainable' but
he takes it all one step further than most. He is also professor at the
École Nationale Supérieure d'Horticulture, housed at the Potager du
Roi, and as well as teaching has designed major gardens, public and
private, all over the world. All in all, he is highly respected as an intellectual figure at the head of France's environmental movement.

You cannot get a car to his house but have to drive across a field
and then park as the track enters woodland and narrows to just a
metre or so. This is deliberate. He has written about the way that all
gardens have lintels that you cross, although we in the West are
rather careless about these. In the East, and in particular Japan and
China, they take great care and deliberation over them. Despite not
consciously paying entrances the due that they deserve, subcon-
sciously we are all aware of them and Clément's point is that it takes
very little – a narrowing, perhaps a log across the path – to make
people stop and adjust their approach mentally and physically.

So I walked through woodland, the path twisting round foxgloves
and mulleins with a kind of elaborate horticultural politeness. An
opening revealed an area of exposed rock, planted with lime-loving
alpines creeping along the fissures. This had not been created by
Clément, who scraped the thin topsoil (by hand so as not to damage
the rock itself) to maximise the range of plants that he could introduce here.

The house appears in the woods. It is very beautiful, a fairy-tale
building made of stone and wood that Gilles built himself over a
period of four years. It looks as though every single stone, every
hand-made wooden tile, has been selected and placed where it is
with the care of someone creating a garden. The log pile looks good,
the fireplace with yesterday's ashes looks dishevelled but poised to
appear in the glossiest interiors magazine. It is a house that fulfils all
the aspirations and dreams of both the chicest Parisian seeking a
country retreat and the most hardy environmentalist wanting to

live as purely as possible in this impure world. Both descriptions fit him exactly of course. He is a man with immediate and impressive style, which he wears with great modesty. This makes him a very attractive figure and it is easy to see how he has become a guru for a new generation of landscape designers and environmentalists.

Sitting over a cup of tea outside the building and above the little wooded valley with the stream running through it that makes up most of his garden (hence the name), he told me about his central philosophy and theme.

It is a kind of anti-gardening. Unlike the building, he tries to exercise as little control as he possibly can over how his plants grow, believing that what happens is always interesting, regardless of the direct cause. He chooses his plants with care, selecting those that he would like to grow and, on the basis of a deep botanical knowledge and experience, that he thinks will be happy.

He loves this area, has visited all his life and owned the land since 1977, trying to look after it as sustainably as he possibly can yet freely introducing plants from all over the world. In fact he rejects the very concept of an indigenous plant because he says that views time in too parochial, restricted a scale. Across the millennia plants have moved freely around the globe and then become isolated and 'local' but that, he says, is a very human-centric view of things. His view is that if a plant will grow happily, then it belongs in that place, regardless of whether it has been planted there deliberately, been transported as seed by a bird or in the hem of a skirt, arrived yesterday or 100,000 years ago. In the greater scheme of things man is no more a significant agent in the dispersal of plants than birds, weather or insects.

He sees ecology as a fluid movement. You can resist it – although that is bound for failure – or go with it. But you cannot know where it is going. All gardens, Gilles said, in everything other than the shortest term, are part of this movement. They will always sort themselves out.

As a very conventional gardener, albeit a longstanding organic one involved in the environmental movement, this is interesting and tricky. For his thesis is based upon all plants, including the knotweeds, hogweeds, ground elders, couch grass, mare's tail, Indian balsam and whatever other invasive weeds happen to be the current or localised bête noir, coming to a balanced ecological relationship with the environment. I repeat: ALL plants. Most things travel eventually. Be part of that and accept the consequences as they occur without forcing any plant on to a place. The only criterion for judging whether a plant is ecologically 'good' is whether it will grow healthily. Either you can see gardening as essentially a denial of this, endlessly bailing out a ship that is remorselessly going down, or see it as a fascinating opportunity to work with nature in a domestic setting.

But, he added, it is not natural. I am not saying leave everything untouched. Every garden must have a gardener.

You can see why the French adore him. There is a frisson of radicalism coming from a highly respected and downright sexy figure. The old order is challenged not by total rejection but by appeal to an even higher order.[1]

So all his carefully selected flowers – the geraniums, seleniums, aquilegias, verbascums, phloxes, alliums, irises, sedums and hundreds more – are happily growing in amongst grass, bracken, creeping buttercup, lesser and giant hogweeds. There are, under this approach, no pests, no weeds, no fungal or disease problems. Everything is in flux and all horticultural problems arise out of not accepting that and working with it.

He gardens with a light touch. I am reminded of Strilli Oppenheimer's head gardener at Brenthurst, her twenty-hectare garden

1 We filmed Gilles and his garden for the BBC and came away enthusing about him and the place and looking forward to seeing it in the edit. However, it never made the final cut because it was felt that the garden looked too unkempt for a British audience to appreciate and that his approach was too intellectual. I am not sure whether this would have been true or not, but the reluctance to use him as part of a film celebrating France for a British audience certainly marks one of the essential differences between the two national cultures.

in Johannesburg, who spoke of not being a 'hands-on' but a 'finger-tip' gardener, nudging and tweaking and essentially trying to do as little as possible whilst keeping the sense of a garden. So Gilles will prune branches for his own aesthetic – and this often means leaving them sprawling. Trees get blown down and he will leave them fallen across what had been a path or clump of flowers and simply mow round them and make a new path, letting the flowers grow through the fallen branches. He is not precious about a local ecology but is constantly adding plants from all over the world. If they survive, then they are at home. If not, then so be it. A 'right' place for a plant in his philosophy is where it will grow healthily with minimal human intervention.

Every April he takes stock of what is growing where and mows the garden paths accordingly. These stay mown until the autumn but will almost certainly take a different route next spring. The design is a reaction to the dynamics of the garden rather than driving it. He says this is because the garden is fluid. Plants move and spread and die. The layout is dictated as much by them as by his imposed design. There are a couple of areas of roughly mown grass, sort of lawns, but there is no flat anywhere so they are banks; these have self-seeded verbascums growing in them which are carefully mown around. A few service paths – to the compostable loo, the vegetable patch and the woods – are kept constant and there are stone steps taking you up and down the valley, but these are as natural and informal as they might possibly be. In his time even the stream has moved, with surges and floods breaking the banks and opening oxbows and leats.

He took me down one of the permanent paths to the meadow he has nurtured over the past twenty years, which is amazingly species-rich, with a combination of annual and perennial flowers. He cuts this in October, leaving the cut material to dry off and wither on the ground. This goes against all received advice for encouraging flor-iferous meadows, which is that you should scrupulously gather all the hay so that it does not enrich the soil as it decomposes, thereby nurturing the grass at the expense of the much more fragile and nutritionally less demanding wild flowers. However, he says that this land is so low in nutrients that no more goes back in than the plants take out and by cutting it so late and letting it lie he ensures that the seeds are ripe and mature well. Although he loves the meadow for its flowers, he has made it as much for the insects, butterflies and moths it attracts as its aesthetic appeal. He sees that all the living components of a garden, of which humans are merely one rather clumsy part, live on an equal billing and looking after plants at the expense of other wildlife is not only bad for the wildlife but inevitably proves harmful to the garden.

The path continues through the oak trees to the steep wooded bank of the long Lac de Chambon, made by damming the Creuse a few kilometres upstream.[2] All you could see in every direction was a great stretch of water, perhaps one kilometre wide with oakwoods billowing down to the water.[3] My swimming pool, Gilles said.

We gave him a lift to the station for the three-hour train journey back to Paris. He said that he hated leaving La Vallée. It was a wrench every time. What was his favourite season? It is all good, he said. I love it all. But then he added, Except the middle of July to middle of September. Too many people.

I agree with almost everything that Gilles Clément says and does. I think his house and garden beautiful. He himself is extraordinarily impressive. Yet it is hard for the dyed-in-the-wool horticultural Brit, even one committed to organics and sustainability like myself, to abandon all the rhythms and rituals of our gardening lives. It

2 The Eguzon Dam that created the lake was built in 1926 to make hydroelectricity and it was for a while the largest dam in Europe.
3 This part of the Creuse valley, between Crozant and Fresselines, was popularised by George Sand in the middle of the nineteenth century and became the location for the Crozant School of painting, inspired both by the landscape and by the work of John Constable in England. It reacted to the grandeur of contemporary landscape painting by focussing on the natural scenery of the place. It gave rise to no great work although Claude Monet spent a couple of months there in the spring of 1889 (by which time Giverny was becoming well established) and made more than twenty paintings.

would be a big step to change my own garden, for example, and run it along the lines of La Vallée, even though I would be fascinated to do so.

There is one other factor too. The nature of La Vallée is that it is a retreat, completely hidden from view, and only accessible on foot down a winding path. It is an escape from the world. Is it merely a very sophisticated, ecologically aware country home for an extremely sophisticated man of letters circling the world giving lectures and seminars, or a still, sane point in a world busily consuming itself, a model for any viable future? The spoiler for both these as with so many of our conundrums comes back to the same thing: too many people.

19

PRIEURÉ NOTRE-DAME D'ORSAN

In September 2011 I was in South Africa, visiting gardens in the Cape, and was sent to visit one between Cape Town and Franschhoek called Babylonstoren.[1] I knew nothing about it but had heard that it had a superb hotel and restaurant, which was incentive enough. That turned out to be true – it is one of the best hotels that you could ever stay at – but I would happily have camped in a tent and eaten my dinner with a spoon from a tin to have the chance to see the garden. It was – is – magnificent.

This was a long-established Cape Dutch farm bought in 2007 by a South African media magnate, Koos Bekker. As well as revitalising the farm with its winery, he immediately set about making a large vegetable garden to supply the hotel that he also created in the existing farm buildings. Money seems to have been no object but a huge emphasis has been put on quality, style and sustainability.

1 One of the initial motives for migration inland at the end of the seventeenth century into what is now thought of as the Afrikaans heartland of Stellenbosch was the arrival in the Cape of French Huguenots, fleeing from France after the Edict of Nantes was revoked in 1685. Franschhoek, where many of these new arrivals settled, is the Dutch for 'French Corner'. Many of the very Afrikaans-sounding names to the modern ear, such as Du Plessis, De Klerk, Du Toit, Terreblanche, Fourie, Le Roux and many more, have obvious French roots.

The result is a very modern place in both concept and per-formance, with amazing food and the kind of perfect simplicity that is the mark of real luxury[2] and a really stunning garden that has edible plants as its priority but by no means its sole content. The garden is heroic in scale – not just in size (over three hectares) but in the scale of its planting, the width of its paths, the structures, rills, and the elaborate frameworks for ornately pruned fruit built out of wood.

I met Koos and his wife Karen and asked them why they had chosen to make a garden like this. The main influence seems to have been a visit to an old monastery whilst on holiday in France. They loved the garden there so persuaded the designer, Patrice Taravella, to come and make one for them. Did I know his garden, the Prieuré d'Orsan? I had not then come across it but I had seen enough at Babylonstoren to want to find and visit it as soon as I could.

So I arranged to visit Patrice Taravella, who was not only the designer of the garden but also the owner. Patrice and his then wife, Sonia Lesot, bought the Prieuré d'Orsan in 1991. In fact they did not know that they were buying a priory – they thought it was just a very cheap set of dilapidated buildings plus sixteen hectares of land for the price of a studio flat in the centre of Paris. The monastic buildings came to light as they cleared and excavated. They did some research, to discover that it had been a priory, Prieuré Notre-Dame d'Orsan, founded in 1107, and was from the outset open to men and women, with the women running it. So their plans to have a small hotel did not seem out of joint with its history and the garden followed the spirit of the original medieval gardens that existed to supply the priory with vegetables, herbs and fruit.

I drove there south from Chenonceau, entering the countryside of Berry which is, geographically at least, pretty much the centre of

2 I have no idea what any of this costs. Probably a small fortune. The South African tourist board was footing the bill.

France.[3] Stopping for a cup of coffee in Le Châtelet, I noticed two things that mark out the quiet provincial villages and towns of modern France. The first was the almost complete absence of anyone out and about and the second was the two or three washed-up middle-aged men sitting on plastic chairs in the tiny bar, supremely drunk at eleven in the morning.

The region, and in particular *Les très riches heures du Duc de Berry*,[4] was a major inspiration for the garden, chiming with the medieval connection to the growing seasons and rhythms of the year. The Prieuré has the substantial, if somewhat low-slung and barnlike, mass of monastic buildings. It is also, in every detail, from the way the car park is ordered to the blackboard with its beautiful handwriting by the modest door into the shop through which you have to pass (of course) to reach the garden, almost painfully stylish. It is a pain I can relish and I instantly liked and admired it, but it does not have even a tiny touch of essential ugliness or kitsch that judders the balance so that you might establish it again for yourself. Wandering round is an experience of passive, if unalloyed, delight.

Patrice Taravella is a rotund, jovial man whose urbanity does not quite hide his intolerance of fools or anything or anyone he thinks is wasting his time. Over a superb lunch of *légumes poché au bouillon d'herbes, cocotte de cabillaud* and a *tarte fine aux pommes* – all, save the cod, but including the oil, wine and lemons, grown here – he explained to me how he set about making the garden. It started, he said, when the first summer was blistering hot. He wanted shade so he planted a tree. If he was going to have a tree,

3 Not that such a thing has ever been agreed upon. In 1855 the Duc de Mortemart built an octagonal tower, the Belvédère, to commemorate the victory of the French army at the battle of Sebastapol but it was retrospectively designated as the marker for the centre of France. It is about twenty-five kilometres east of Prieuré d'Orsan.
4 *Les très riches heures du Duc de Berry* was a book of prayers that were said at appointed canonical hours, or offices of prayer to be said throughout the day. It was made between 1412 and 1416, with over 130 astonishingly vivid and detailed painted illuminations (some added nearly seventy years later) illustrating the courtly life of the Duke throughout the year.

then, although he wanted it to be beautiful and have flowers, it also had to produce something to eat, so it was an apple tree. He had never gardened before but was a working architect so treated the design and layout of the garden as a series of architectural problems to be solved. The monastic tradition supplied the content along with his own love of food. (I am of Italian descent, Patrice says to explain this – as if this trumps any French obsession with the table. It probably does.)

Now they supply the hotel, the restaurant, their staff and themselves, with any extra going to visitors. They never buy vegetables. This inevitably means, he says, some periods of monotony. If we have a lot of cabbages, then we eat a lot of cabbage. So it had better be good cabbage.

So, twenty years on, I ask that hoary question, What would you have done when you started the garden if you knew then what you know now? His answer was immediate but surprising. More walls and fewer hedges. It takes 1,400 man-hours to cut the hedges that are principally hornbeam, but also yew and box. Spread that out over even ten years and it makes them more expensive than walls. Even if the initial costs of building walls may seem very high, you soon get it back and also you have the finished structures the moment the work is done, whereas with a hedge it takes five to ten years to get the same structural effect. Far better to spend the capital and save the costs unless you are sure of the income to maintain it.

Yet the hedges *are* the garden. Replace them with walls and it would be something else altogether. But there speaks an architect, seeing the place as a series of carefully defined volumes rather than plants woven together. Nothing could be more different from Gilles Clément's view of gardening, or indeed Gilles Clément's garden.

Although the actual garden is not especially big – most of the sixteen hectares are still fields – it feels complicated and much bigger than it is, in an unoppressive way, because so little is revealed at any one time and because every area is curtailed and hemmed in by

hedges and structures and yet also has tantalising glimpses of more through doorways and windows cut in the hedges. Every space is human, and never has the overused garden expression 'outdoor rooms' felt more apposite. The organisation of space – compressing it, expanding it out again, stretching it – is masterfully done. There is also much medieval imagery and many monastic references, via the labyrinths, the tracks that lead you astray and the paths to salvation, which almost all visitors will not even recognise as being present but are there.

There is a huge amount of treillage and structure created with chestnut poles. Patrice said that he has two large lorry loads delivered every January and the whole garden is reassembled with them. Their unmachined, hand-cut shapes and textures are an essential part of the way that the garden feels as well as looks. The result is extraordinary, with every kind of cradling basketry and screen for every kind of top and soft fruit, tomatoes, roses, vines, gateways, pergolas and fencing. It adds a playfulness to the garden that stops it disappearing up its highly sophisticated nether regions.

On the lawn in front of the main building where the guest rooms are lie two large rectangular beds – bigger than the grass itself, one with a crop of standing wheat and the other with maize. The wheat is harvested for bread – everything in the garden that is edible is eaten – but looks stunning. Tomatoes are planted underneath a latticed roller coaster that they will be trained through. Squashes have square raised beds walled with woven willow, and rhubarb woven willow guards, the giant leaves sticking out of the top of waste-paper baskets that both protect and blanch them. Paths and seating areas are floored with sleepers, massive and geological yet soft-edged. Giant mangers made of split chestnut (it rives and cleaves beautifully, allowing interplay between different thicknesses and textures by latticing the grain of a cleft rod with the bark of a whole one) splay out to hold raspberries and gooseberries, picker-friendly, supportive and damned handsome.

It is no wonder the hedges take so much cutting. They are often layered two or even three deep, each one a different height. They are crenellated, curved, buttressed and quoined. Stone envy.

The vegetables are good. It shows that although you do not need anything other than a slightly scruffy field to grow expert veg you can combine the best culinary and aesthetic tastes if you choose to do so.

When I was there at the end of May there was very little colour but lots of light. There were roses but they were nearly all pale, and the fruit and vegetables would surely glow in their various colours in late summer and autumn, but at that time of year the green of the hedges and grass dominated everything, leavened by the pale browns and grey of the wood. It made me think that green is not just the saving grace of a drab northern sky: under this light – not too harsh and yet bright, sparkling – it is all the colour you need.

20

CHENONCEAU

In one of the classrooms of my little prep school was a picture of Chenonceau from the air. Beneath was the caption 'Châteaux of the Loire'. Note the plural 'x'. We were told that the Loire was adorned with châteaux, each a gem in its own right, bejewelling the Loire valley. That was it. No one ever mentioned that the Loire is not noticeably in a valley or that Chenonceau is not on the Loire at all but the river Cher.

The Cher rises around 300 kilometres south-east of Chenonceau, in the Auvergne, quickly becoming a navigable river that joins the Loire the other side of Tours at Villandry, about fifty kilometres downstream. Unlike the Loire, it rises and falls significantly, hence the great river walls and the height of the arches above the water, save when the river is in spate. It muscles through the landscape.

The river dominates Chenonceau, even though all approaches are now by road with the river effectively tucked away behind the château. Were it not for the iconic image of the library with its piers straddling the water somewhere between the most elegant of bridges and a paddler with his trousers rolled to his knees, the river would be a scenic backdrop, appearing from the edge of vision on the one side and conveniently dropping out of view on the other.

But the river is the thing. That white-stoned, turreted, fairy-tale castle of a bridge is not an architectural extravaganza but a homage to the river gods. The château had been originally built by the river in the thirteenth century, both for protection from the south and access by boat which was to remain the easiest and quickest form of transport, especially for goods, for another 600 years. This building stood where the forecourt is now and there were various rebuilds, of which only the early fifteenth-century donjon tower, reeled around with nesting swifts, survives. In 1512 Chenonceau was acquired by the financier, Thomas Bohier, who built a new castle actually in the water, the footings[1] sunk deep beneath the river bed. This is central to the iconography of the place because the whole building is reflected, always double its shimmering self as it rises out of the water. After Bohier's death in 1535 the estate was forfeited to the crown in lieu of debts and the king, Francis I, used it as a hunting lodge. His son, Henri II, gave it to his mistress, Diane de Poitiers, when he took the crown in 1547. By the time she built the bridge in 1556, so she could ride across the river and hunt the forests on both sides, she was making a statement of her own power in the land, the relative safety that meant the château did not need such fierce defences and her power over the river, that she could cross it dry-shod.[2]

To get the measure of the river's hold over the château it is best to see it first from the other side. Unfortunately this means a long excursion as there is no entry across the drawbridge and through the doors of the gallery back to the keep. I first visited on a grey, bleak day in winter and the river coiled round the piers like a fat brown

1 The château is actually built upon the site, and presumably some of the foundations, of a previous mill.
2 Between 1940 and 1943 the river was the border between Free France and the Occupied zone. So the front door of the château was in German-controlled territory and the back door, at the end of the gallery, in Free France and many people were smuggled into the Free territory via the gallery.

snake. But I went back to the château in late spring, with the sun shining and the trees all fledged and fat with leaf, and had the privilege of being allowed through the gallery at six thirty in the morning.

This was after a strange night. I stayed just outside Amboise, in a hotel with a long drive through a golf course and fields arriving at a substantial building with a courtyard. The nearest habitation was a couple of kilometres or more away. I checked in, with a sulkily pretty girl taking the information down very slowly and carefully, using a broken English even worse than my own French.

The room was typical of so many that I have stayed in. Almost grand but also rather seedy. It was comically overstuffed with furniture so that the doors of the big wardrobe couldn't be opened without pushing the bed hard against the wall, and even then the only way to get anything in or out was to stand on the bed and squeeze an arm round the half-opened door. If you wanted to sit at the desk there was not enough room to get your body between the desk and chair without shunting the bed as tight as it would go against the wardrobe, sucking in your tummy and somehow wedging your knees under the table top.

This odd lack of attention to the needs of the visitor is not unusual. It is all part of the French desire to display, first and foremost, how good they are – lovely furniture, nice house – rather than working out what the guest might need or want. I went to eat in Amboise and when I came back at about eleven the whole place was dark and there was no one around. The front door was open, but the place was completely deserted. I found my room in the pitch-black corridor and went to bed. I got up and checked out early the next morning with still no evidence of any life at all.

I went into town and stopped at a café, busy at that hour with street cleaners, doctors and lawyers pausing for a coffee on their way to work. Suddenly the best of France, its civilisation, its style and dignity and refusal to surrender its values in the teeth of much of modern life were again to the fore. The café had not yet received its delivery of croissants so I went in search of some and saw a van loading up with bakeries from a door in a side street. It turned out to be the kitchen entrance to a hotel but I asked if they could sell me some croissants and came away with a bag still warm from the oven. To sit on the street of a small town by the Loire, drinking good coffee, with flakes of croissant spangling your shirt while the church bell strikes the early hour is enough to restore anyone's love for this complicated, awkward, beautiful country.

No one was about at Chenonceau either, although gradually the flower arrangers and gardeners arrived, calmly readying the place for the visitors that would jostle in at nine. But whereas spending a night in an empty hotel is creepy, having a grand château to yourself is a fabulous treat.

Out on the other side of the river the cuckoo's call had a particular flutey resonance in the silence of the morning and the soft echo amongst the trees. Looking back at the château from that side you realise the connection that the bridge makes, rather than just seeing the gallery as a room with a watery view.

These woods are lovely but now unremarkable, save that they are clearly a plantation rather than a carefully managed loose jumble of coppice woodland. The trees, mostly young, are planted in rows although their upper branches tangle. However, a drawing by Du Cerceau[3] from the late 1570s shows this southern side of the river laid out as two formal gardens or orchards, flanking the approach to the bridge (and the drawing shows it as a bridge without the gallery that was later built on top), the ghosts of which can just be made out on the ground.

Although these gardens had been laid out and there is evidence of treillage work on the north-west side of the river in this Du Cerceau illustration, the gardens at Chenonceau really became interesting

---

3 *Les plus excellents bastiments de France* (1576) by Jacques Androuet du Cerceau showed a range of buildings and, critically, their gardens. He was a favourite of Catherine de Medici (who owned the château after Diane de Poitiers), which is probably why Chenonceau appears in the volume.

when Diane de Poitiers took over. Her garden is still there much as
she made it, and although the planting owes more to an early
twentieth-century municipal parks department than sixteenth-
century France, the site is sound and it would take very little to
accurately restore it to its Renaissance glory.

Diane was one of the more attractive figures of the French
Renaissance. Born in 1499, at the age of fifteen she married a man
forty years older than herself to whom she bore two daughters
before he died in 1531. She wore black widow's weeds – set off
only by pure white – for the rest of her life. Beautiful, sophisticated,
learned and clearly irresistible, she was part of the Court and had
known the royal princes, Henri and François, as children and in
1538 she became the mistress of nineteen-year-old Henri, who was
exactly half her age. By this time Henri had been married to
Catherine de Medici[4] for five years but his love affair with Diane
continued unabated until his death in 1559. For twenty years Diane
was the most powerful woman in France – much to Catherine's
fury.

Catherine, twenty years younger than Diane, was the only surviving Medici when the family was thrown out of Florence in the late
1520s. Married off as a child-bride to a husband she had never met
and forced to live in another country, she adored Henri and loathed
Diane. But it was no contest. Whilst Catherine was titular queen and
bore Henri ten children, Diane was not only his true love but also
effectively ran him and therefore, when he became king, the country.

4 The marriage was arranged by the Medici Pope Clement VII, Giulio de Medici, who
was pope from 1523 to 1534, to try and make allegiance with the winning side in a
Europe made chaotic by war between France and the Holy Roman Empire. Giulio de
Medici lived in interesting times. He was pope during the sack of Rome in 1527 and the
expulsion of the Medici family from Florence. It was under his watch that Henry VIII
broke away from the Catholic Church and established the English Reformation. He is
believed to have been the father of Alessandro de Medici, first Duke of Florence, who
was murdered and replaced by his cousin Cosimo de Medici, who went on to become
Cosimo the Great, maker of the superb garden at Villa Castello and the Boboli Gardens.
Clement/Giulio also ordered Michelangelo's painting of the Sistine Chapel, although he
did not live to see the work begun.

Henri gave Chenonceau to Diane when he succeeded to the throne in 1547[5] and she loved the place. As well as commissioning the bridge that conquered the Cher, she made a huge fortified garden. The fortifications were against man, beast and the river. The latter's tendency to rise hugely in the early months of the year necessitated the enormous retaining walls, like ramparts protecting the raised area against flood and making a great buttressed quayside for the stream of deliveries that would have arrived daily to the château by river. The other two sides were moated and walled so that nothing and no one might enter unbidden, be it truffling *sanglier* or rude peasant after illicit fruit. Thus, whilst easily viewed from the castle, the garden was enclosed and protected and designed to look inwards and, for the privileged few inside the château, to be looked into.

The work, which began in 1551 on a one-hectare site just to the north-east of the château, was well documented. The records show the purchase of hundreds of plum, pear, apple and mulberries, whereas the only flowers mentioned are lilies, musk roses and violets. A great raised walkway ran right round the perimeter so that Diane and her ladies-in-waiting could promenade, looking down on this ornate array of beauty and productivity. The latter would have been as highly valued as any conventional floral beauty and one thinks of Italian gardens of the same period, where the citrus and vegetables, including peas, artichokes, leeks, cucumbers, melons and onions grown amidst ornate parterres, were carefully cultivated, first to feed the household and then, importantly, to sell to raise an income to run the garden.

This was an enormously extravagant enterprise, akin to building another château, and was intended both to impress people with its opulence and to pay its own way as far as possible. Thus the moat and walls are as substantial as a castle keep. This was a fortified,

5 In fact there was a complicated charade of ownership whereby Catherine contested Diane's legal right to the château. It was temporarily reverted to the Bohier family and then repossessed and put up for auction, when Diane bought it for 50,000 livres.

defended garden against, I suspect, the imagined horrors of historical precedent rather than a practical security assessment.

You must remember all this when you walk round the garden (entering by the lovely sixteenth-century Steward's House), because it does not reveal itself through the rather half-hearted planting. This is despite the 130,000 bedding plants (all bought in, despite the magnificent potager, used mainly for growing cut flowers for the house) and vaguely Victorian topiary. It is as though no one is interested enough to engage with Diane's garden as thoroughly as they have done with the château itself. Nevertheless, it is completely fascinating, and perhaps the last great fortified garden to be made in Europe.

But disaster struck in June 1559. Henri, aged just forty, was killed when a splinter from a shattered wooden lance pierced his eye and brain whilst jousting in what is now the Place des Vosges. He took a painful month to die, during which time Catherine took control. When he finally expired on 9 July he was succeeded by his fifteen-year-old son, Francis II, husband of Mary, Queen of Scots. Francis died within the year and was followed in turn by his ten-year-old younger brother, Charles, who lasted until 1574 and was replaced by yet another brother, Henri. This meant that Catherine effectively governed France from the death of Henri II in 1559 until her own death thirty years later in 1589.

She took sweet revenge on Diane. Knowing how genuine was the love between her and her husband, she banished her from the deathbed. Then she demanded back all the jewels that Henri had lavished upon her and then, more precious yet, Chenonceau, forcing her to exchange it for the château at Chaumont, about twenty-five kilometres north on the banks of the Loire. Diane visited this once and never returned, retiring to her Château d'Anet in Normandy.

Catherine took over at Chenonceau just as she did in government. A fortune was spent on the château as it was on other crown buildings. Diane's bridge became the base in 1576 for the two-storied gallery and library that stands there today. Instead of taking

over Diane's garden and changing it, Catherine let it stand as it
was – suggesting that it was too important as a provider of fruit and
vegetables to be tampered with – and built her own garden, of which
a small part remains on the other side of the entrance.

The symmetry of two powerful women vying for the love of one
man – one the mother to his ten children but spurned, the other
deeply loved and lavished with gifts but never possessor or even
sole mistress – is played out like a duel with gardens as the symbolic
weapons. Apparently Catherine's, surely influenced by the gardens
being made by her cousin Cosimo in Florence, once had grottoes
and boscoes, menageries and aviaries, but all that remains is another
municipal layout around a central circular pond. But walk quietly
there, by the banks of the Cher, the great château catching the
evening sun, and imagine Catherine scheming and planning, running her sons and the country from here, as she did, perhaps
plotting the St Bartholomew Day's massacre,[6] perhaps planning the
elaborate fêtes for which she was famous.[7] In any event, it seems that
she used her garden as a kind of chamber in which to scheme, and
politic and plan. Catherine died in 1589 and a few months later
her third and favourite son, Henri III, was murdered, bringing the
Valois dynasty to an end. His successor, Henri IV – who had married
Catherine's daughter Marguerite – was the founder of the Bourbon
dynasty that was to rule for another 200 years, through to the
execution of Louis XVI in 1792.

Chenonceau is fascinating and beautiful in itself. But to the student of French gardens it has a special role through the pattern of
history. Diane's garden is the most visible example of the fortified,

6 This took place on 23 August 1572, when many leading Protestants were gathered in
Paris for the wedding of Catherine's daughter, Marguerite de Valois, to Henri III of
Navarre, who was himself Protestant. Somewhere between 5,000 and 30,000 Huguenots
were slaughtered.
7 We know of at least three elaborate festivities held at Chenonceau, in 1560, 1563 and
1577. The first was to celebrate the visit of Francis II and Mary, Queen of Scots; *cabi-
nets, berceaux,* pall-mall *allées* and a large *jeu de balle* were all created by the banks of the
Cher for the occasion. In 1563 the first recorded firework display in France was held at
Chenonceau.

inward-looking garden that is a hangover from medieval times, defended against man and beast, cultivated to supply food and income for the household, enjoyed essentially from the outside looking in, or more specifically, down. Catherine's garden mirrors this but on a lesser scale, although without the full range of Italianate grottoes, cascades and aviaries we can only have a partial glimpse of it as it was. At the same time she was making the gardens at the Tuileries, which were to become the setting for the garden-maker who would change everything for ever. Rather than turning inward against the horrid world, André Le Nôtre took the gardens of Catherine de Medici's French High Renaissance and blew open their doors, reaching out to dominate and include everything to the furthest horizon.

But that is still a hundred years away and 250 kilometres to the north-east. First there is a journey to be made down the Cher to the point where it joins the Loire, at Villandry.

21

VILLANDRY

Were you to leave Chenonceau by boat, travelling on down east towards the sea, the river widening as it flows south of Tours, you could sail on down until some twenty kilometres east of Chenonceau, you could moor your craft and walk a few hundred metres to the little town of Villandry, with its château bounding the western edge.[1]

Villandry has become, through a combination of its extraordinary scale and maintenance and some very good marketing, the prototype of the potager, to British eyes at least. Rosemary Verey, who I suspect is not much read nowadays, was one of the first to actively translate its vast regimented beds into the average middleclass kitchen garden with her version at Barnsley House near Cirencester, which she wrote about extensively and I remember one of my first television assignments in the 1980s was to film it, and she subsequently became a good and wise friend to me.

---

1 Should you take the TGV from Tours to Paris, think fondly on the Cher because the stretch of line at Tours was built using it was sand dredged, in the late 1980s, from a boating basin made by diverting the river twenty years earlier that was used to make the stretch of line at Tours. The only time I tried to catch the train there, the taxi followed satnav rather than any map or local knowledge and we got lost and I missed the train. I spent a freezing hour waiting at Tours station, missed my flight home and finally got to the airport at ten, spent an unplanned night there, missed all kinds of meetings the next day and arrived home twenty-four hours late.

Until then the British vegetable garden had styled itself almost exclusively on the dream of a Victorian kitchen garden, surrounded by high brick walls. With its greenhouses and cold frames on one sunny side and fruit lining the others, this was really a rather smart allotment, with the vegetables grown in straight rows in large beds, perhaps with gravelled, box-lined paths but fundamentally a place where the earth was managed for maximum productivity, and everyone, from a pensioner picking runner beans by a railway line to the banker buying a rambling rectory in the country, could identify with it.

But by the end of the 1980s the potager,[2] with its small, box-lined geometric beds, was all the rage. The vegetables were chosen for their colour as much as taste, so there were lots of ruby chard and red lettuces, purple kale, purple and yellow beans as well as green ones, crimson-flowered broad beans and lovely rich chocolate-coloured mangetout peas. It was intended to be as elegantly ornate as it was productive and was the garden accessory every aspiring homemaker wanted. I am not mocking this. My own vegetable gardens have been and still are strongly influenced by this, and the idea of the formal, decorative kitchen garden is a beautiful one.

The potager is rooted in the medieval monastic gardens – Diane de Poitiers's garden at Chenonceau was essentially a potager – but gradually became increasingly decorative as the formalism of the seventeenth century spread and dominated all kinds of horticulture. The result is a strange mishmash that is hard to pin to any age. I suspect that all gardens carry the influences of the previous generations, as much in its rejection of as its replication. They change and evolve and it is only because box is so very long-lived and hardy that the structure of gardens tends to survive and be regarded with such

2 And the word 'potager' was not to be translated or said with an English accent. If you did not understand all the subtle distinction between potager and kitchen garden then you were distinctly outré. In fact the word stems simply from 'potage' or soup and referred to the place where one could gather the basic ingredients for the simple soup that was the mainstay of most people's midday meal.

significance. What written evidence there is from Renaissance gardens shows that vegetable gardens often contained lots of flowers, and formal parterres housed fruit that was carefully cultivated to provide an income even to the very wealthiest of houses.

There are two things to know before consigning Villandry to that section of theme-park France that houses potagers. The first is that the garden is so much more than just ornate veg – in fact I would argue that the potager is the least successful and interesting part of the garden – and the second is that it is an elaborate and brilliant twentieth-century reconstruction of the idea of a Renaissance garden. There is nothing to suggest that it is in any way unfaithful to the original but equally no one is suggesting that it is a careful reconstruction.

The château was built in the 1530s on the site of the earlier castle[3] known as Colombiers which Jean Le Breton demolished save the Keep, which he kept, and replaced with an elegant three-sided building with an open courtyard and with arcaded ground floors, and high mansard roofs set with gabled windows. This was one of the last of the great flush of Renaissance castles to be built in the Loire valley and is typical of the light, elegant simplicity that now exemplifies this line of great buildings along the Loire and Cher. Jean le Breton had been finance minister under Francis I (the father of Henri II whose mistress was Diane de Poitiers). He was also French ambassador to Rome during the papacy of Clement VII. This was a time when there was an extraordinary flowering of Italian High Renaissance gardens, initiated by Cosimo de Medici's Villa Castello in Florence. Jean Le Breton drank deep of that air. He studied the buildings and gardens of Italy and was clearly influenced by them when he came back to build his own castle and grounds.

3 Where, on 4 July 1189, the dying Henry II of England met King Philippe of France at the castle and signed the Peace of Colombiers, and raged against his son, Richard, later Richard I of England and known as 'Coeur de Lion', who had fought against him for the French side. Henry died just days later.

The château was not then called Villandry but Jean Le Breton got royal permission to change the name of both town and castle and it became a sign of his rise in status and rank until his death in 1556. His descendants kept the name, at a time when France was going through political and religious turmoil, with his grandson being made Marquis de Villandry.

The château was radically rebuilt after being bought from Jean Le Breton's descendants by the Marquis de Castellane in 1754. It was modernised. The Keep suffered the indignity of having casement windows cut into it. Renaissance was not sexy any more, just old. Then came the Revolution and the estate was confiscated. Like so many of the best buildings and houses in Europe, it became the property of the Napoleon family. In 1810 it was bought by the Hainguerlots, who owned it for the rest of the century and replaced the formal garden with an English-style landscaped park. Where there had been parterres, potagers and tightly clipped topiary, were now sweeping lawns and mature trees. The three distinct levels of the modern garden were graded to one flowing slope and the large pond at the top level was filled in to make a bowling green (giving rise to my favourite French word, *boulingrin*).

'English' gardens based upon the work of Capability Brown and Humphry Repton were very trendy in nineteenth-century Europe, but this was also politically expedient. Formal gardens were associated with the pre-Revolutionary aristocracy and turning them into parkland removed any taint of their hated rule. By the time this ceased to be so much of a problem, perhaps the middle of the century, the new gardens were established and changing them would have been an enormous undertaking. However, this is precisely what happened next.

In 1906 Villandry was bought by Dr Joachim Carvallo, a Spanish-born doctor who had emigrated to Paris in 1879. In 1899 he married an American heiress, Ann Coleman. These two foreigners bought Villandry – presumably with her money – with the intention of restoring it from its rundown state, with an overgrown landscaped park, to their idea of what they considered to be its Renaissance glory. It was an immense undertaking, involving excavating, rebuilding and replanting all six hectares. The moat was dug out, the courtyard, which had been closed in the eighteenth-century rebuild, was opened up and, despite the scale of the undertaking, everything was done to an astonishingly high standard. There were no half measures.

Some of the restoration is based upon archaeological evidence and descriptions, much is guesswork and, indeed, simply reflects the taste of the Carvallos. I do not think this matters at all. The garden carries its history lightly, as all gardens must, because the only certainty is that they will change. I once asked the head gardener at Levens Hall in Cumbria, made in 1694 by a Frenchman, Guillaume Beaumont, and the oldest surviving garden in the UK, which is famous for its massive, monumental and surreal topiary, how long it would take to create this from scratch. About thirty years, he said. That's all? About that. For nearly 300 years all we have been doing is holding it back, working hard to stop it growing.

It takes four gardeners at Villandry two months just to prune the 1,200 lime trees. The box hedges in the potager take four men three weeks to cut. Cutting back. Restraint. Control. Having done the initial groundwork setting up any garden and allowing it ten to thirty years to establish, everything from then on is the art of curtailment. This is the essence of gardens like Villandry. One can see why the ideas of Gilles Clément at La Vallée are so radical and provoking.

Visitors all come to see the potager, but the place to start is up Jean Le Breton's tower to get a bird's-eye view of the garden. Go on a wonderful June morning, as I did five years or so ago, and it is stunning, with the garden laid out like an ornate quilt, its patterns and layers and volumes revealed in a way that can only be guessed at from the ground. Go on a day when it is pouring with rain, as it was on my last visit, and peer from under the brim of an umbrella, and it still looks good.

The most interesting things about Villandry from the point of view of garden design are its volumes. The British, caught up in an obsession with plants, their provenance and individual performance, often fail to understand the power of volume in a garden, regardless of which plants create it, overlooking the wood for the trees. Villandry is a masterclass in volume.

The garden is broadly laid out on four terraces coming down the hillside,[4] although the 'terraces' are each as big as a park. The highest terrace, bounded by tightly mown steep grass banks with a line of pruned limes at top and bottom – Villandry does these grand, landscaped repetitions so well – is the Sun Garden. It was made in 2008 by the current owner, Henri Carvallo, to celebrate the centenary of the start of restoration of the gardens and designed by Louis Benech. Unlike the rest of Villandry, it has huge borders themed by colour. I visited in 2007 when the area was being prepared by planting hedges, and the proposed borders were sown with green manure and cereals. It looked rather wonderful just like that but now the curving grass paths – in themselves extremely unusual in a French garden – and mature beds have a twenty-first-century, or at least unashamedly modern, panache and energy built out of colour, with a blue, white and pink garden and a yellow and orange garden.[5] The borders are all really generous and soft, with the soil mulched so there is no bare soil and they feel exciting and a genuine expansion of the garden. Certainly shackles have been thrown off in its making.

The second terrace is the water garden, based around a large pool

4 The site actually slopes both east–west and north–south and the east–west level is created by an enormous stone retaining wall holding back the hillside with woods above. I have been to Villandry three times over the past few years and each time this wall strikes me anew as a piece of architectural and landscape genius, both sublimely beautiful as well as astonishingly bold. But then I do like a wall.
5 The subdivision of gardens is always a descriptive minefield. I feel comfortable calling any separate, enclosed or defined area a garden, even if it clearly is connected to other gardens and they all are set within a garden. There are tougher things in life to deal with.

surrounded by grass plats and broad gravel paths, which acts as a reservoir for irrigation and to feed the canals that tumble down the slope into the moat. It is an empty, calm place, a space for the mind.

Then you cross the lovely path, lined by silver-trunked limes, that swoops in a long shallow curve right across the width of the garden and look down on the ornamental or Music Garden. This is one of my favourite pieces of horticulture in the world.

Bounded on the east by the long canal and its vine-covered oak walkway that divides it from the Garden of Love and on the west by walls and tiered hedges with the Bowling Green and Maze above, the Music Garden was designed by Joachim Carvallo and qualifies him, in my opinion, as a great garden designer. It is very simple. Great blocks of box, cut dead flat, are divided into segments, quadrants, diamonds, triangles and oddments, with a few sentinels of yew topiary like chesspieces marking the board. The box is interspersed with lavender, santolina and, on my last visit, a couple of rather eccentric segments of marigolds, but it does not need any floral addition. They distract. Shape, form and volume are the things and they amount to a sculptural presence that is breathtakingly inspiring. It works both as a flat piece of broderie, looked down on from the upper levels and, when you are walking amongst it, as huge blocks of green. This is because the box is clipped off at waist height, giving real substance and weight. I wondered how on earth they managed to reach the inside of these slabs of green, thinking one would have to dangle down from a hoist, but I was told it is much simpler than that. The gardeners simply wade into it, up to their waists in hedge, the green parting before and closing behind them.

The final tier, on the same level as the moat and the château, is the potager. This is the one part of the garden where the volumes do not work well because the hedges, made out of the dwarf box (*Buxus* 'Suffruticosa'), are too low for the area they are set in and the proportion of path to border is too great. This looks fine in two dimensions from above but feels too open and unarticulated on the ground. It is, in every sense of the word, flat. That it exists undoubtedly adds to the gaiety of nations, but walking through it is disconcerting. Gradually, and slightly shamefully – because, as a keen gardener one surely should be delighted with it, should admire and respect it – I realised that it is rather dull. The lack of structure means interest has to be found in the plants on the ground and these simply do not sustain interest. Once you have taken in the patterns and configurations and established what the vegetables are, then there is nothing more to see or know. There is no becoming, no dynamic, no sense of growth into something other than the blank face that it presents at that moment.

This is not helped by the knowledge that the vast majority of these vegetables will not be eaten[6] and being purely decorative robs them of most of their meaning. They become like silk flowers in a vase. And if a vegetable garden is not directly connected to food – potager to potage and kitchen garden to the kitchen – then it has no soul.

The potager at Villandry is the horticultural equivalent of one of those meals – and there are depressingly many – that arrive with every variation of dribble and roulade, jus, velouté and refinement of the food to the point at which it functions less as a meal and more as a decorative display of the chef's arrangement and skill. It is as if the ego of the chef has swallowed up the spirit of generosity and hospitality, chewing it over and then regurgitating it in spatters and morsels, as often as not served on a slate or square plate. The central task of serving delicious food as simply as possible, so that it connects directly with the appetite and desires of the eater, seems to have been replaced by a slightly sulky, truculent offering that demands more than it gives. It was not always like this. Forty years ago, nine out of ten meals in any restaurant in any part of France were a celebration. Some were better than others but almost all were

6 The vegetables are not harvested until they need replacing so as to maintain the overall unity. When they are all gathered up and replaced they go to the restaurant and the family of the household and gardeners but the head gardener told me that the overwhelming majority go onto the compost heap.

good, and almost all were a shared experience between cook and diner. I wonder when this started to break apart, when the diner became such a passive recipient of the chef's performance?

Function and form in a garden do go hand in hand, even if the only function is to be beautiful. Lose the function and the form starts to become questionable. So this one-dimensional view of a garden coupled with the two-dimensional layout leaves the visitor reduced to admiring the statistics rather than the thing itself.

Mind you, the statistics are worth bandying about. Some 150,000 plants are grown in the potager every year, including 30,000 lettuces, of which half are grown by the gardeners and half bought in, but every one is raised in a container and then individually planted out. In the whole garden three times that number of plants are used for the bedding in the parterres. I was allowed to have a mooch around the greenhouses (greenhouses, potting sheds, tool-sheds, hardening-off areas: these are all the most informative bits of a garden, where you see how it is really run, and Villandry is run very well indeed) and saw one greenhouse entirely filled just with celery plants. Three thousand identical tufts of green lined up in row upon row of black pots. System. Order. Method. It is all undeniably impressive and really does have a rhythm and balance that is beautiful. But it comes with a horticultural health warning. Walking round the garden I started noticing, in a finicky, nit-picky way, a few weeds, some suckers from the standard roses, stray leaves and untrimmed corners of box hedging. I realised that amongst all the immaculate pursuit of perfection I was looking for fault and that things that I would forgive and even encourage in the hurly-burly of a garden that wore its failure on its sleeve had become irritating. I suppose if you live by perfection and order then you must die by it too and be judged on terms that would otherwise be unnecessary and unfair.

On the other side of the potager from the château, up another level, is the bowling green (I think in practice a croquet lawn, but that is more nit-picking) which, after all the intricacy and intense maintenance, is wonderfully calm and simple. Green grass, green pleached limes and a green hornbeam hedge surrounding it. A garden needs very little more than this.

Although the garden is designed to be viewed from the top working down, I strongly advise starting with the potager, getting it out of the way and slowly working up to the top and then coming back down by a different route, finishing with lunch or at least coffee and a bun at the very good restaurant. Go thinking that Villandry is a potager with château attached and you will be disappointed. Go to see one of the great gardens of the world which includes a highly, slightly absurdly ornate vegetable garden and you will find it there in all its glory.

22

LE CHÂTEAU DU GROS CHESNAY

Drive a hundred-odd kilometres north of Villandry and you are in another country, entering the flatter, greyer twenty-first-century France, whose white edge-of-town hyperstores and factories – and they look identical – seem to sprawl uncontrolled in a dystopian presentiment of the future we deserve.

Just outside Le Mans I stayed in one of those hotels that are decorated like a modern hospital waiting room and make no pretence of being anything other than a stopover for lonely underpaid businessmen and lorry drivers. They are often clean, quite cheap and quiet. They are often the least worst option. Holed up in your room you can usually make them perfectly comfortable. But their corridors and lobbies make my heart plummet. At breakfast, rainy darkness outside, a drinks machine with buttons serving variations on the theme of tepid brown liquid, Rice Krispies, tinned grapefruit segments and pots of sugared yoghourts on ice set out in wavy-edged glass bowls, with a covered dish of baked beans and another of congealed scrambled egg floating in its slightly scummy water, the besuited men ate with their eyes fixed on the television on the wall. There are times when the greatest gift for any traveller is a kind of blind cheeriness.

It was worth making the effort. I wanted to see a set-up – half-garden, half-market garden – that supplies L'Arpège, the Parisian restaurant of the chef Alain Passard. I could not begin to afford to eat at L'Arpège,[1] but when I read about the chef's commitment to fresh, organically grown vegetables and that he bases his entire menu around the produce of the day – literally of that day – I was intrigued. A man after my own heart.

Twenty minutes south-west of Le Mans, along the river Sarthe that twists through the flat willow-banked countryside, the rain becoming mist through which the willows and villages lurched, was the vegetable garden I wanted to see. This area is one of those contradictions that you find all over France once outside the great cities. On the one hand there is the appalling face of modern life squatting by the side of big roads and on the edge of towns, on the other there is the France that has remained similar for hundreds of years, if not millennia, where the countryside swallows up people, villages, communities so that they almost disappear. Right up to the end of the nineteenth century the Sarthe department had 20,000 communities with fewer than fifteen people, each self-contained, each barely more than a family. These people effectively lived in another land from Paris and that sense of remove still exists. Yet this plot just along the river from Fille is operating as the back garden of a restaurant in the most sophisticated centre of Paris. It is a curious juxtaposition.

Passard has three separate gardens that he owns to supply the restaurant, each with a different soil type. This one is dedicated to growing the produce best suited to the sandy, light soil of the Sarthe.

---

1 This is not true. I could. But whereas a Frenchman with my income would feel as though it was a luxury that he had worked hard to enjoy every once in a while and that it was a celebration both of his own success and the supreme sensual, intellectual and cultural joys of haute cuisine, as an Englishman I simply could not bring myself to pay as much for a meal as I would normally spend on food and drink in an extravagant month. It would feel as though I was taking money from some other part of my life that needed it in order to satisfy an indulgence that could almost certainly be equally well satiated for half the price – and still be excessive. Eating out in France is expensive at the best of times and colossally so on occasions. It is a huge cultural divide.

Vegetables like carrots, potatoes, salad crops and asparagus. There is also a plot in the clay of Normandy and a third in Le Manche with silty, alluvial soil that specialises in herbs. It is a refinement of *pays* and *terroir* to go and choose the ideal locations to become the source for your desired ingredients rather than selecting the ingredients that will grow best where you happen to be. As I say, it takes the concept of *terroir* and turns it on its head through the speed and ease of modern transport and yet preserves all the essential qualities of it such as being true to the specific geography, climate and geology of a place that in themselves are inextricably bound with local culture and even society. Unlike La Chassagnette in the Camargue which has the garden out the back, it spreads Passard's plot right across France. It is the power of the chef – manipulating food, designing the plate – spreading to the garden. Perhaps.

I arrived at Le Château du Gros Chesnay, the sandy-soiled and first of the great chef's vegetable gardens, as the rain dribbled to a stop. I think I expected to find a version of the over-embellished plate, all spatters and reductions, imposed on to a garden. So much for prejudice and preconception. I could not have been more wrong.

For a start the château, although lovely, is modest and was a full-blown building site, the grass muddy and uncut and the car following the ruts like tramlines. Then, when I began to explore the growing area, set to one side, it was downright scruffy – but good scruffy. Scruffy because no one was trying making it look good for others' eyes. All the time and energy of the five full-time gardeners was going into growing vegetables and fruit as well as they knew how. Added to that there is a commitment to a holistic, organic approach which integrates all life as part of the process of putting the best possible food before M. Passard's customers. Long grass, brambles, nettles and hedges are carefully encouraged to provide habitats for invertebrates, birds and mammals, while ditches and ponds attract amphibians, and all combine to create a balanced, sustaining health. This is not hippy shit but straightforward practical production. I do it myself. It works.

Everything served in the evening in rue de Varenne, some 200 kilometres away in the centre of Paris, is harvested the same day. Nothing is stored even overnight. This means that only produce which is at its exact best for eating is harvested. This makes the restaurant extremely unusual, but it is in fact no different from nipping out into the garden, seeing what is nicest and readiest and constructing the dish or meal from them. I, and lots of gardeners, do that for half the year. But we have no pressure and few expectations. Simplicity is the greatest domestic culinary virtue if the ingredients are good. But the French, especially those who run or frequent restaurants adorned with Michelin stars like American generals, do not celebrate simplicity unless it is the result of fantastic and convoluted skill, trouble and expense. The integration and umbilical connection between garden and kitchen that La Chassagnette and certainly scores of restaurants now practise is made into high drama because it has to be winged to Paris. Of course if the château were the restaurant, then it would be even fresher but it does show how Paris is where it is truly at. Anything outside the centre is still provincial.

In truth the habitué of the 7th arrondissement that early March morning would have found the provinces pretty dirty and bleak. There was not a lot to see. There would not be in any vegetable garden in the northern hemisphere. But any experienced vegetable grower can smell when things are done right, can feel it in the soles of their muddy boots. A good vegetable set-up has a rhythm and energy that is evident at any time of year and in all that it does. The polytunnels, horrible things that they are, sheltered from the cold wind, were already filled with rows of young rocket, mizuna, chard, spinach, pak choi, mustards, cabbages, early lettuce, peas climbing pig wire strung between bamboos and held up with baler twine and potatoes[2] already

---

2 Everywhere I went I asked what potatoes people grew and almost everywhere the same answer dominated: 'Charlotte'. Occasionally there would be some 'Belle de Fontenay', but 'Charlotte' was by far the most popular. Given that both are a waxy, essentially boiling, second early potato, it says much for how the French like to cook and eat them.

breaking the surface of their ridges. In the outside beds everything is grown in long temporary raised beds, narrow enough to straddle splay-legged, with just room to walk single file between them, which will then be planted with individual seedlings raised by and large in soil blocks.[3]

The ground is cultivated entirely by two Pecheron horses, Devine and Gabrielle, and a pair of slightly bad-tempered donkeys. This is ploddy and slow but faster than any machine that would be small enough to do the work and the horses are gentle on this light soil – as well as gentle on this self-consuming planet. The whole place takes pride in reusing, mending, adapting and treasuring the old that serves well, be it a horse or a hoe.

Perhaps the food is less than the sum of its parts and perhaps the prices are ridiculous when you consider that a well-run allotment – and there are tens of thousands of those in France – will produce vegetables you eat the same day more cheaply than can be bought from any shop, but it was all terribly impressive and inspiring, not least because it was being done at all. To combine ethics and food in a commercial enterprise is painfully rare.

I left not with a burning desire to dine at L'Arpège and try some of M. Pessard's craft (I realise I risk being branded a philistine – his Art, his rarefied, brilliant Art) but to try some of what I had seen in my own garden. That is about as high a recommendation as I can give.

---

3 Soil blocks are made by making a seed compost mix that is dampened to the consistency of thick mud and then either cut into squares with a special blocker and carefully lifted and placed into some kind of container or moveable surface, or else the mix is put into a container like a seed tray and divided up with a knife. A seed is sown in each block which then dries, contracts and separates from the others like chocolate brownies in a cake tin. The virtue of them is partly that they do away with the need for thousands of plastic modules or pots but mainly because the roots are air-pruned as they reach the edge of the block. This makes them denser, tougher and quicker to grow when transplanted.

23

COURANCES

Over the years I have played a game which is futile, self-indulgent and tinged with a dubious cast of envy, but it whiles away the empty moment or two. It goes like this.

I choose a passing building, usually uncommonly big or beautiful or desirable in some way. A six-storey house in Mayfair or Manhattan, perhaps a mansion set in a landscaped park or a Scottish estate. A critical factor to the choice is that it must be somewhere that I have never remotely had an opportunity to live in but which is conventionally, even irresistibly desirable. And – this is essential – it must be wholly and unreachably beyond my means and sphere. Once selected, the building is, in the same moment, owned. I may never have seen it before (but there are favourites) and it may just have been glimpsed as I pass, but it is now mine.

I explore this thought a little, weigh up the implications, wander, if you will, the empty building with a proprietorial air. If this takes root and I am on a long journey or it is three in the morning and my brain can neither sleep nor properly wake, I will take my time about this. Poke about. Admire the view. Take in the furniture, paintings, fittings which are left exactly as I have seen them. View the horizon and know that my new lands stretch beyond the eyes' scan. Then the decision has to be made. Would I live there if that were the condition of ownership? If not, then game over. If, however, I feel I could, then I wander through my life as it might become in this new, utterly unplanned and inappropriate setting. At this point the game usually fizzles out, because I have yet to find anywhere I want to live more than my own home. A variation of the game is that I have the choice to live there all the time or sell it. That option sets up another whole train of fantasy whereby I suddenly have oodles of money to embellish and improve what I already have – the best of all worlds. Power without responsibility, the stuff of all dreams.

But just occasionally I come across a building that confounds the easy indulgence of this daydream and Courances is one. Because although I am not sure I would want to live there all the time – and thus leave my home – I certainly would not want to sell it. I regard it as one of the loveliest houses and gardens I have ever seen.

There is nothing about Courances that I would want to change. It is, in a profoundly satisfying way, integral and immutably itself. Château, gardens and woods are all inextricably bound to make as magical and beautiful a *domaine* as can be found in the whole of France. Yet the thing that has made it so complete and at ease with itself is that it has steadily changed and evolved and continues to do so.

You take the road from Le Mans to Chartres, perhaps stopping to visit the cathedral (which I have yet to do, despite taking that road a number of times) and veer off towards Fontainebleau. In fact I veered off a little further to make a little speculative sub-visit to the village of Milly-le-Forêt, where the garden of Jean Cocteau is in the process of being restored. It was not up to much. There is a collection of apples, all cleverly pruned, but then all fruit trees in France are well pruned. In general the place seemed uncared for. I was told that the gardener was 'learning'. It was cold, showery, lunchtime and sometimes gardens just do not engage, like reading a book which you know, within the first five pages, you are not going to finish. If Cocteau is important to you, then it is a pilgrimage that is probably worth making, given that it is so close to Courances, Fontainebleau and Vaux le Vicomte. And there is a good shop that is much better stocked and tended than the garden. I consoled myself with a dish of kidneys and a glass of wine in the only bar open in Milly-le-Forêt.

Courances is just five minutes up the road, with the château set back behind fine iron gates and down a long drive. Stop, peer through the bars and the only reasonable reaction is to smile, because it is so stupendously, exactly, as a French château ought to be. A dead straight approach, paved in sets,[1] is flanked by long mown lawns, a pair of canals and then a double avenue of mature plane trees. It contains all the elements of the classical French garden. Proportion, balance and harmony using symmetry, straight lines, water, grass and the repeated rhythm of trees whose wriggling, sinuous branches are reflected in the dark water adding depth and an essential touch of movement. This is hardly uncommon. You will find similar entrances all over the country – but none better than this.

The driveway leads to a seventeenth-century brick building, the courtyard before it flanked by two brick and stone pavilions, each one a perfect little house. For a moment the game kicks in. Swap one of the pavilions, maybe on its own, in a wood? With a view? But you cannot break the whole up, even in fantasy.

The first house was built in the Middle Ages to go with the seigniory and when Francis I, father of Henri II and arranger of his marriage to Catherine de Medici, transformed the hunting lodge at Fontainebleau into a palace and his favourite royal residence, the area became fashionable for the Court. Courances was bought by Cosme Clausse, the owner of the Château Fleury-en-Bière, in 1548. The land began to be shaped and water controlled and moved.

---

1 The pathmaker in me immediately thinks of the physical business of laying each one, as deep as it is wide, a heavy block of stone needing two hands and strong arms to lift and place just so, and the scores of lorry loads to bring them in and sand to set them in, and the gentle but exact camber that is held along its length. No machine can do this. A hand-made road.

Water is the key to Courances. There are seven springs rising on the land and the basic layout of the Renaissance water garden still remains. When one thinks of the extraordinary lengths that gardeners of the period went to in order to get water into gardens – Louis XIV planning to divert the Loire to Versailles with a specially built canal and half-building an aqueduct to carry water from the Seine, or in Italy, Cardinal Ippolito d'Este diverting the river at Tivoli to supply his fountains – this is hugely important. Water in all its forms was the most effective display of power, money, control and taste that a Renaissance or Baroque gardener could employ. So to have it in limitless supply was the greatest advantage that any site could possess for a prospective garden. Even the modern visitor, blasé with sheets and plumes of water everywhere, is still immediately aware of the generosity of the water here. Unlike other gardens of the period, and in particular Versailles, it is not the fountains and play of water that is so impressive as the generosity of the stretches of light rippling back from the surface of the moats, ponds, rills and canals. This brings a palpable sense of calm and stately charm.

In 1622 Courances was bought by the Gallard family and the present château was built in the 1630s. In 1768 the Nicolay family married into Courances and lived there in style, but father and son both lost their heads in the Revolution and the estate was confiscated for a while.

During the nineteenth century the château was unoccupied for forty-two years and in 1871 it was sold to Baron de Haber, a wealthy banker. Courances was both an escape from the rampant anti-Semitism of Paris and also his entrée into an aristocratic lifestyle, a move which was helped by marrying his only daughter to a Comte Octave de Béhague. Even with his bankers' millions, the restoration was a tall order. The house was practically falling down, with a tree growing up from the dining room through the roof and the garden an overgrown marsh. The Baron cleaned out the canals and ponds, put new stairs on the front of the house and built another wing. He died in 1892 and left Courances to his granddaughter, Berthe de

Béhague who married Comte Jean de Ganay. It remains in the de Ganay family.

The Germans took over the château in the Second World War and used it as a driving school and they covered the lawns with barracks and concrete. Then the Americans occupied it, before Field Marshal Montgomery took up residence, from 1949 to 1955, when he was commanding the NATO troops based a few kilometres down the road at Fontainebleau. Philippine de Ganay, the current *châtelaine*, says that she remembers him as rather a cold and formal figure who nevertheless was relaxed and kind with her small children.[2]

Philippine, Marquise de Ganay, is one of those formidable but utterly charming women from a generation now growing very old and seemingly not being replaced. She was born Philippine de Noailles, niece of Charles de Noailles, maker of the Villa Noailles and its Cubist garden at Hyères, and recalled 'such amusing' parties there before the war. She had a British nanny and her perfect English is peppered with prewar expressions straight from P.G. Wodehouse. Do you know X? I overheard her being asked. Oh yes, she replied, he is a peach! So, most surely, is she.

She had always loved gardens and on her frequent visits to England after the war would go and visit gardens such as Hidcote and Sissinghurst – at a time when the French were not that interested in gardening. She organised local garden visits to generate interest and she and her sister would set off in a car with a ladder on the roof so that they could climb up and look over garden walls to vet a potential garden. If they were no good they could slink away without the owner going through the indignity of knowing they had been rejected.

2 This recalls an odd story I heard from a fellow of my college when I was a student. He was at a prep school in Wiltshire in the late 1950s when the great Field Marshal, Britain's most prominent war hero, paid a visit. He took a shine to my supervisor, then aged about eleven or twelve, and invited him to tea. The following Sunday a chauffeur-driven Daimler appeared to whisk him to Monty's home. Tea was taken, rather formally, and kindly but stilted conversation shared. Then the car drove him back to school. That was the end of the experience. In an age of paedophile paranoia this might be deemed as creepy but I think it a lonely, sad story.

Philippine and her husband had feel. They understood what the place needed to be, or perhaps more aptly, what is was trying to become, so their touches, although involving major work to both house and garden, were all light. They gave it a helping hand rather than taking a grip of it. They instinctively understood that Courances had a life flow of its own that ran through them and would, with a little help, continue to run long after them too. When you think how so many formal gardens attempt to pin nature down and hold it in place as an act of colossal, although often beautiful, hubris, theirs is an approach of intuitive wisdom. She told me how she and her husband repaired the garden after the various military occupiers had done their worst, taking up huge areas of concrete and then gradually changing the gravel paths to grass. It is this extra greenness that softens and deformalises it and, with all the extra light bouncing from the water, gives it a rich emerald glow.

The neglect in the nineteenth century and its wartime travails are probably the best things that could have happened to Courances – that and the care and money that have been lavished on it across the centuries, usually just in the nick of time. So the bosquets, which would have been planted as neat, little wooded boxes of delight with high clipped hedges, have changed utterly. Now the trees have grown enormous and mature so they soar up cathedral-grand. The walks have become woodland rides but are flanked by trimmed box hedges at about head-height. So there are long, wide green grass paths, deep green box hedges and a dark green understorey of yew and other trees, filled with unseen birdsong, towering heavenward, filtering out the sky as their leaves emerge at the end of April and greening the light. This is not what anyone intended. This is not how any garden-maker or planner wanted it to end up. It has all gone completely wrong in the best and most joyous way imaginable.

Of course, this is less than all, or even most, of the story. Four and a bit gardeners work hard to keep what needs keeping properly kept. Immediately outside the house the parterre, pleached limes and hornbeam hedges are immaculate. The mowing alone must take days every week. I know myself that cultivating an artful naturalness is just as much work as strict formality.

There is a large Japanese garden, begun in 1908, around the time when, following great Japanese exhibitions in Paris and London, Japanese gardens became immensely fashionable. It must take a great deal of maintenance. To a visitor trying to absorb as much of a country's culture as possible through the medium of its gardens, the elaborate recreation of another style, be it Japanese or English landscape, can never be more than an admirable exercise or pastiche. Clever but pointless.

Infinitely better is the long open sweep of the *miroir* with its wide grass lawns and statues set against a wall of clipped yew under the trees or even the mown grass beneath the clean trunks of the chestnut quincunx. The bridge over the leat from the 600-metre-long Grand Canal that is lawn above and clean stone slabs below, the lovely pair of hounds that guard the avenue of water steps of 'Les Nappes'.

Now the château is lived in by four generations of the family in a series of *appartements*. Children run and play and ride bikes and ponies, and the tapestries and pictures remain on the walls. It holds together by its looseness. Courances has escaped imprisonment in its past yet has absorbed influences and accidents of history and made them its own and by accepting them and taking them in has resulted in a garden that is grander, simpler, more accessible and more charming than any other.

24

VAUX LE VICOMTE

On 17 August 1961 I was six.[1] It was a Thursday. On Thursday afternoons the ice-cream van came round and we would hear its
approaching chimes in time to run and beg the sixpence needed for a
lolly. I, a twin, was still always we. Within a year I would be sent away
to boarding school and nothing would be the same again. It was the
last summer of innocence. I had a strawberry Mivvi. She a choc ice.
We shared them both. It was the highlight of our week. Party time.

Three hundred years earlier, on 17 August 1661, Samuel Pepys, his
morning's work done, was hearing about the ribaldry at the newly
established Court of Charles II.

> At the Privy Seal, where we had a seal this morning. Then met
> with Ned Pickering, and walked with him into St. James's Park
> (where I had not been a great while), and there found great and
> very noble alterations. And, in our discourse, he was very for-
> ward to complain and to speak loud of the lewdness and
> beggary of the Court, which I am sorry to hear, and which I am
> afeard will bring all to ruin again.

1 I wrote these words on 17 August 2012. I only realised the connection a few hours
later.

From what we know of Pepys, he was not sorry to hear of it at all, but absorbed the salacious gossip as he walked around admiring the improvements to the park and garden of St James with titillation, envy and admiration.

Yet the fear of bringing all to ruin once again is real enough. Less than two years earlier the British state was in danger of falling apart. State and Crown had been fighting, with appalling, catastrophic consequences, for twenty years. Oliver Cromwell was dead, his son Richard clearly not up to governance, Parliament riven and Charles II, uncrowned and hitherto unwanted, sulking in Holland. His restoration returned colour to a monochrome Britain but also, and much more importantly, order. To risk that through lewdness and beggary, however exciting, could provoke a return to puritanism and revolt – bringing all to ruin again.

Across the Channel, on the hot afternoon of 17 August 1661, Charles's first cousin, Louis XIV of France, was making his way north along the appalling roads from the royal palace at Fontainebleau. The weather was glorious. He was going to a party and he expected that it would be magnificent in every respect. He knew this because there had been another party at the same location, the new château of Vaux le Vicomte that was about halfway between Fontainebleau and Paris, about a month earlier. The King's brother and his wife, Henrietta, the younger sister of Charles II of England, as well as her mother,[2] had been guests on that occasion and returned with accounts of the brilliance of the festivities and the magnificence of the house and garden.

2 This was Henrietta Maria, the widow of the beheaded English king Charles I and thus the mother of Charles II and Louis's aunt. The blood connections between the courts of Charles and Louis were of the closest kinship. Louis was ten and had been king for five years when Charles I, his uncle by marriage, was beheaded and the state taken over. At that age he was smuggled out of Paris to the refuge of St Germain during the *Frondes*, the French civil wars between 1648 and 1653. He therefore had a very personal understanding that the possibilities and dangers of Pepys's 'ruin again' were real and present.

Louis was twenty-two years old and had just taken over the personal control of government after eighteen years as titular king whilst France had been governed by a regency council controlled by a handful of powerful men, latterly and most powerfully of all, Cardinal Mazarin. Mazarin had just died and Louis was now taking the power of his own throne.

The man appointed First Minister to replace Mazarin was one of his trusted aides, Nicolas Fouquet. Under Mazarin, Fouquet had been superintendent of finances. He was already wealthy through marriage and skilful acquisition and had various houses and estates other than Vaux. This wealth was made all the greater by his rise up the rungs of power. The post of superintendent of finances involved negotiating and broking the king's borrowings with financiers over Europe, with all the possibilities of commissions, bribes, kickbacks and rake-offs that still attach themselves to all the sleek middle-men fixing deals, converted his existing wealth into vast riches. This made him enemies.

The coaches of the royal party, including the Queen Mother, Anne of Austria, and her niece, Maria Theresa, the young Queen, six months pregnant beneath the ribbons and bows of her party finery, bounced and heaved through the royal forests, over the Seine and along the road that still runs to the great gates of Vaux le Vicomte, the road that, as they and any new visitor is heedless of, runs in at the same level as the hall, running through the house and on to the giant statue of Hercules right across the valley of Vaux that the garden crosses. This is not happenstance. Nothing at Vaux le Vicomte had happened by chance. It is an expression of mastery over nature and – unluckily for Nicolas Fouquet as he awaits the visit of the King – over man. Today is the greatest of honour of his forty-six years. And his world is about to tumble around him.

As you enter from the high road, the house is set back, and flanked by brick and stone stables that are mini-châteaux in them-selves. The house avoids vulgar pretension. It is elegant rather than palatial, the honey limestone glowing even on the grey overcast days that I visited. In the late summer sun of 1661, freshly hewn, it would have positively gleamed. The King's carriage would have crossed the first courtyard, then the moat into the inner cobbled yard where Fouquet and his wife waited. It was six o'clock. The sun was still hot but its shadows began to add body.

Fouquet had bought Vaux twenty years earlier, as much for the status it gave him as for the château or estate as it was. But when he was nominated superintendent of finances in 1653 he began work by knocking down the existing house and buying up surrounding land. The project was under way.

Fouquet did not design Vaux le Vicomte, any more than Pope Julius II painted the Sistine Chapel, but he did deliberately foster an environment where artists, poets, philosophers, gardeners and musicians could meet and work together. His genius was in combining the complementing skills of the architect Le Vau, the painter and designer Le Brun and the garden designer Le Nôtre to create the first fully integrated house and garden. Every detail, from the earth moving and damming of the stream that ran down the shallow valley, to the huge dome sitting over the entrance hall, and the painted ceilings or the statues flanking the *allées*, were all of a piece. Every aspect was integrated, harmonious and spurred a connection to the next delight. It was, and is, a supreme masterpiece of integrated design conducted by Fouquet.

The cost was colossal. It is said that it took 18,000 men to build. At one stage Fouquet had the surrounding wall hastily built to hide them from passers-by, lest they should notice the incredible resources that he was able to muster and begin to question the source of his wealth. Although his role as superintendent of finances was open to every kind of corrupt manipulation, there is no evidence that he availed himself of these opportunities any more (or less) than his contemporaries. There was a torrent of money flowing in his direction and if his hand dabbled in the till he was nevertheless a longstanding and loyal servant of the crown. But Louis, chafing in his minority, was growing suspicious of him. Fouquet's real crime was to display his wealth in such lavishness and, in the King's eyes at least, flaunt it so openly.

We now think of the display of new money as vulgar and tasteless and like poor salacious Samuel Pepys hearing of the revels of the Restoration Court, we cannot help ourselves wanting whilst simultaneously despising it. But Vaux le Vicomte that August night was the height of all that every visitor regarded as the perfect taste. To the modern eye, the Baroque world in its pristine state would have seemed shockingly gleaming, brash and gaudy, channelling the spirit of Vegas or a dictator's palace more than our notion of refined constraint. Vaux on 17 August 1661 brilliantly summarised and paraded all that was admired in architecture, art, design and – tellingly – horticulture. This was better than anything anyone had ever set eyes on before. It had the panache and showbiz of an Olympics opening ceremony with the dignity of a state banquet.

There was an elaborate dinner in the garden for the 6,000 guests, followed by a play, *Les Fâcheux*, especially written by Molière and a ballet with music composed by the King's favourite composer, Lully. The King, of course, was celebrated as a dancer himself and at that age was at the peak of his balletic powers. The night culminated in a huge firework display that involved a life-size whale floating up the canal amongst the explosions and eruptions. It is said that Fouquet was particularly proud of the whale.

This immense fête had the effect of sending Louis into a tyrannical rage of despotic envy. A few weeks later, on a visit to Nantes, Nicolas Fouquet was arrested by a captain of the musketeers called d'Artagnan. He spent the rest of his life imprisoned in the fortress of Pignerol in the Alps.

This was just the start of Louis's revenge. With Fouquet locked away he systematically looted Vaux of everything that could possibly be removed. Tapestries, furniture, statues, paintings and plate were all shipped away and eventually placed in Versailles.

Even – especially – the garden, the scene of Fouquet's crime, was stripped. Topiary, statues, fountains, orange trees all went to Versailles. Thousands of shrubs and hedging plants were stored in nurseries. Louis's main objective was not to punish Fouquet, although he did that with all the petulant viciousness of a tyrant, but to remove every possible element from Vaux that he could use himself.

Not only the objects but the people that made them were taken. The main designers, Le Vau, Le Brun and Le Nôtre, were hired for the new palace and gardens at Versailles. La Quintinie, the lawyer turned gardener who was in charge of the potager at Vaux, was taken to establish the Potager du Roi. The fountaineer Claude Robillard, the stonemason who made the grotto, the sculptors Anguier and Girardon who, with their team of masons made the scores of statues, even the flower gardener who planted up the parterres, all were poached by Louis to make him a palace and garden bigger and better than Vaux le Vicomte which would arouse the envy and respect that Fouquet had briefly touched before his wings were burned and he crashed ignominiously to the dark ground of a dank cell where, deprived of books, writing materials or access to the outdoors, he remained for nineteen years until his death in 1680.

There is no evidence to suggest but that they all went willingly, honoured by their call. Le Nôtre and La Quintinie not only became feted as the very best in their profession but remained lifelong friends and intimates with Louis, who trusted them above his courtiers.

Fouquet's wife regained possession of Vaux in 1674, then sold it in 1705. In 1875 it finally reached the hands of the Sommier family, whose fortune was made through sugar refining. They bought it at auction, completely dilapidated, and have gradually restored it to its 1661 glory as best and as faithfully as they could.

Sugar financed restoration in England too. There were huge

profits to be made from it, either through converting it into jams and marmalade, as my own Keiller forebears did, refining the cane cut by slaves in British or French colonies or simply trading it as sugar to be used in the house, as became increasingly common through the nineteenth century. The Keillers' marmalade money ended up being largely spent restoring the monoliths of Avebury in Wiltshire. It was money well spent. My granny was the youngest daughter of one of the Keiller brothers that built up the firm and a really substantial personal fortune in its Victorian heyday. When she died I received a bundle of shares, including, I recall, Tate & Lyle, sugar refiners, which I sold the same day for just under £7,000. I used the money to put a deposit on a house where I made my first garden. Not Avebury or Vaux but the right idea.

The Sommiers needed their fortune even to consider restoring Vaux. Apart from the planting and maintenance, all the hydro systems, pumps, piping and fountains had to be repaired and replaced. In 1968 the house and garden were formally rated a *Monument historique* and opened to the public, recouping some of these costs. The trade-off and dynamic between making the place pay and preserving its fabric – let alone its soul – continues. Patrice de Vogüé, the father, is determined to hold Le Nôtre's garden pure. Alexandre, the one of his twin sons actively running Vaux, agrees but knows they have to make money any way that they can. The other brother, whom I have not met, seems to want to cash in more overtly commercially. There is tension.

I have visited Vaux when it has been deserted, save for a couple of companions, with the sky a bleached grey and a cold wind cutting a chop into the canals and smearing the fountains across paths and parterres. The dome was wrapped in a plastic carapace around scaffolding and a white marquee pitched for weddings and marketing jamborees flapped uninvitingly. Yet the magic was still there. It is still regal even with its worst face on. It is not hard to see how the Sun King felt eclipsed.

Although subsequently dwarfed by Versailles, Vaux is an enormous garden, thirty-three hectares in its full extent, including a 3.5-hectare walled garden that is no longer used.[3] As you walk through the front door, across the hallway beneath the cupola, glimpses of black and white diamond marble floors stretching either side with gold and glass catching the light within the brocaded recesses, towards the tiny figure of Hercules on the horizon directly ahead, you arrive at a vast rectangular plat, gently curving away, bounded by tall trees on either side so there is nothing visible but garden or sky in every direction. The ornate *parterres de broderie*, the low box brocade patterned against red gravel, flank a central path that seems to lead directly to a grotto at the foot of a grassy slope. But it is a long way away. There are pools and fountains, topiary and, in Fouquet's day, before Louis got vengeful, statues lining the path.

Broad canals, hidden from the house, turn left and right from the

---

3 The main reason for the abandonment of the potager is because the produce would be potentially poisoned by industrial pollution: Louis's curse lingers

first central pool, leading to the Grille d'Eau in one direction and the entrance to the walled garden in the other.

The *miroir*, a huge square basin in which the house is perfectly reflected (or so I am told. It was cloudy and sunless on both occasions that I visited) is invisible as you walk down, yet looking back at the house from it, it seems to be the centrepiece of the entire garden that everything else revolves around.

The garden on the one hand seems laid out with complete visual accessibility, like a monstrous parterre, but on the other hand is constantly revealing itself and unfolding. Drop below it to the *basin de cascades* at the bottom of the huge grotto and the enormous Grand Canal stretches right across the garden.

To get to the grotto and Hercules, now looking down on you from the other side of what has revealed itself to be a gentle valley, you have to walk right round one of the ends, although on the night of Nicolas Fouquet's party Louis and other favoured guests were ferried across in a boat. I went right round the western stretch, which is a long and, had it not started raining hard, beautiful walk. Had I checked my map I would have seen it is better to go up to the Confessional with its massive grass platform flanked by broad hedges on stilts and then walk down to the eastern end where the round pool (so boats can turn) filled with enormous brown fish thicker than a thigh, leads you round either back to the grotto or diagonally up through the trees to the clearing before Hercules.

The garden at Vaux is based upon surprise as the main element of delight. Surprise itself as a weapon of garden design had been used for the previous hundred years but Le Nôtre broke the mould at Vaux by the scale and ease with which it is done. Rather than just spraying the visitor with water or having fountains play music or any of the other canards that his contemporaries used across Europe, Le Nôtre took order, symmetry and control and made them almost playful. He reorganised the landscape drastically – a village and two hamlets, a church and water mill were all destroyed to shift and accommodate his design – and yet the result seems given, almost geological.

At every turn you think you are seeing the whole and yet at every further turn more is revealed, so that the picture seems more complete, more fulfilled, with the final grand scene from the base of the enormous statue of the Farnese Hercules back towards the house and, were your eyes keen enough, through the hallway, across the entrance yard to the gates and the road that leads to the château. The end evenly balanced with its beginning.

According to Alexandre de Vogüé, the French rarely visit Vaux to see the garden. Most will walk outside when they have looked at the house and, if the weather is good, stroll down the first parterre to the circular pool or, if they are feeling adventurous, the grotto. However, anyone wanting to understand Le Nôtre's design or experience any of the range of the garden must walk up the grassy slope to Hercules.

It was from here that Louis apparently said to Nicolas Fouquet, 'I'm surprised.' Fouquet, failing to read the menace in the remark and instead thinking it a suitably Baroque compliment, replied, facetiously, 'And I am surprised that you are surprised.' Anyone else reaching that point without fanfare or exaltation should be not so much surprised as impressed – which is probably what Louis really felt. It is the perfect template for the ordering of nature, the triumph of the straight line over the site's subtle slopes that slip both sideways and away from the house.

This is what Louis understood and was determined to take that night, the knowledge and means to suborn nature in such a way that it seemed both majestically conquered and yet natural. What could be a better manifestation of his own reign? And how did Fouquet dare to assume such dominion?

In this light the party, the garden, the fireworks, the life-sized whale floating down the canal, the gold plates on which the food was served to the guests, the subtle and brilliant hydraulics that powered scores of fountains flanking the paths, the way that the château was exactly mirrored in the central point of the square basin that itself was invisible as you descended through the parterre and appeared as a sheet of sky set perfectly square on the falling ground and in turn revealed the grotto on the other side of the valley where the waters fell in a celebratory dance of fecundity, power and – the damning fact – majesty: all were a challenge so flagrant that the only wonder is that Louis waited two weeks to have Fouquet arrested and flung into his cell. But then the date of his arrest was 1 September, Louis's twenty-third birthday. It was a special present to himself. Party time.

It marked the beginning of Louis's extraordinary expansion into gardening and mastery of nature and set down a marker for all the other courtiers and politicians, fins circling the royal waters, that Louis was *capo dei capi* and his revenge was terrible. From now on both man and nature must bend to his rule or consider well the fate of poor Nicolas Fouquet, the man who dared to fly too close to the Sun King.

I walked through these gardens knowing the story and looking for ghosts of that night, laughter behind a hedge or wisps of Lully's music filtering through the breeze, but was accompanied only by the moaning buzz of two gardeners strimming and the folding splashes of fountains landing and flopping in the wind. The shape of the garden is wonderfully faithful, as far as anyone can definitively tell, but the substance is inevitably completely renewed and renewed again. I went down a shaft to see the hydraulic workings of the fountains where the water, stored in a vast reservoir beneath Hercules, is piped to successive fountains with great wheels to open and close the valves and sluices. The pipes look magnificently old but are part of the early-twentieth-century restoration and due, as soon as the money can be raised, for replacement. Hardly anything of Robillard's hydro system remains. Without constant renewal the centuries eats these things up.

Gardens are transient things, ready to run to wilderness and seed in the span of a war or messy divorce. Holding them in place is not so much like cleaning a statue as restraining a high-spirited horse. It wants to bolt. Much of the stone structure remains but these are not the same yews, box, hornbeam, planes or oaks. These are not the chippings that scrunched beneath Louis's elegant little shoes with their extra-high heels, nor this the water that he was ferried across to Hercules to save the modern walk around the transverse canal. It is all gone, along with the display and roister of the party.

Part of the power of gardens to capture and evoke history lies in this transience, the way in which we know that nothing can be fixed, that everything will be different if we return tomorrow, let alone in 351 years' time. The fact that they cannot be preserved entire for solemn appreciation is, paradoxically, what makes them bring the historical moment so powerfully alive.

And what remains is still more extraordinary than almost any other garden in Europe. It remains the masterpiece that defines French formal gardening, the yardstick against which all other such gardens must be measured.

25

ANDRÉ LE NÔTRE

In January 1679 André Le Nôtre travelled to Italy. His coach bowled out of Paris on one of the new roads ordered by Colbert, Louis XIV's first minister and employer of Le Nôtre at the Tuileries and his own château at Sceaux. This would have been at least twenty-two metres wide, with a further eighteen metres cleared on either side, and more or less straight and more or less paved. The edict of 1607 that detailed minimum width also instructed that signposts be put up at crossroads. Many of the crosses were of stone and still exist, a mark of civic obedience rather than piety.

Louis always travelled with his own team of road menders, which indicates their constant need for repair as well as his need for a fantasy state of perfection, rather like towns and streets being unnaturally spruced up before a modern royal visit. But within a hundred kilometres the royal route out of Paris would have deteriorated, maintained only by parish labour[1] and within 200 kilometres

---

1 In 1738 the corvée was introduced, whereby the male (save, of course, the gentry and priests) population aged between twelve and seventy had to give so many days (usually about a week) to working on the roads in their parish. The main purpose of this was to make the roads fit for carriages. None of the workers who forcibly made the roads had carriages. This was hated and inefficient but it made the roads a little better for travellers like Le Nôtre.

it would have been little more than a muddy track. It was a long, uncomfortable and frightening journey. Crossing the Alps would have involved dismantling his carriage so that it – and he – could be portered through the mountains by mules. That famous painting by David of Napoleon at the St Bernard pass on his rearing white charger was a piece of revisionist fantasy. Napoleon, like everyone else, crossed on the humble but much surer back of a mule.

Having crossed over the mountains Le Nôtre stopped at Pignerol in the Alps to visit his disgraced former employer, Nicolas Fouquet.[2] Was Fouquet glad to see him or did he resent his garden designer's subsequent royal favour? Despite the act of loyalty from Le Nôtre the difference in their fortunes must have sat heavy between them. Fouquet died just a year later.

Le Nôtre was on his way to Rome to see the Pope but stopped, it is said, at Villa Torrigiani, near Lucca. This was the home of Marquis Niccolao Santini, who was Lucca's ambassador to the Court of Louis XIV at Versailles. Santini accompanied Le Nôtre and they stayed for three days at Torrigiani and – although, as with all Le Nôtre's work – there is very sketchy evidence of this – Le Nôtre is said to have roughed out plans for the garden while he was there. Everyone wants to claim that their garden is by Le Nôtre. He is like Chippendale furniture or Stradivarius violins. But I would like it to be true, partly because I have visited Villa Torrigiani twice and think it one of the most charming late-Baroque gardens in Italy (and by definition that also means in the world) and visiting places that a shadowy figure has been to fixes them a little, makes them a little more corporeal. What is without doubt is that Santini, who spent fifty years remodelling the house and gardens along French lines, was hugely influenced by Le Nôtre's work at Versailles.

His influence did not travel to England with anything like the same effect. In 1662 Le Nôtre drew up plans for a grass parterre for

2 Pignerol was, in modern terms, on the Italian side of the Alps and only briefly French, reverting to the Turin-controlled state of Savoy under its previous and subsequent name of Pinerolo in 1696, sixteen years after Fouquet's death.

the newly planted park at Greenwich but, although implemented, this seems to have been quickly neglected. He also drew plans for Windsor at the end of his life. Some sources say that he visited London and was responsible for alterations to St James's Park although if so it was after Samuel Pepys 'found great and very noble alterations' on 17 August 1661. But there is no evidence and it seems inconceivable that diarists like Pepys and Evelyn would not have mentioned it if he had, given that he was a Frenchman and gardener to the most garden-obsessed, despotic monarch that Europe has ever seen.

But we tend to view influence through a modern eye. Anyone successful in the twenty-first century has that success recorded and broadcast within months or even minutes. Last year's achievements are old news. In the 1660s, most people rarely travelled more than twenty-five kilometres in any direction in their entire lives. A minuscule number ever went abroad. So it took a generation for influence to spread beyond the immediate circle that were touched by it.

In Le Nôtre's case it was not until the publication of *La théorie et la pratique du jardinage* in 1709 by Antoine-Joseph Dezallier d'Argenville that the dissemination of the style of French garden design that he dominated became widespread and international. The book covers the siting of the house, the layout and proposed plans for parterres, avenues, bosquets, fountains, cascades, ponds, canals, treillage and the most appropriate siting for sculpture.

I have looked through a 1722 edition (the third) of this work in the library at Versailles. This lovely, slightly scruffy building has that dusty, stony smell I have only encountered in French townhouses and reminded me exactly of the smell of my first lodgings in rue Cardinale in Aix. It is the fragrance of leather, polished tiles, metal stair railings, plaster, the slight mustiness of an unheated building, of dark corners lit by natural light on the turn of a stair and heavy fabric in tall rooms. It is a completely unmodern smell, unmodified by supermarkets, central heating, deep freezes, television, computers or mobile phones. I love it.

Going through any book published nearly 300 years ago, with its beautiful type on handmade paper, is a precious, almost sacred experience but as a garden writer, I marvelled at the clever, cool simplicity that has taken the vast and completely overwhelming complexity of Versailles and filtered it down to accessible, imitable stages. Dezallier was not himself a gardener but an aristocrat who presented the work in the language of his readers. There is no attempt to tell or show how to do any of its contents – merely what and where to instruct others to do it for you. I can imagine Santini poring over it at Villa Torrigiani. It is a manual of regal gardening for the affluent professional classes and lesser aristocracy and it sold incredibly well, running to thirteen French editions, as well as German and English translations. It also documented, for the first time, Le Nôtre's work.

I flipped through Le Nôtre's work at the Tuileries, Vaux and Versailles with the ease of the modern traveller, visiting all three within two days. I could have done so on the same day if I had timed it to avoid the appalling traffic getting out of Paris. I have read about, thought, photographed and revisited these gardens. But I am not sure that I am much closer to the man. He eludes three dimensions.

Contemporary reports variously ascribe to him a naïve bonhomie very atypical of the Court. For example, Louis said that Le Nôtre always kissed him when he returned from a military campaign, and he kissed and hugged the Pope when he visited him in Rome. But at the same time his letters show an almost sycophantic civility and courtliness towards his patrons. All we know is that he seems to have lived a long life without making any enemies and to have remained the friend, as well as servant, of a fickle and autocratic king who almost everyone else was terrified of.

26

VERSAILLES

At a certain size a thing becomes something else entirely even though every component might be the same. A ten-metre-high chair clearly ceases to function in the same way as a comfortably huge one but this is true even if the function is identical. A parking space for six cars is clearly different from one for 6,000, even if each parking bay is identical. Completely different responses are needed.

Versailles shouts its bigness by repute before you arrive. You brace yourself for it and therefore are predisposed to overlook the personal and intimate – which is the key that unlocks any garden worth visiting – which is nevertheless there to be found, albeit in a sea of enormity. Inside the sweeping grandiosity, the clipped hedges, canals, allés, gravel walks and massed battalions of bosquets, *boulingrins* and *berceaux* is the safe haven of the man who would be king and yet felt threatened at every turn. Inside the county-sized garden that needed an army of gardeners is the genuine interest in horticulture and design of the king who remained on easy terms with his chief gardeners – Le Nôtre, La Quintinie, Le Brun – when the aristocrat at court could be summarily ignored on the slightest pretext.

The truth is that, beneath all the hyperbole, much of Versailles is rather dull. There is too much, too many directions, too little proportion or sense of place. It marches impressively but never dances. The interesting question is not so much what or how but why?

GALERIE DES GLACES

It is best to start indoors and look down on the garden from the Galerie des Glaces. This is one of the great interior spaces of the world, as breathtakingly impressive now as it surely must have been when first completed. However, in 1678, when work began on building the vast chamber from an existing suite of rooms and a terrace, mirrors were enormously expensive and Venice was the only place in Europe that had the skills to melt glass at sufficiently high temperatures to make high-quality mirrors. But the First Minister, Jean-Baptiste Colbert, who always rather resented the money spent on Versailles and had tried to persuade Louis to make the Louvre his primary residence, insisted that all materials and manufacture had to be French. So the 357 mirrors in the seventeen alcoves opposite the seventeen huge windows were a triumph not just of design but the first time that mirrors of this quality had been made in France by Frenchmen.

Mirrors are so ubiquitous in modern life that we pay them no attention at all as we intensely inspect our reflections. But in the latter part of the seventeenth century all reflective surfaces – water, glass, metal – were subject to the same intellectual and artistic fascination and scrutiny as telescopes, microscopes, prisms and all optical instruments and phenomena. To understand the impact of the Galerie des Glaces you have to put yourself in the shoes of people who saw themselves in a glass darkly and who celebrated Le Nôtre's great canals as marvels of reflection rather than reducing them to numbingly prosaic 'water features'. Light, in a world lit only by candles and the sun, was powerful magic. The Sun King lit the world he bestrode and this great gallery, effortlessly catching light and reflections within the darkness that was habitual in even the most magnificent seventeenth-century interiors, was a celebration of both his and France's new magnificence. It still is.

I was there early, before the crowds endlessly photographing themselves in the glass, before the attendants' bored toleration, before any of the thousands of visitors began to seep into the garden below whose flat, slightly deadened enormity is laid out before you, statues and sky bounced down into the vast stretches of water and the horizon still essentially one forest cut through by great swathes of path and water. From this room nature is suppressed, cowering before the radiance of the Sun King. At least that is the intention.

Yet even from this elevated, protected position that does not quite work. There is an underlying puniness about the puddled, empty walks and still water, the tiny ranks of topiary and statues made anonymous by distance and time. So much work was needed to make it and so much more to keep it there, and yet even a modest storm, let alone time, can make a mockery of it all. This, of course, is true of all grandiose gardens, but truer at Versailles because none other ever set out to be grander.

So much for the empty garden at dawn. It is strangely more at ease with itself when filled with the thousands of visitors. It is a garden made for crowds, be they sycophantic seventeenth-century courtiers or twenty-first-century Chinese tourists with expensive cameras.

The garden is reflected back around the room, contained in glimpses broken by sunlight and cloud, bedazzled, lost, almost sky, jinking back at you from handmade glass, within one astonishing chamber. I kept thinking of the 1919 Paris Peace Conference, which was signed in the Hall of Mirrors, and T.E. Lawrence, dressed, slightly madly, in Bedouin robes accompanying the Saudis to watch the Middle East being carved up between the victorious Allies.

It is a room of whispers, voices rebounding in the mirrors ahead of sight. Sound remains long after the ear has used it all up. If sound dissipates exponentially then the ghost of everything ever said remains in a white noise of history. T.E.L's surprisingly high-pitched laugh along with Louis's chilly commands and the sycophantic laughter of over-eager courtiers. Footfall and coughs. The scrape of a chair. Some rooms are more resonant than others. Some sounds hold longer. Good gardens team with ghosts, mostly at the edge of the eye, seen beyond description, heard clearly enough without sound. Stand quietly in the Hall of Mirrors and Versailles speaks.

Behind the Hall is Louis's bedroom, with its sequence of ante-chambers so preciously manned in the hierarchy of his Court, where to attend the King's rising was as great a mark of favour and influence as any. This was a court where every detail of the king's day, from the ornate ritual of the levee in the morning to his retirement at night, was conducted as an elaborate stately procession or dance. Rather like the Chinese court of the late nineteenth century, where the rituals became so labyrinthine that they barely left time for the most basic human activities, the details were minutely observed and attendance at the various stations of the day – such as holding the royal candlestick or watching the royal bowel movement – were awarded as titbits and inducements to the courtiers, who were obliged to hang around Versailles waiting for preferment. Absence made Louis's heart grow chilly and not to be seen at Court was self-imposed banishment, so an absurd level of performance filled the echoing boredom of the courtiers' lives. It was a clever and cruel way of making the aristocracy – who, unlike a hundred years later, were the ones with the potential to revolt against the crown and thus needed to have an eye kept on them – sycophantically dance and jerk to the slightest twitch of their strings by Louis.

It is both significant and somehow moving that this most splendid and formalised suite of rooms was the King's emotional safe house, his own bedroom almost untouched within the heart of his father's original modest hunting lodge whilst the palace grew around it. The Sun King, answerable only to God, ruthlessly holding dominion over all of France and much of Europe, never lost the comfort of the safety of his childhood bedroom.

Most of the work was done by Le Vau – who had designed Vaux le Vicomte – although the building is a hotchpotch with the clumsy hand of a committee steering it, an unsatisfactory affair that lacks any cohesive identity, especially in relationship to the monstrous enormity of the gardens, where it appears with all the presence of a louche bungalow at the edge of a vast suburban lawn.

THE ORANGERIE

The South Parterre, filled with bright flowers (tulips, daffodils and wallflowers on this particular day but specialising in Mediterranean plants in Louis's time)[1] is the first thing that the visitor to Versailles sees, but it faces sideways from the main façade of the palace, looking southwards to the Pièce d'Eau des Suisses, the lake dug by the regiment of Swiss Guards in 1678. Most visitors funnel in, immediately have their picture taken with the building behind them in a desperate attempt to make the experience real by clipping it to Facebook, and head west for the Royal Walk and the Grand Canal. But if you walk through the flower parterre to the balustrade at its southern edge you look down more than ten metres to the 2.8 hectares of the Orangerie Parterre which, with the incredible Orangerie building itself, are the best things at Versailles. If the garden consisted of nothing but this then it would be worth making a special journey to see.

Come in winter and it is primly stark, the paths and stone the same lovely golden colour, six great plats guarded by sentinel cypresses and wasp-waisted yews clipped into tightly corseted forms.

---

1 It is a mistake to think that parterres were solely ornate patterns in box infilled with gravel. Most were always intended to be filled with flowers. Louis's First Minister Colbert had a network of nurseries established to provide plants, mostly around or, like the one near the Tuileries, in Paris but there was also one near Toulon, established to raise plants and seeds bought in from the Middle East and north Africa, and to raise Mediterranean plants and bulbs for Versailles.

There is a spareness about it, a restraint and proportion, that is lacking from most other parts of Versailles, and it is beautiful. But come after the trees have been lined out in spring, albeit, in my own case, a spring day of squally, petulant weather, and it is transformed by the citrus and palms set out by the thousand in their boxes. The wide paths are now flanked by a crowd, albeit in meticulously ordered, straight rows. It is made curiously vulgar and overblown but is exactly as Versailles should be – that strange mixture of refinement and brashness where Baroque money and power, perhaps all money and power in all times, always end up.

As you go down the enormous flight of a hundred steps from the Floral Terrace, on either side of the Orangerie, not just as deep as an Aztec temple but as wide as a street, you realise that the buildings you can see either side of the Orangerie Parterre are merely the flanks of a three-sided façade, as grand as a château and roofed by the parterre above it.

There had been an orangerie on the site as early as 1664, designed by Le Vau to house the citrus that Louis had plundered from Vaux le

Vicomte. Twenty years later, after much further work on the palace, it was out of alignment and considered inadequate so Jules Hardouin-Mansart,[2] Le Vau's successor as Premier Architecte, designed another twice as big. It is a work of architectural glory to match most cathedrals and by far the most beautiful garden building of any kind that I have ever seen. From the outside it forms an elegant, colonnaded rhythm of huge arched windows, painted to blend into the ochre of the St Leu stone, forming three sides to enclose the parterre – the only truly satisfactory enclosed space in Versailles. But for all this the real magic is inside the building. Going through the enormous central door, you enter into a huge vaulted chamber that is a joyous mixture of cave and nave.

By complete chance I visited on the day that they were taking the 1,100 citrus plants in their crates out on to the parterre. They had been waiting for the rain that I was sheltering from because a rainy spring day would wash the accumulated winter dust from the evergreen leaves and outside little white puddles were forming under the trees already in position. There were four tractors and in all perhaps thirty men, working in sequence, each with an attachment like a chariot that both lifted and grasped the oak and steel planting boxes and then lifted the whole thing – and some of the citrus were really large trees hundreds of years old – so they would not be damaged and yet could be driven through the huge double doors, out from the dark of the Orangerie into the cleansing rain and their allotted place in the parterre.

Other than the tractors this was a scene that had been replicated every year since the Orangerie was built and the building has resisted every kind of adaption, transformation or change of use despite time, wars, revolutions and lack of interest. If it were British it would be a tea room and gift shop by now. Its continuity is there in the air and shape of the light of the building. You breathe it in.

2 Mansart gave his name to the tall mansard roof, with each face having a double slope, the lower one steep and often with dormer windows, that is so ubiquitous in France.

The summer emptiness seems to be part of its function, like a barn before the harvest is in, but during the Paris Commune of 1871 it was used as a temporary prison. But it was unthinkable that the citrus should be left out to brave the autumnal cold, so come October the prisoners were taken out and many executed to make room for the oranges and lemons.

When I walked through the door it was half empty and far down the other end of the building the team was already starting to gather the lorry-loads of dead leaves that had fallen over winter. But the other half was dark and huddled with the remaining trees. Outside they looked like props in a film lot, waiting to be taken to a set. But inside they had a kind of secret magic like an attic filled with generations of treasures.

By the time I left they had all been moved and the building was completely empty for the first time since the previous October. At one end there were crates being repaired and stacks of oak boards for the job. The air in this section was a lovely rich, musky mixture of tannin and citrus. The Versailles crates, which come in three sizes, are a heavy, strong metal frame like a square brazier or grate topped by finials, with the sides made from thick oak boards cut from the Versailles woods. The whole thing is enormously heavy and therefore stable. Planting the trees in wood means they can be handled and moved without breaking and when they need repairing, which is winter work done in the gloomy warmth of this end of the Orangerie, two sides are changed one year and the other two sides the next, so that the roots are not unduly disturbed. It is then all painted in the Versailles duck-egg, Cambridge blue.

Joel, the head gardener, not a tall man but almost completely square, monitored the moving of the trees like a sergeant major overseeing a complicated piece of drill. Occasionally he shouted. Mostly he silently watched, knowing every single plant. When it was done he said that now we could all go and have lunch. He said that he loved the Orangerie. Truly loved it. He said an English duke had come to France especially to see him the other day to ask his advice on how to manage his own – very inferior – orangery back home. An English duke! And he slapped me on the shoulder with the smile of a man who knows his luck.

BOSQUETS

The bosquets that flank the central *allée* at Versailles are a series of theatres, in full view but deliberately placed far enough away from the palace to entail a special visit, where the performances range from orchestrated drama and dance to tableaux coyly posed as the setting for a tryst. It is the horror of the wildwood made tame by organisation, order and strict control and exemplifies both the extent of the triumph over the landscape that Versailles set out to achieve and display and, almost incidentally, everything that is good about gardening. They define space and volume, need skill and control to establish and maintain and yet use plants that must be responded to sympathetically and not bullied into submission. They are beautiful in themselves but are also magic woods with almost endless scope for transformation and elaboration.

A bosquet is an area of woodland, usually straight-edged and bounded by neatly clipped sides or hedges, and often containing elaborate fountains, statues, lawns, ponds, mazes, theatres or retreats, according to fashion and whim. The prevailing species used for the woods at Versailles were oak with a few chestnut, beech, ash and wild cherry, but oak does not clip or train well so bosquets were more usually planted with lime, elm and chestnut, sometimes mixed and sometimes as single species, as well as yew to provide evergreen form.

The magnificent hedges that link the bosquets visually and line the broader *allées* were nearly always hornbeam and these are still used superbly, training the trees up tall canes so that the hedges grow as slim as a pencil but up to ten metres tall. This creates beautiful spaces that would be more likely in the aisles of a cathedral than in a garden, and are none the less awe-inspiring.

The French have always used hornbeam freely for hedges and training in treillage and pleaching, whereas the British reach more readily for beech. I don't know why this is. In bosquets hornbeam could be trained to arch over frames or have alcoves and niches cut into it to house statues. Of all the trees, it is the easiest and most rewarding for this kind of work.

From the outside, bosquets are closed woody fortresses, but inside they can be whatever you want them to be. The Italian equivalent, the *bosco*, evolved from hunting grounds, especially for small birds, that gradually became domesticated throughout the sixteenth century into gardens. Their magic lies in the relationship between the trees and memory of woodland and the formal control of hedges. In modern France woods remain the defining feature of the landscape, whereas in Britain it is the hedge that measures and maps the landscape. You can drive for miles throughout northern France without seeing a single hedgerow but blocks of woodland appear mysteriously in the great plains of maize and wheat, four-square and clean-edged, monstrous agricultural bosquets guarding the memory of the forests that they once were. In the seventeenth century, when Le Nôtre was making the bosquets at Versailles, France was still a country of vast, impenetrable, unknown and unknowable forests, where hundreds of thousands of people lived without any contact with the outside world. Despite the horrible clearance of much of agricultural France, it still has much, much more woodland than Britain and is a country that understands and responds to woods with a practical eye. The neat stacks of firewood outside a million homes are a testament to the continuing role of wood as something practical and useful in everyday life. You grow, gather and store wood carefully and with respect when it matters to you. The chaotic jumbles of logs and branches on a British farm are a measure of how incidental wood is to most Britons, how peripheral. Then again, perhaps the neatly trimmed hedges in a million British back gardens are the same line of memory for the long-lost fields of our agrarian, pre-industrial past.

The surviving bosquets of Versailles are – and were from inception – deliberately as mannered and as far from the wildwood as might be imagined. There are two I like particularly.

The first is the Bosquet de l'Encelade.[3] This was commissioned in

3 Enceladus was a giant, one of the sons of Gaia who led a rebellion against the Olympian gods. In the battle Enceladus was struck by a bolt of lightning thrown by Athena. When he hurled rocks at the gods they buried him for his audacity beneath Mount Etna in Sicily, whose volcanic flames were said to be his breath – and he is breathing still, because I have seen those flames.

1668 and revolves around a huge figurative fountain set in a round pool, designed by Le Brun and made in 1676 by Gaspar Mercy. The gilded figure of Enceladus, cast in lead and engulfed in lava, struggles vainly to throw a rock as he disappears beneath the weight of Olympian wrath and stone. A massive jet of water spurts five, ten metres from his mouth, and lesser fountains bubble furiously from the rocks. The whole thing is a watery shout of frustrated rage.

The dates are significant. This bosquet with its grotesquely dramatic sculpture was finished at just the time Louis was moving his Court to Versailles. The message that it sent out to his courtiers was unmistakable: witness your fate if you dare to mess with me. This was not the language of the elegant, ballet-dancing, Baroque Apollo but of a despotic tyrant. Louis wanted the Court at Versailles so he could keep an eye on them. He wanted them terrified and if the price of that was entertainment, then it was a small one to pay.

Actually not so small. The really, astonishingly expensive aspect of Versailles – and most Baroque gardens – was their water. To enable Enceladus to vomit water so powerfully took hydroengineering on a municipal scale.

Before work began in the early 1660s Versailles was a marsh, and huge amounts of water had to be removed from the site, with more than thirty kilometres of dry drains dug. These *pierrées* were trenches nearly a metre deep, backfilled with hardcore and rubble. They are still used and work well, although we call them 'French' drains. I have dug plenty of them myself. Then water had to be brought into the site. One proposal, which was only scotched at the last moment, was to build a chain of canals a hundred kilometres in length to link the Grand Canal in the garden to the Loire, with boats sailing right up to the palace. In any event, water – controlled, accurately directed water – was needed on a huge scale. By 1672 there were over 1,000 fountains to be fed and eventually, if you include every jet in every part of the enormous garden, they numbered more than twice this.

Water, more than any other single feature, was the measure of wealth and power in an age when clean drinking water was a luxury to which most people scarcely had access. It was currency, and the more that Louis could display it, the greater his wealth in the eyes of his subjects and the world. So he wanted Versailles to have more and bigger water features than anything hitherto seen in Italy, which, with gardens such as Aldobrandini, Villa d'Este, Lante or Farnese, was his only potential rival. Versailles had to break all moulds.

To this end water was pumped from sources all around Versailles but these were never adequate. Famously, gardeners would be situated ahead of the King as he progressed, semaphoring his movements with flags and whistles to others controlling the water supply, so that fountains could be turned off as he left them, to enable those that he was about to visit next to have sufficient flow. There was a scheme to bring water from the Seine and even an aqueduct half constructed. The river Bièvre was dammed and diverted to the garden. Windmills were used to raise water from the canals and send it back round the system but they were subject to the vagaries of the wind. In 1674 a superb pump was built, powered by three horses, but for all its efficiency there was still not enough water for it to shift. A header tank was built on the roof of the grotto that held 580 cubic metres of water – enough for all the fountains to perform simultaneously for a couple of hours. By 1677 there were ten windmills and a team of 120 horses of which forty were working at any one time.[4]

Around the outside of Enceladus's pond is beautifully restored

4 The statistics at Versailles are always dizzying. There was an extraordinary amount of pipework conveying the water round the garden – lead near the palace where it was less likely to be stolen and iron in the further reaches. Of the total of 80 million livres spent on the garden, 3 million were spent on these pipes alone. To put that in context, a livre – which had no actual face value other than that which was decreed at any particular moment – was worth something between £3 and £8 in modern money. So the gardens cost around £400 million and the pipework supplying the fountains around £15 million.

rose-covered oak treillage that was Le Nôtre's contribution to the display. If the fountains are on – and they were turned on for ten minutes so that we could film them – then one side is a sheltered walkway to admire the display and the other a water-lashed cage as the wind catches the fountain and spins it off sideways, soaking everything within that half of the bosquet. But even this lack of control is impressive because it extends the threat. You don't want to cross me, it says, because you might unleash something that even I cannot control. I might get angry – and you would not like me when I am angry.

The other bosquet that I particularly like has none of that simmering threat. It is said to be the last work of Le Nôtre at Versailles and was begun after his return from his jaunt to see the Pope in Italy. This is the Salle de Bal or Ballroom, begun twenty years after the Bosquet d'Encelade, in 1688.

You turn into the bosquet at what proves to be the bottom end and then kink sideways to enter the interior, so nothing is revealed and there is drama from the moment that you are part of it. It is not so much a ballroom as a theatre, where plants, water, hugely expensive vases, shells from remote corners of the globe as well as the dancers and musicians that would perform for Louis and the Court are all on display. In fact I approached from the top, let in by a security guard with a gun and dark glasses barking orders on his phone. It turned out to be to his mother about the time he would be home for his lunch.

I came to the top of the cascade, taking the path that the forty-odd musicians of the Grande Écurie would have shuffled down clutching drums and fifes, cornets, crumhorns, viols, violins, serpents, sackbutts and trumpets, and perhaps the newfangled *hautbois*, knowing that they would have to saw and blow prodigiously to rise above the roar of the cascade that tumbled below them. However, given that they performed not only on public occasions at Versailles but accompanied the king in all public events – including war – this probably would not have alarmed them unduly.

On three sides below them were the tiered seats made from grass, now lined with clipped box, which looks wonderful but means the seats cannot be used. A very French way of politely telling the public to Keep Off the Grass.

I can see the influence of the water theatre at Villa Aldobrandini in the way that the water cascades down the amphitheatre steps in layers like flowing millefeuilles and in the magnificently kitsch sense of dancing girls high-kicking in unison that is present in the wonderfully true Baroque restoration. The urns and vases on gilded plinths add swaggeringly to the shamelessness of the display. If Baroque is not slightly absurd then it is not true to itself. The tank for the water apparently took two days to fill and only worked long enough for a performance of the ballets that Louis loved so much. Originally there was a moated island in the centre of the arena that served as the stage but now it is an open, empty space.

The point about this bosquet is that it is playful and frivolous and yet magnificent in a way that all the fist-thumping somehow is not. It is a wonder that it has endured, because the shells, all gathered from Madagascar,[5] and *rocaillage* that adorn it are fragile. There was a court *rocailleur* at Versailles, called Berthier, who made the volcanic rubble that surrounded Enceladus and who now encrusted Le Nôtre's cascade so that it was like an open, streaming grotto.

THE POTAGER DU ROI

The modern town of Versailles is padded with the comfort of money. The tourists swirl through it without really touching the sides, the only obvious mark being the price of hotel rooms – eyewatering – and most of the tourists, arriving in the coaches, never set foot beyond the palace and the town shrugs them off easily enough. Strolling through the streets is a relief from the bedlam and five minutes' walk from the palace takes you to the unassuming entrance of the Potager du Roi. Take a detour, make it fifteen minutes, do as I did and have lunch, scribble some notes and read a guide and let the enormity of the palace and gardens settle a bit before taking on even more information and experience. But come back and visit the kitchen garden. It is worth it.

The potager at Versailles, designed by Mansart and built between 1678 and 1683, is truly enormous. It was created on what had been a rather boggy, unlikely site to the south of the main building, detached from the rest of the ornamental garden, using the spoil from the Swiss pond (Pièce d'Eau des Suisses) dug by the regiment of Swiss Guards from the stinking marsh that lay to the south of the Orangerie, which was constructed at the same time. As the lake

---

5 Louis ordered his entire fleet – every single ship that was able to make the journey – out to gather and ferry back these shells.

covered nearly sixteen hectares, there was an awful lot of soil, stinking or otherwise, to lose.[6]

Although open (albeit slightly erratically and out of kilter with the main gardens) to the public, the entrance looks and feels forbiddingly private and, compared to the frenzy of the main palace and gardens, devoid of any of the language or behaviour of tourism. Nothing could be nicer. Private enough to feel special and privileged and public enough to allow you and me inside and seemingly hardly anyone else. In fact when I went it was pouring with rain, which might have explained the scarcity of visitors. The potager covers an area of almost eight hectares with twenty-nine separate enclosures divided by high walls. Each wall, of course, is ideal for supporting fruit of some kind, according to its aspect. The walls are high enough to support the fruit and no more and do not shield the town, so houses and the cathedral of St Louis, built a century after the garden by Mansart's grandson, loom over the potager. It is the exact opposite of Le Nôtre's long vistas cutting into the horizon.

As well as fruit trained tight against the ochre render of the walls – and there are a couple of dozen of these, each with two sides – there are rows of martialled fruit trees within each individual walled garden. Only the central area (only! It is enormous, but one tires of thinking about the scale of Versailles: anything less than gargantuan would sit oddly) is reserved for vegetables. Otherwise the space is filled with row upon row of fruit trees. Apples, pears, plums, cherries, apricots, peaches and nectarines all grow in precise formations, scarcely a leaf out of line. After the grandeur and parade of the main garden this is strictly, almost shockingly utilitarian. But there

6 To make all and any of the earthworks at Versailles involved staggering amounts of hand labour. As well as hundreds of wheelbarrows, 600 baskets with straps were purchased for soldiers to carry the soil on their backs like donkeys, back and forth to the potager. There was also raised wooden trackway, like a kind of railway, on which carts of soil were pushed. All this continued without pause for years, and deaths to the workers, mainly from illness bought about by exhaustion, were so common that every night carts piled with bodies were taken away for burial.

is a rhythm to this, an accumulation of precision that is a deeply satisfying and soothing wave of controlled vigour. I went in spring as
the blossom was rippling through and must one day return in late
summer when all the fruits are ripening.

Louis XIV loved his food and took a real and personal interest in
how it was grown. Amongst the team that he plundered from Vaux
le Vicomte was the lawyer-turned-gardener Jean-Baptiste La
Quintinie, who had been responsible for the establishment and
management of the walled kitchen garden there. Although in charge
of all the fruit and vegetable production for the King and Court at
Versailles, La Quintinie's real obsession – the one that had made
him give up his legal career – was the growing of fresh fruit.

The word 'fresh' is really significant, because outside the summer
months fresh food was invariably limited in both quantity and
variety. It may seem obvious, but it is worth reminding oneself that
there was only limited refrigeration (although ice houses very
effectively provided ice throughout the year) and almost no
importation of fresh food at all: food was only as fresh as the time
it took to go from source to the table. Seasonal treats were truly
luxurious for king and peasant alike. So the greater the range of
treats, the longer their season could be extended and the more
unusual the produce produced on one's doorstep, the greater the
acclaim for the producer. We have grown careless about this, but
even food that we regard as so common as to be unremarkable was
a rare seasonal treat. For example, peas were only introduced to
France in the beginning of the 1660s and they became a fetish of
Louis XIV.[7]

La Quintinie provided the King with not just the rarest fruit and
vegetables of the time but also always the earliest. Having the first
cherries, asparagus, peas or whatever was as much an obsession then
as it is today, and it was an assumption that the King would be ahead

7 Mme de Sévigné wrote, in a letter, that 'the pea business still goes on. Impatience to
eat them, the pleasure of having eaten them and the hope to eat more of them are the
three questions constantly discussed . . .'

of the nation in this as in everything. So with a combination of glass cloches and hot beds made from layers of soil and fresh manure, along with the protection of the walls, La Quintinie was able to produce strawberries in March, beans in April and asparagus in December.

Since 1874 the Potager du Roi has been the home of the École Nationale Supérieure d'Horticulture. This trains head gardeners to go and run gardens although, in the French way, theory and research is valued more than practicalities. Students are expected to know such things as pruning techniques, but ideally they go on to lecture and research them rather than suffer the obvious mark of failure of having to actually do them for a living.

There are nineteen different styles of pruning formation that the students have to master, and any freedom of expression is not only frowned upon but apparently unsought. I spoke to the head

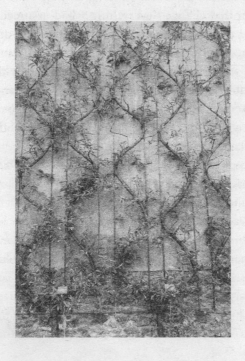

gardener, Antoine Jacobsen, who said that pruning suits the French character as it is based upon an assumption of an agreed order. There is a correct way of doing things – an etiquette of pruning. So if you have the skill and you apply yourself to get the recognised qualification, then you automatically earn the respect you deserve. Both the action and the knowledge support the status quo and all the thousands of disciplined, ordered trees reinforce that. The student learns the existing styles and only a Master can introduce a new one and thereby add to the recognised order rather than digress from it.

The French, he said, warming to his subject in almost perfect English spoken with a broad American accent, love Cartesian values. Mathematics, harmony, straight lines and, above all, order. To buck this in any way is revolutionary and, for the most part, deeply disturbing.

So much for the theory. Then he gave me a piece of practical information that changed everything I had assumed about the French, and particularly Baroque, way of growing things. I had thought that the pruning of fruit trees had reached its most elaborate apogee at the end of the seventeenth century, in line with the extreme control and manipulation of plants and the landscape that Versailles exemplified. But this was not the case, because until the end of the eighteenth century all pruning was done with a knife, *la serpette*, or saw. This changes everything.

Try it. Roses, fruit trees, vines all cut with a knife. For anything that is not rigid – and in pruning terms that means anything less than about three years old – you need one hand to hold the material to cut, to steady it and provide resistance to the other hand, which holds and directs the knife. However sharp – and having spent my entire life sharpening blades from the largest axes to delicate wood-carving chisels, I see no reason to suppose that any age has been better at sharpening blades than our own – force is needed, either towards or away from the pruner, and the greater the force the less the control. This means that, in an age that revered ornamentation and embellishment, all shaping and training of fruit trees was surprisingly crude.[8]

Secateurs, which of course is a French word, were apparently invented after the Revolution by the Marquis de Moleville, although it is hard to find good evidence for this, and it is inconceivable that the marquis would have felt the need to use them himself. *L'art de tailleur* was the craft of an artisan not an aristocrat. So all the more complicated and ornate shapes and styles of pruning come from the nineteenth century when, secateurs in hand, the *tailleur* was able to reach, bend, snip and cut with a precision and delicacy unobtainable by the seventeenth-century gardener.

As a result an orgy of fruit training and restriction, all based upon maximising production, with every bud and fruit receiving as much light as possible and growing in such a way that it, rather than the wood of the tree, took most of the tree's energy, became part of the gardener's armoury. Espaliers, cordons (both upright and angled), fans, goblets, *palmettes U double* and *palmettes Verrier*, *losanges*, *L'arcure Lepage*, *quenouilles*, *pyramids*, *candelabres* – they all had to be mastered in order to show yourself properly trained. All can be seen perfectly executed in the Potager du Roi.

Had La Quintinie had access to secateurs rather than a *serpette*, would Louis have been impressed? Certainly. He loved the practicalities of his garden. But not as much as he loved another bowl of fresh peas.

8 Parterres, which we now think of as the watchword for neatly clipped containment, would have been cut with small billhooks – effectively large knives – which means that they would have had a slightly rounded profile. I have seen this done at the amazing garden of Castello Ruspoli at Vignanello in Italy and it is almost impossible to swipe a four-square edge. So the original Baroque parterre was a softer, more rounded thing altogether than the modern machine-trimmed version.

27

PALAIS ROYAL

At eight o clock in the morning at any time of year the 1st arrondissement is very quiet. At the end of August, when Paris is still on its holidays, it is practically deserted. In rue de la Sourdière a woman dressed as though about to shop round the corner in rue Saint-Honoré washes the front of a building, dipping a brush carefully into her bucket of water as though she is painting it clean. A girl in an apron stands in front of a shop window that contains a gold table on which there is a single small handbag. She shifts her weight on to one leg and cocks her head then reaches for her phone, talks animatedly, sighs and goes inside and turns the bag about ten degrees from horizontal before coming back outside to the pavement to scrutinise it again.

Next door a discreet plate screwed to the wall by the door says '*Détective Privé (depuis 1994)*'. A slim figure, hair and beard one stubbly fuzz, wheels his bike into the next door along and disappears into the back. A sign in Greek, Mandarin, Russian and English says 'Tailoring, Repairing, Alterations Professionally Done'. He reappears with a cigarette in his mouth and sets up his bench with its sewing machine in the window, winding a length of deep purple thread and carefully pulling it taut before snipping it free. He catches me looking, is used to it, continues the performance and I move on.

I had been told that there was an exceptional flower shop here but it is closed. The window has a display of brambles, cardoons, roses and lichen. Peering into the recesses of the shop I see a vase filled with cut cardoon leaves and a row of tin vases filled with pink hydrangeas. Do the locals buy these? Greeks? Russians or Chinese picking up their mending? I'd certainly like to see someone walking down the street, perhaps with a little dog and a bag containing a bag so special that it needs a whole shop window to itself, clutching a bouquet of brambles and cardoon heads.

I turn left into rue Saint-Honoré and walk down to the Place Colette, past the façade of the Comédie-Française to go into the deep shade of the entrance into the Palais Royal in the far corner. Although right in the middle of Paris, a stone's throw from the Louvre, many tourists never visit and yet the garden is one of the best places to get away from noise and people and bustle. I wish I had known about it when I was younger.

The Palais Royal was built by Cardinal Richelieu but became a royal palace when he died in 1642. It was where Louis XIV spent his early regency years, and he fled from the mob from there in the middle of the winter of 1649, when he was ten and as soon as he had the choice he moved from it and never returned. It was this traumatic incident which has been ascribed to Louis's love of order and control, his hatred of Paris and the establishment of Versailles as his main home, and the crushing control that he exerted on his Court and Empire. Perhaps. In any event the palace became the home of his younger brother, the Duc d'Orléans, who made the gardens[1] that became the centre of Parisian courtly society for the next hundred years.[2]

1 Although no records exist, it seems almost certain that André Le Nôtre, in charge of the gardens a stone's throw away at the Tuileries and heavily involved at Versailles, was involved in their creation. He was also gardener to the Duc d'Orléans and Anne of Austria, the King's mother, who lived at the Palais Royal.
2 But not, of course the Court which was firmly being established by Louis at Versailles.

In 1781, the Duc de Chartres, heir to the house of Orléans and cousin to Louis XIV, began turning the gardens and grounds into a kind of commercial pleasure ground. When he was finished in 1784 there were over 200 shops and galleries around the great palace courtyard. It was said a man could buy any item of clothing for himself or his mistress, have his wig dressed and powdered, dine superbly, see a magnificent firework display, gamble away his fortune and dissipate his flesh according to whatever fancy took him, without leaving the grounds. Crowds came every night to partake in some or all of these activities and to observe others do the same. The finest goods from all over France and its dominions could be found there and anyone with any pretension to society made it the centre of their Parisian life. Pickpockets, whores, hustlers and thieves thrived within its palatial bounds. They probably still do. It became the byword across the whole of Europe for debauchery and gave Paris the aura of naughtiness that my grandfather, visiting the city for the first time in the first few years of the twentieth century, still spoke of with a gleam in his eye seventy years on, almost 200 years after the Duc de Chartres opened its doors.

The colonnaded arcades still run round three sides, looking stately rather than thrillingly wicked, and create an immense, long courtyard containing lawns, ranks of shady trees, walks, a fountain and pool in its centre and beds spilling with roses in the late-summer morning. If no longer the place for a good debauch, then it is the best place in the centre of Paris to sit and eat a sandwich or read for a while. The innate sense of proportion that the French seem to crave means that simple things like the double avenue of limes that runs down either side of the garden creates a kind of delicate harmony that hundreds of gardens filled with the rarest and most horticulturally demanding planting never attain. Just trees, trunks trimmed to the same height, apportioned just so, the pale gravel below spangled with light, make an entire garden. It is deeply satisfying.

It is a short walk, broken by a stop at Café Nemours for coffee

or a mid-morning glass of something more suited to the spirit
of the Palais Royal, across the rue de Rivoli to the Gardens of
the Tuileries.

28

THE TUILERIES GARDENS

The Tuileries gardens are in the centre of Paris between the Louvre and Place de la Concorde. They are so called because they are on the site of the tile kilns (*tuileries*) used by the tile makers that Francis I had brought to Paris to build a palace, completed by Catherine de Medici in 1572. This ran across the front of the Louvre, on the site of what are now the Carrousel gardens, set on a level above the rest of the Tuileries. The building was burnt down by the Communards in 1871 and was not rebuilt but the gardens, all twenty-six hectares, remain.

I first went there in 1970, when I was fourteen, to go to the Jeu de Paume, the building on the corner made by the rue de Rivoli and the Place de la Concorde, that originally housed a real tennis court, to see the collection of Impressionist paintings. I don't think that any visit to any art gallery has been so thrilling since. My grandfather had regularly taken my brothers (and occasionally sisters – he felt that girls could only absorb culture in smaller doses than boys) to galleries in London and instilled into us the sanctity of the Impressionists as the summation of painting in the previous hundred years. As a nineteen-year-old, in 1904, he had gone to work in Paris and seen these works both in galleries and, most memorably, in the windows of private dealers. I picture him as a figure in an Impressionist painting, his tall slimness, stiff collar, hat and cane distilled into an essence of colour but still recognisably him, who was always an old man to me, his white, bristly moustache dark then, perhaps softer, leaning from the waist to see better through a shop window whilst women with huge hats and corseted waists, above skirts that dragged the Parisian streets, passed him by. It is astonishing to think that Monet or Cézanne, on a rare trip to Paris in his old age, could have occupied the same street as this man I knew so well.

A friend once told me that she was walking the streets of London listening to Tom Waits on headphones and, distracted, she bumped into a man and dropped her bag. The man stopped and helped her gather the spilled contents, apologising. It was Tom Waits, on an extremely rare visit to London to play a concert for which she had been unable to buy a ticket. Overcome by the shock of recognition she merely mumbled thanks and apologies and went on her way. Perhaps Grandpa bumped into Cézanne, just as he was looking at one of his paintings through a window, who then apologised to this tall young Scot. My grandfather bought paintings all his life but almost all of them were dark and terrible, hanging gloomily on ill-lit panelled walls. He left a third of them to me and I tried hanging them on my own walls, but they brought with them the darkness of his house, so I sold them all. They made practically nothing. He told us that he could have bought a large Monet painting of water lilies at Giverny for £200. I wonder if he knew it was special, and if so, why he never bought any of the thousand imitations or derivations that lay within his means. It might as well have been £200,000 for me then, he would say, shaking his head as though still feeling the pain of deprivation. In fact, accounting for inflation until 2012, it was the equivalent of £20,000, which, even today, might as well be ten times that amount to the average nineteen-year-old for all its remoteness. This, in the mid-1960s, was at a time when Monet's water lilies were either reckoned to be the most valuable paintings in the world or one had just been sold for a million pounds or some such marker of unobtainable wealth.

At fourteen it was the suffering and devotion and social rejection that attracted me to the Impressionists more than the rising value of their paintings. And they were as unstuffy, unchurchy, unacademic as any hopelessly entrapped fourteen-year-old could wish. I loved them but until then had adored singly in the National Gallery in London or in books. To see scores of paintings by the incredible roll-call of Manet, Monet, Renoir, Degas, Sisley, Pissarro, Cézanne, Van Gogh, Gaugin all under one roof was intoxicating. I could scarcely breathe for the excitement. But the Tuileries were merely the back-drop, the space that surrounded the gallery, which in turn existed for me then only to house the paintings. And to a large extent Paris only existed to house that building, because I could not absorb more than them in one dose.

I remember visiting the gallery again, on my own, a few years later, when I was nineteen and, as is the way, effectively another person. It was entirely another experience. I had the whole day to kill and practically no money, so spun out the Jeu de Paume for as long as possible before sitting in the Tuileries. It rained. I was lonely and anxious. I remember killing time, walking through the centre of the gardens towards the Louvre and back down rue de Rivoli, returning through the gate at the Place de la Concorde end and round again, taking a side avenue this time and returning along the opposite side of rue de Rivoli. Like a dog pacing a kennel. When you have money you easily forget the luxury of being able to sit and order a coffee or *citron pressé* without it being a trade-off against a meal or a ticket on the metro. The gardens, with their rather listless throng sifting in at one end and dispersing again at the other, became oppressive. Loneliness, even in one of the most beautiful cities in the world, is, after all, still loneliness.

I had forgotten all of this when I visited the Tuileries as a garden, wearing my much older, much-travelled garden-expert head. But it leached back in. We all leave traces of ourselves behind and they remain, like a strand of wool on a thorn. Overwhelmed, anxious, uncomprehending bits of me were scattered beneath the marshalled trees where the incessant flow of walkers and tourists paraded. Back in the 1970s hardly anyone took pictures. I have none of that visit although I recall almost all of it with hallucinogenic clarity because the experiences were so intense and fresh.

This time I came at seven o'clock on a Sunday morning when the rain fell with cinematic, absurd power. You got soaked putting up your umbrella. Only joggers were about, clutching water bottles whilst the rain ran in rivulets round their mouths.

On the Grande Terrasse le Long d'l'Eau along the garden's boundary with the road beside the Seine, the water formed huge pools that spilled down the steps like cascades, brown from the sanded paths. Even so, dodging the deepest puddles and hunkered down beneath an umbrella that tugged and concertinaed in the wind, this raised walkway is magnificent. It is wide enough (nearly thirty metres) to have two lines of limes cut with easy but exact rectilinear precision to a uniform maximum height of 2.2 metres to make an unbroken raised hedge running down the centre in a broad avenue, and leave wide paths on either side. The limes lead to the Louvre at one end and, crossing the Allée de Castiglione that bisects the gardens by steps that miraculously disappear to make an unbroken walkway within metres of ascending them, stretches down to the Orangerie and the Place de la Concorde nearly 600 metres away in the west.

This Grande Terrasse was designed by André Le Nôtre. The Tuileries were his home territory. His father, Jean, was *jardinier ordinaire* at the Tuileries Palace. This was not, as the name implies, some lowly post but a Master Gardener, with employees, responsible for maintenance. André grew up in a house attached to the Tuileries and, as well as taking on his father's profession (and position), he studied architecture, geometry, painting, poetry and literature. He was a learned and accomplished man who was, by modern definitions, a fully qualified landscape architect by the time he established himself as a gardener in 1635, aged only twenty-two, for the brother of Louis XIII, the Duc d'Orléans at the Luxembourg Palace. In 1637 Jean Le Nôtre retired as *jardinier ordinaire* at the Tuileries and André took over his role. So by the time that the reworking of the gardens began in 1664, he knew the Tuileries better than anyone.

Although owned by the King, the Tuileries were then, as now, open to the public and a place for people to promenade and meet. The Allée de Mûriers Blancs (the Mulberry Walk) was situated on the opposite, northern side of the garden and Le Nôtre, always looking to impose symmetry and harmony on an unruly site, made his great terrace to balance this. His plans removed the existing road and wall between palace and garden and centred the terrace on a line running west, along what is now the Champs Élysées, and on out into what was then open country but is now the great arch of La Défense. It is worth joining the queue to go up the Arc de Triomphe to look back down this central approach to the Tuileries and see it as a harmonious whole, which cannot properly be appreciated from the ground.

Three avenues splayed out from where the modern Place de la Concorde now sits. The central one, to Saint-Germaine-en-Laye, follows the Champs Élysées, the one on the left was to be the start of a new road leading directly to Versailles and the one on the right to Faubourg Saint-Honoré. It was entirely typical that Le Nôtre seamlessly took parterres, plats and ponds and linked them to the larger landscape, to take in literally all the eye could see.

To make this with the modern armoury of diggers, graders, bulldozers, laser levellers and CAD modelling would still be extraordinary but Le Nôtre just had a workforce equipped with wheelbarrows, picks and shovels and a graphometer. This had been invented in Paris sixty years previously and was an essential piece of surveying kit by the middle of the seventeenth century. It consists of two alidades, one semicircular and curved and the other flat and straight, fixed to a pole via a socket and ball joint. There were two sighting slots, one at either end of the straight sighting rule, each with a taut hair centred for the exact alignment of two points. Once aligned, the angles on the curved second rule could be used to measure angles and distance against existing features. With this, Le Nôtre could both survey the landscape and lay his plans on to it with real precision – which of course he had already done at Vaux and was beginning to do on an even larger scale at Versailles.

Back on the ground, at camera-lens height, the paths, blocks of trees, lawns, parterres and ponds create a rhythm and counterpoint that has the inevitability and charm of the best Baroque music. Le Nôtre seemed to instinctively maximise the possibilities of order from a site without a particular stroke of genius or drama. People do not walk there just because they can. They go because it draws them. It is a good place to stroll or sit if the sun is out. Children play and toddlers are safe despite the inevitable weaving joggers. It is big and generous enough to accommodate the thousands of tourists taking pictures of each other – again – and scarcely noticing where they are. No one minds. There is enough space left for everyone. The rain stops and the bare trunks shine black in the new sunshine. It would not be such a bad place to kill half a day now, almost forty years on from the restless young man heading south.

29

MALMAISON

The widow Rose Beauharnais rarely smiled. Now in her early thirties, she was nevertheless still a beauty and cut a figure in society despite her bad teeth and a life that had already known dramatic change, execution and imprisonment. She was christened Marie Joséphine Rose Tascher de la Pagerie but everyone knew her as Rose, which was appropriate, because roses were to be the second great passion of her life.

Born in 1763 and brought up on a sugar plantation on the Caribbean island of Martinique – which probably accounted for the wreckage of her teeth – she came to France when she sixteen, apparently speaking French with a Creole accent. This did not stop her marrying an aristocratic general, Alexandre de Beauharnais,[1] to whom she bore two children. Alexandre sided with the revolutionaries after 1789 and became president of the National Assembly but

---

1 He had also been born in Martinique whilst his father was governor there. Catherine, Joséphine's younger sister, was originally engaged to Alexandre but she died so Joséphine stepped into her shoes.

it was not enough to stop him losing his head to the guillotine in 1794. Rose was thrown into prison with every expectation of going to the guillotine herself but, after she had been incarcerated for four months, Robespierre was overthrown and guillotined, the Reign of Terror ended and she was released.

Rose was a survivor. In the following year she met a young general from Corsica. He was just twenty-six years old, brilliant, intense but penniless and famously devoid of social graces. He was, of course, Napoléon Bonaparte. Despite the age difference – she was six years older than him – his gaucheness and poverty, and her mouth full of rotten teeth and almost pathologically extravagant spending habits, they fell passionately in love and in 1796 married. Napoléon did not like the name Rose so called her Joséphine. So, thereafter, did history. But the rose could not be wholly suppressed.

In 1799, as Napoléon's victories brought wealth and increased status, Joséphine Bonaparte bought herself the Château de la Malmaison on the western outskirts of Paris, with an estate of around sixty hectares, that had formerly been owned by Cardinal Richelieu. Napoléon became First Consul and at the turn of the century Malmaison was the centre of social and state life. Joséphine was, unusually, even eccentrically, a keen gardener and amateur botanist. She collected rare plants and from the outset Malmaison was more of a botanical garden[2] than a conventional formal château garden laid out in perfect order and symmetry around the house. She collected plants from other gardens, aided by the botanist Étienne Pierre Ventenat, and bought many plants from Jacques Philippe Martin Cels, who was one of the few Parisian botanists. He had a nursery at Montrouge, just south of the 14th arrondissement,

2 From 1804 Josephine employed her own full-time botanist at Malmaison, the magnificently named Aimé Jacques Alexandre Goujaud dit Bonpland, who had accompanied Humboldt on his exploratory journey to South America between 1799 and 1804 and in the process collected over 4,500 plants, of which 3,600 were new to cultivation.

for exotic and unusual plants brought into France by the expanding number of plant hunters and naturalists, where he propagated
and grew them. We take this sort of thing for granted now but
the influx of new plants from the end of the eighteenth and first
half of the nineteenth centuries was to dramatically change the
way that our gardens and landscapes looked. By encouraging
and being part of this Joséphine was in the vanguard of modern
horticulture.

After driving for ages, thoroughly lost, cross, tired and hungry,
I finally found Malmaison, almost hidden in leafy suburban
backstreets. The château is a low building of white stone, one
room wide, with a jutting wing at either end, not grand, modest
even, but set back from a long wide drive flanked by beds filled
with pansies, tulips and roses breaking into leaf in between a
line of flanking yew cones. Everything thus far is unexceptional.
It could be the house of a wealthy banker or minor dictator
wanting ostentatious privacy within easy access of the centre of
Paris.

Walk round the side of the house and the garden is conspicuous
by its lack of attention. Grass is uncut, borders unweeded and a
half-hearted straggle of rose bushes, admittedly amounting to scores
of different varieties, are unpruned and sitting in a mulch of couch,
dandelion and shepherd's purse. It is the end of April. Clearly no one
cares very much.

Round the back of the building I found a group of men and
women in cheap jackets, hunched over cigarettes, in the process of
being issued with brand-new hoes, forks and spades. They had
creased, weatherworn, stubbly faces with soft overweight bodies and
spoke to each other in a language I could not place. A supervisor or
gang master was instructing them in the process of weeding and
edging the main wide path, scraping and hoeing the moss and grass
that spread on to the gravel and loading it into a tractor and trailer.
This reluctant team of unskilled labour seemed to be the extent of
the gardening.

But the garden, like the curate's egg, has parts that are both lovely and fascinating. The whole area behind the house is devoted to a tree-fringed meadow that is beautifully done. Meadows, despite their appearance of being an effortless amalgam of grass and wild flowers, are never easy to make or sustain. They depend upon a very careful management regime that keeps nutrients as low as possible, to discourage the grass from swamping out the much more sensitive flowers, and yet for best effect the grass should look like what it is aping – a lush, grassy, undulating flower-filled field. This did, with cowslips,[3] buttercups, wild geraniums, clover, daisies, scabious and mulleins liberally sprinkled through the sward, the delicacy of which exactly mimicked the leaves emerging on the limes, chestnuts and plane trees around the meadow's edge.

One of those trees, nearer the house, was a Cedar of Lebanon. At that time wildly fashionable and exotic, it was supposedly planted by Napoléon and Joséphine in 1800, to commemorate his victory at the Battle of Marengo earlier that summer.[4]

The meadow is not a modern rationalisation of a previously formal layout but a faithful and extremely good recreation of Joséphine's original garden. This was a radical, revolutionary, change from the garden style pre-1789. But then everything had changed post-1789, and any hint of an aristocratic garden would have been unthinkable. It was the aristocracy and their châteaux with Le Nôtre-inspired gardens that had been overthrown as much as the Bourbon monarchy. After all, Joséphine's husband had been sent to the guillotine just six years earlier, despite enthusiastically siding with the revolutionary regime. He was an aristocrat and a symbol of the old repression and that was enough to condemn him – as it

---

3 I love the French for cowslip, 'coucou,' summoning at once the lemony softness of the flower and the cuckoo's call that usually appears at the same time.

4 The battle was not just a victory over the Austrians, thus securing all of northern Italy for France – and subsequently half of Napoléon's family – but also consolidated Napoléon's position as First Consul and paved the way for his total control of France. He was just thirty-two.

would surely have condemned her by association had Robespierre lived.

A new regime demanded new horticulture. A meadow, soft, untrammelled, bucolic and flowering with tousled abandon, was a clear statement of a new age. Any of the government officials who came to see Napoléon would look out on to a scene as different as was imaginable from Versailles.

The interior of Malmaison has been meticulously restored to the period 1800–1814. Napoléon's presence dominates, although he was not there a great deal, with dark, strong colours. Blacks, deep reds and golds are everywhere, in a curious mishmash of Egyptian, ancient Roman and modern Directoire French, with a touch of furious Corsican gangster thrown in. There is nothing of the seventeenth century and the Sun King at all. I would hate to live in it but as a historical artefact it immediately whisks you back 200 years.

Joséphine was crowned Empress on 2 December 1804 but when

her grandson – the child of Napoléon's brother and her daughter Hortense – died in 1807 Napoléon actively looked for an alternative marriage that would produce an heir and they were separated from the end of 1809. Napoleon married Marie-Louise of Austria in 1810 and she bore him a son a year later. Joséphine retired to Malmaison and cultivated her garden, dying there, aged fifty-one, in 1814.

By this time it had become a large estate, extending to over 700 hectares[5] with a menagerie, hothouses and an extraordinary botanical collection, but Joséphine's overarching passion was for roses. She set out to collect and grow every rose in the world at Malmaison. To that end, Napoléon had ordered his generals to search out and bring back any roses they saw on their campaigns and Joséphine was in contact with all the major European rose growers and breeders. She had a rose garden made, which contained about 250 varieties when she died. At the time, it was the largest collection ever assembled. But practically nothing of it remains. Despite her private botanists and dedication to collecting, no written catalogue has survived. Perhaps this is why the rose collection at Malmaison has not been gloriously and proudly recreated and maintained. But that is a feeble excuse. Surely it should be a national treasure? It would be much easier to do than the meadow.

As it is, we do have the work of Pierre-Josephe Redouté. He had illustrated Vententat's *Le jardin de la Malmaison* in 1803, with 120 plates made from watercolours. He also made 486 engravings from watercolours to illustrate eight volumes of *Les Liliacées*, published under the patronage of Joséphine between 1802 and 1816. But the work that has made him famous and which is still reproduced in a million place mats and prints hanging in a million homes is his three-volume book *Les Roses*, with 170 colour prints made from his colour engravings. This was published after Joséphine's death

5 By 1896 it had been reduced to less than six hectares. It was donated to the state in 1904.

in thirty instalments between 1817 and 1824. The text was written by Claude-Antoine Thory, whose work in untangling the genealogy of roses still largely holds true today. Most of the roses in the work were from Malmaison, but some came from other sources, and we do not know which is which. This confusion is compounded by the nomenclature, which has changed considerably for many of the roses since then. If it is a muddle then it is a glorious one, because Redouté's work remains the best imagery of roses ever made and the best memorial to Malmaison in its brief heyday.

I have memorials of my own to Joséphine, growing in my garden. The first is 'Souvenir de la Malmaison' which is a Bourbon rose. Bourbons originated from the French island of Île Bourbon, now known as Réunion, which was an important refuelling and trans-shipment port for French ships going to the Far East. Roses were commonly used as hedges on the island and the result of a hybridisation between two roses growing in a hedge, the Old China 'Old Blush' and the damask 'Quatre Saisons' (which I also have growing in the garden) became common on the island. It was recognised as unique and seed was sent back to France in 1819 and grown as 'Bourbon Rose'. Redouté painted it in 1822 with slate pink flowers, hooded petals and strong, abundant foliage. This strength and generosity of flower made the Bourbons extremely popular throughout the Victorian period in both Britain and France and it was the forerunner of modern favourites such as 'Louise Odier', 'Gypsy Boy', 'Madame Isaac Pereire' and 'Souvenir de la Malmaison'. This latter was not bred until 1843 but is a lovely rose with satiny white petals with a touch of the palest pink. There is a climbing form too, which I have growing on a west-facing wall, although a south-facing one would have been better as it really needs lots of sunshine to perform well and hates wet weather. It is worth growing both on its own account and as a floral tribute to the vanished glory of Malmaison.

Joséphine started a trend that took off dramatically in the years after her death and an intense period of breeding followed. What we now think of as 'Old' roses, which would have dominated her collection, along with species – the Gallicas, Albas, Bourbons, Centifolias, Damasks, Portlands and Mosses – were usurped in popularity by Hybrid Perpetuals and, overwhelmingly, Hybrid Teas. France was the centre of European rose breeding, not least because it had a climate in the south that many roses much prefer to the rather soggy, grey north.

Although Malmaison is not the place to see roses grown, a thirty-minute trip to L'Haÿ-les-Roses in the southern suburbs of Val de Marne will make a fair substitute. I went at the end of May, when the roses had not really hit their stride, although I suspect just a week or two later, in the first or second week of June, is the very best time to go.[6] It can be confusing to find because it is often referred to as Roseraie de L'Haÿ but calls itself Roseraie du Val de Marne. Roseraie de L'Haÿ was made in 1899 by the founder of the Bon Marché department store and claimed to be the first garden in the world devoted exclusively to roses. It is indicative of the fecundity of the rose-breeding programme that had taken place throughout the nineteenth century that, eighty-five years after Josephine's death, when her collection of 250 roses was the largest in the world at that time, the number of roses in this new rose garden had grown to 1,600. By 1910 Roseraie de L'Haÿ claimed to have 8,000 roses, which was every single type known to man. Most of those would have been the innumerable varieties of Hybrid Teas. There are now around 3,200 varieties and species growing in the garden.

It is set in a public park and parents and children in buggies wander round in the same spirit as they might look at a range of curtains or a display of frocks. Few seemed to regard the roses as

6 You would think that someone who writes and broadcasts about gardens would choose the best moment to visit a garden, to make the most of its virtues. But life is more complicated, not to say compromised, than that.

possible plants for their gardens, if they had one, but most relished them as colour, scent and shape. The truth is that although roses are lovely, dedicated rose gardens are a bit of a bore, just as any garden based around a large collection of only one type of plant is a bore. A collection quickly ceases to be a garden and becomes a work of reference and should be treated as such. I confess I was completely happy because I was able to go round and identify scores of roses I had read about but never seen growing before, but then I am a rose geek.[7]

I tried to ignore the weeds – I have them abundantly and at times rampantly in my own garden after all – but found myself becoming pernickety and over-fastidious. Weeds everywhere, distracting from the roses. I think that if you have bedding or a monoculture, then you have to match that with a purity and discipline that mulches thickly and weeds regularly. I was never quite able to work out whether the weediness was a sign of lack of resources or whether no one really cared and never able to square it with all the indications of style and flair, such as the way the roses were tied with withies rather than twine or, worse, rubberised stuff, which would be quite likely in an otherwise perfectly weeded British garden of that ilk. The arbours, treillage, seats and pergolas were simply lovely too, with a generosity and scale that few gardens north of the Channel would dream of.

At Malmaison I had seen an original Redouté engraving of the rose 'Rosier du Bengale (cent feuilles)' and at Roseraie de L'Haÿ there it was, in flower, not spectacular or showy but quietly, richly opulent. That connection, from remote historical figure, her home, the engraving of a rose she grew hanging on the walls she sat in (albeit done after her death), to the real flower cupped in my hands is as powerful as a hundred history lessons.

---

7 A few years ago I had over eighty different types of rose in my garden. This has reduced down to about fifty, but the visit to the Roseraie filled pages in my notebook with lists of ones I would love to grow. However, I integrate mine with other plants rather than display them as specimens.

30

COURSON

If you travel around France making a stately but erratic progress from garden to garden, the historic patterns reveal themselves clearly enough, as do the passions for food, order, mastering received methods and the ease with which everyone seems to conceptualise and enjoy intellectualising ideas that would leave the average British gardener uneasily shifting from foot to foot or hunting out pretension. So far so general a nationalistic sweep. But I remained confused as to what French people wanted from their gardens. It is easiest to put this into the context of what the British want, which is possession of place, plants, soil and territory. The last and first bastion against which creeping industrialisation and bureaucracy can, if not flounder, at least be hidden out of sight. An Englishman's garden is his castle.

You don't quite get that across the Channel. There is the lack of hands-on engagement and love of growing things for the sake of it, the lack of generous privacy – which is to say a privacy that one delights in inviting chosen ones to share and admire. Visit only the gardens of the great or the good – and just sometimes both combine – and you have a much more formal picture, where a superb display is put on although horticultural detail is often neglected in an almost careless way.

I was mulling these things as I made my way out of Paris on the road towards Chartres before turning off to the Château de Courson.[1]

I was going there to see the plant fair that has been held in the grounds of the château for the past thirty years, figuring that if I went to a garden that was displaying what people wanted to buy for their own gardens, I might get a little closer under the skin of the French gardener.

Les Journés des Plantes de Courson take place twice a year, for three days, over the third weekends of May and October and is a big event, with tens of thousands of visitors and nurseries from all over France and Europe showing there. Nevertheless, what struck me immediately as I parked in a field and strolled up through the château's stableyard, was the atmosphere of a large, jolly village fête. There was not a whiff of the solemnity, not to say pomposity, that struts busily about British flower shows. There is a collusion between those like the Royal Horticultural Society that put on such shows and the visitors, many of whom are members of the RHS, to treat them as an event where class, society and an accepted code of behaviour form a vague, unspoken alliance that is comforting to those who readily observe and read the smoke signals but constraining and even bewildering to those who do not. It appeals to the best and the worst of the British character.

The really interesting thing at Courson was how one instantly realised that none of that was there. The relief was tremendous. Over 200 stalls were set out under the trees of the park with the same informality and confidence as tables on the street outside

---

1 Courson was originally built in the sixteenth century, but the modern appearance is down to substantial changes made in the 1820s by Jean-Thomas Arrighi de Casanova and it now looks like a larger version of Malmaison. The connections go beyond appearance. Casanova was a Corsican married to Napoléon's cousin and fought with him throughout his military campaigns. Napoléon made him Duke of Padua. Padua's botanical garden, made in 1543, was the oldest in the world and he inherited Courson through his marriage. After Napoléon's fall he was exiled from France until 1819 but on his return made Courson his home and completely renovated the château and estate.

a café. There was little or no attempt to dress the stands other than with the plants themselves, yet an easy elegance and confidence against the backdrop of the mature trees and outbuildings of the château meant that it all looked as stylish as any British equivalent that I have been to. And I have been to a lot.

There were significant factors involved in these differences. For a start everyone was buying. Every stall and display was there to sell its wares. There was no fetishisation of the 'show gardens'. The few that there were served only to jolly things up a little. As far as I could make out there were no awards or prizes involved. People walked about with bags of plants but I never saw a camera or notebook come out, whereas in Britain the same event would have had an air of studiousness, as though visitors were going to be quizzed on it at some later date.

One of the curiosities of British flower shows is that the show gardens are judged with absolute solemnity by a group of self-appointed judges and the results are waited on with bated breath by the press and entrants, yet any real analysis or aesthetic judgement of these gardens is frowned upon as bad form. In other words it is perfectly acceptable to criticise how it is done but beyond the pale to criticise what is done. It would be like having an exhibition in an art gallery where the only comments permitted were on the application of the paint or the staging of the pictures. This denial of serious criticism makes British flower shows, despite their horticultural solemnity, curiously juvenile. Criticising them is like criticising performances in a school nativity play or the food offered to you by your dinner party host. Of course this is only in public. In private, behind people's backs, every kind of judgement is passed but because it is sotto voce it never has to be scrutinised or tested so assumes a kind of bitchiness that undermines any serious criticism. It becomes the worst of all worlds. Do away with that and suddenly things are more grown-up and cheerfully honest.

I expected none of this. Everything about French life had led me to think that any French flower show would have a measured, codified structure. This looseness and flexibility was both a surprise and a delight. Because it is held in the gardens and grounds of the château, rather than relegated to a field or section where the great unwashed will not frighten the horses, it is not crowded although very busy. There is freedom to wander about without looking for anything in particular. The rain fell steadily but it did not put many off. The umbrellas came up and people sheltered under the trees but without the stoical bravado that would be almost aggressively displayed in a similar British situation.

So I looked at roses and irises and paeonies, all in their full sumptuous flower, and a plant stall selling rheums for planting along the margins of a pond that also offered rhubarb (*Rheum barbartum*) for sale in bunches '*fraîche direct producteur*'. This is like a stall at Chelsea that displayed prize ornamental ribes also selling red currants by the pound. I can't think of anything nicer.

The really refreshing thing about Courson was that it felt like an event created and run for the maximum enjoyment of amateur gardeners. In a country where professionalism and qualifications are so admired, this is surprising. In Britain, where the code of amateurism is normally celebrated, hardly any flower show can do this. This is because for a very long time professional gardeners were not allowed to show under their own names. They would grow the roses, carrots, rhododendron or whatever and the exhibits would be labelled as being shown by their employer, who took any prizes and plaudits going.

Professional gardeners were servants. A good head gardener was highly valued and respected, but was never on equal social terms with his employers. This meant that, as well as widening the social divide and establishing a set-up whereby the employers – by definition those with large gardens or estates – ran shows and attended them in the very mannered fashion that resembles a public school speech day, professional gardeners looked down on amateurs and created their own strict hierarchy. At my own village flower show, when I was a child, there were classes which professionals were not allowed to enter so as to clear the field for amateurs. It was as though the bar was lowered to give people a chance.[2]

To make it more complicated, the professional gardeners increasingly manned the endless committees organising shows and provided judging expertise. For many of them this stroked the martinet within and they as much as anyone supported and upheld the system and its rotary-club bureaucracy, whilst still being treated as other ranks by the controlling elite. Above all, they policed and promoted the celebration of skills and techniques above aesthetics.

2 Even now, I sometimes find myself referred to as 'the nation's head gardener', as though that was the highest accolade. The irony of course is that I am an amateur through and through and have always been much more interested in the way that gardens look than the details of how they are grown. Because I am self-taught, I realise that there are lots of 'correct' ways of arriving at the chosen effect. The means is nearly always much less interesting than the end.

To treat gardens in a grown-up, critical manner needs an intelligentsia at ease with serious but open discussion of abstract concepts and not concerned whether their opinions will affect their professional status. The French have that and welcome it, but the British still shy from it – especially in horticulture. Paintings, music, buildings, clothes, utensils are all allowed to be assessed on their artistic as well as practical merits, but gardens are still taboo.

So what do the French want from their gardens? Colour, flowers, herbs, vegetables and fruit. Some order. Somewhere to sit on a pleasant day. But not, on the whole, very much. This lack of urgent horticultural edge makes them much more relaxed about the whole thing. It matters less. And because it matters less they can be easier about their gardens, less protective and that, coupled with an inclination to be analytical, makes them enjoy gardens as statements, symbols and art as much as horticulture.

31

ALLOTMENTS, AUBERVILLIERS

The *banlieue* of Aubervilliers is not somewhere that the tourist – let alone the garden tourist – would normally visit. You are advised not to travel alone, not to travel after dark, not to carry cameras or wear wristwatches, not to wear expensive clothing or to look at maps. In short, it is not safe.

This bleak suburb in the north-east of Paris is typical of the dis-enfranchised New France, where Arabic and African immigrants form a second-class, simmering community, occasionally exploding into violent riots. These are the people that Nicolas Sarkozy, fanning the embers of the bourgeois vote, called *racaille*.[1] As one youth was quoted as saying, while he prepared a Molotov cocktail, if you are treated like a dog then you tend to behave like a dog.

In 1775 it was noted, as part of a Paris–Rheims map describing what the traveller might encounter, that Aubervilliers was an area devoted to the growing of vegetables to sell to Paris and I braved the hostile natives, who were slightly wary of me but not in the least bit unfriendly, to visit some modern allotments.

In 1935 eight hectares with eighty-five plots of *jardins ouvriers*

1 Which can be – and was – interpreted to mean scum.

(workers' gardens or allotments) were established on a winding strip of ground alongside the enormous Cimetière de Pantin and the Fort d'Aubervilliers, which had been built, along with fifteen others, a cannonball's range from Paris.[2] The workers' gardens[3] were originally created to improve the quality of life for the workers, but they now function mainly to improve the lot of the unemployed. They are overlooked by high-rise towers and the sinuous curves of the vast Courtillières housing estate, built as a model of post-war modernity but long since sunk into a model of modern slum, but, once through the permanently locked gate, I found as charming, bucolic and just plain pretty an allotment as any anywhere might aspire to be.

2 Twenty-five years after it was built, during the Paris Commune, that range was put to direct use by the Prussian forces besieging Paris, who set up an artillery battery in the fort during the winter of 1870–71 to pound the city.

3 The *jardins ouvriers* were initiated in the 1890s (a good hundred years later than British allotments) and were originally intended for male factory workers, partly to provide a source of fresh food for their families and partly to give them some fresh air. Women and children were only allowed to go there at weekends. As in Britain, it was illegal for allotments holders to sell their produce: the intention was to provide a means of keeping their families fed and healthy. Allotments are cheap to provide and run – it has been calculated that they cost about a fifth as much as a municipal park on the same sites, parks which, although having obvious virtues, are also often unsafe areas for women and children. Despite their advantages, there is a huge shortage of allotment sites.

There is a language of allotments, verbal, visual and even auditory – a murmur and clink of people working, overlain with conversation that rolls across afternoons and even days. I have visited dozens of sites around the world and they all share this. It is, I suspect, to do with the communal space that does not inhibit private and often eccentric expression and activity. The balance between sharing and owning seems to be almost perfect.

Many British allotments are devoid of trees but here many plots had mature fruit trees – figs, plums, apples, pears, apricots and cherries with whitewashed trunks – as well as large bays, rosemary bushes and vines, rampant on the sunny side of the buildings that ranged from huts to glorious little summer houses, as big as, and in many ways much nicer than, the flats the owners lived in. Bright red roses scrambled over a doorway into one plot, supported by a scaffolding pole. Irises and paeonies popped up for their week or so in the limelight on plot after plot – next to potatoes, onions, carrots and chard.

Most of the plot holders were not born and bred in Paris but came to the city from the countryside, looking for work. For most these plots are the link to their rural upbringing and there is a strong sense of *paysan* practicality and ethos. I met José, who came to Paris from Portugal for a few months forty years ago, married a French girl and stayed. He still spoke with a strong accent. He has had his plot for over twenty years and spends most of his days down there.

José took me round the back of his shed, with its table under the tin verandah set with a plastic cloth and bowls of broad beans to be podded, past the dozen large blue water butts that he had piped together in series – the site has no water, so all rainwater is carefully gathered and treasured – to show me his hens and hares. The hens were a fairly mangy bunch but he assured me that the three fat hens laid well and the six pullets that were skittering against the wire would eat even better. His hares were huddled in the back of a shockingly small hutch. José was oblivious to my obvious qualms and pulled one out. It was sweet in a fluffy bunny way but also pretty bedraggled. There were eight more compressed into the darkness. 'I killed the mother yesterday,' said José. 'My wife will make her into a nice terrine.' I am not squeamish. I eat meat with relish. One of the best pasta dishes I have ever had was *pappardelle sulla lepre* one cold night in Florence thirty years ago. I rear animals which I kill and eat. I profoundly believe in the morality of eating every scrap of any animal one kills. But I have wept as cattle I have raised from birth are loaded for the abattoir and the least one can do is rear animals with respect and dignity. When I see mountain hares, which I am lucky enough to do regularly, I feel heart-soaringly blessed. Dear God, of all magical creatures, hares should not be stuffed into a urine-soaked small cage to be fattened for terrine.

Inside the two-roomed hut linked by the verandah – almost a little courtyard – herbs were drying from the ceiling. A faded pin-up girl, cut from a magazine twenty years ago, was sellotaped to a cupboard. Did his wife come down here? Oh yes, at weekends, when she was not working. She was a cleaner and had two jobs. He had not worked for a long time. But most of what they ate came from this allotment.

Everything was growing well, everything perhaps a week or two ahead of Britain. His tomatoes were planted out in rows, each with a square stake ready to bear the load of the fruit. Right across the allotment, tomatoes were being grown outside, something that is rarely worth doing anywhere in Britain. I also noticed that he grew his potatoes in a block, with no rows or ridges, just spaced as one mass of ground-covering foliage. Was this a particularly French secret to getting the very best potatoes? Nope. It just saved space. In fact as I walked around I saw that an awful lot was grown with much closer spacing than the average British allotmenteer would be told was correct. Horticulture is horribly hidebound.

Every plot had a table and rackety plastic chairs, usually sitting in a patch of unmown grass, often in the lee of a vine or fruit tree. There were no children, but quite a few North African faces, a lot of old men, a few women. It was a quiet Tuesday and those that had work were busy.

The paths between plots were a wheelbarrow's width wide, every centimetre used. Everything has to be wheeled or carried in from the road – perhaps as much as a kilometre to the furthest plot. This has shaped everything. The place has not been bullied into blandness by the combustion engine. If a man – an elderly, retired, unemployed, worn-out man – could not lift and carry it, then it could not be there. So the allotments have a human scale and everything, from the way that the ground is cultivated to the materials for the sheds, is a patchwork of time and effort, dictated by human means. It is the exact opposite to the sprawling, vast white hyperstores and warehouses fringing the ring roads of most French towns and strangely ancient, on the scale of medieval towns with the lanes, tracks, burgages and buildings accruing through long, patient handwork and maintained only as far as needed to function well.

There is a ramshackle, shanty-town element to allotments the world over that has an inbuilt flexibility and strength that comes both from their productivity and nurturing of the earth and from the resilience that comes with having to make do and mend. A spade, rake, hammer and nails and something to hold and carry water and any allotment in the world can function as well as the most expensive gold-medal winning garden in any flower show could ever hope.

A series of dull thuds accompanied by the occasional clash of metal on metal rose over a couple of hedges. The sounds came from a small square of beaten grey gravel. This pétanque[4] pitch was part of the allotment and for general use by the allotment holders. There were three men and a girl in wellies. It was her turn to throw the bright *cochonette*. It went just a metre or so. Her father squeezed her hand and gave it a little kick. The others nodded. No group of sportspeople ever looked more shabby or down at heel.

4 Forty years ago I seem to remember that people in Paris would speak of boules and those in the south of pétanque, and it is a Provençal word. In fact pétanque evolved at the beginning of the twentieth century at La Ciotat near Marseille from boules, which in turn had evolved from bowls – hence the sevententh-century *boulingrin*.

No game was ever played with more concentration or seriousness. One of the men, forearms like hams, was better than the others and whilst the hollow metal balls mainly skidded to a backspun stop too short or shot too far, his, pitched in a high arc with a wristy underhand flick, precisely clattered and elbowed the other balls away and consistently nestled up to the *cochonette*. The other three did not seem to mind. The girl's mouth was slack-jawed and drooling, her face registering no expression at all and her throws rarely going more than a metre. No one commented. She was offered no favours. Just included.

Further down the mown grassy track that curved round to follow the fort's pentangular outline, I found Elaine Daviaud's plot, down steep steps to a lower level that itself edged on to a sharp drop into the defensive ditch, now filled with trees. Like José, Elaine is not a Parisienne, but she has had this plot for thirty-nine years and it is clearly her garden rather than just a productive patch. She is seventy-seven but gardens it all unaided and has the bubbling energy of someone half her age. There were roses, aquilegias, irises, cornflowers and clematis, as well as gnomes and sinks filled with water for the birds. A lily waited to flower in a pot on a little table. It was where she lived much of her waking life.

Elaine talked nineteen to the dozen, explaining exactly what she grew, bustling, describing, pulling a weed, tying in a pea tendril. It was all 'bio', all natural, all the food was good. And she shared. That was the important thing. Everyone came to her for advice – Elaine, why are my courgettes not flowering? Elaine, how do I stop the slugs from eating my lettuce? Elaine, the leaves on my raspberries are yellow, what am I doing wrong? And they give me things and I give them the things I don't need. It is easy to forget that this is one of the poorest, scariest places in France although just the other side of the moat from Elaine's allotment and hidden by the trees, inside the remains of Adolphe Thiers' fort designed to keep the enemy from Paris, there is stationed a unit of the gendarmerie's riot force, handy for dealing with the *racaille*.

I said goodbye and she rushed into her shed and came back with a bulging plastic shopping bag that she pressed upon me. I demurred. I couldn't possibly ... She insisted. *Tenez, tenez.* Thank you for coming to see me. We all share. She smiled and waved vigorously as I climbed the steps back up to the mown path.

I looked inside the bag. It contained jars of her rhubarb chutney and raspberry jam, a lettuce kept cool in a newspaper, and a bundle of herbs. The sun shone. The sirens wailed.

32

HERMÈS ROOF GARDEN

I battled through the hordes of inching tourists in Montmartre, up the steps to Sacré Coeur, retracing my previous visit forty years ago. The view was all but obstructed by couples posing for each other. I suddenly could not face going inside the basilica. It was one of those days when I spoke to no one all day other than a shopkeeper when I enquired about the price of a pen. In fact this one tiny conversation gave me a little insight into the cultural chasm between French and English.

I stood in the little shop on rue Durantin, waiting whilst he dealt with another customer. I made eye contact and nodded in the abbreviated greeting that would pass muster as friendliness anywhere in the UK. When he was free I asked the price of that pen in the window, the one on the left. He stared at me. I started to ask again, suspecting my clumsy French, before he interrupted with a loud and very pointed, *Bonjour, M'sieur.* It was then I realised my solecism, apologised and wished him a suitably contrite good morning. Having been through these motions he duly told me the price of the pen. I bought it and left, his huffiness not much mollified.

The truth was I had been, in his eyes, just plain rude. His position as keeper of the shop – let alone another person I was addressing –

demanded the respect of a formal greeting. That day-to-day formality underpins all behaviour and is based upon an absolute respect for positions and roles which, by entering the shop, I was fully endorsing.

On the other hand, once due form is enacted, a warmth can establish very quickly. My companions and I spent four nights in Montmartre and ate in the same restaurant on rue des Abbesses each night. On the first night service was absurdly slow but we were tolerant, had a day off to follow and the food was good. Nevertheless it was agreed that the people serving us were a caricature of rude Parisian waiters. The second night we only went there because it was very late and other places were full. The staff recognised us and we were treated a little better. The food was still terrific. On the third night we were greeted like friends and on the fourth like family. As a tourist you instinctively feel that you ought to be trying different places and that it is a kind of cop-out to return to tried and tested ground, yet it is almost always true that if you find somewhere you like you should stick to it until you have exhausted all its pleasures, as it is likely to get better and better.

Despite my social gaffe, I spent a perfectly happy day in the rain wandering around the steep streets of Monmartre, peering over walls and through railings, trying to get an idea of what people were growing in their gardens. A lot of trees. Box of course. Wisteria and acacia and the occasional Banksia rose breaking into flower that wet, cold April. But the next morning I set off to see a garden both as private and as public as the centre of Paris could offer.

In the 1980s I had set up a company, with my wife, designing and making costume jewellery. Almost by accident we found ourselves, by the spring of 1982, working in the world of fashion and living our lives to the rhythm of spring and autumn collections. Over the next six years we made jewellery, belts and all kinds of accessories for many different fashion labels, as well as pop groups and stars, a couple of big films, opera, theatre and television. We had our own shop in Knightsbridge and sold through big stores all round the world and we were right at the centre of the world of London fashion, at a time when that was an exciting thing. But exciting was based upon being young, fresh and a bit whacky. When it came to elegance, style, confidence and sheer class London could not hold a candle to Paris.

Sarah and I went to Paris to design a collection for Chloé in the 1980s and had a taste of the engrained confidence – not to say sense of superiority – that ran through the French fashion business. For all the energy and iconoclastic verve of London, one could not help feeling a bit of a larrikin.

By the mid-1980s I was beginning to begrudge any time that took me away from my garden and when a series of disasters, both beyond and within our control, brought financial calamity, it was with some relief that I could devote all my energies to gardens in some form or other and not have to pretend to be fascinated any longer by the fashion business. But it left me with a love of clothes and fabrics and an insider's knowledge of how that world works. Occasionally fashion and gardening combine, although they make uneasy bedfellows.

I remember interviewing Karl Lagerfeld – who in the early 1980s was the most influential and sharpest of all French fashion designers (albeit a German) – when he came to the Chelsea Flower Show and 'designed' a garden[1] under the auspices of Chanel. The brand identity was spot on. Nothing could be more French and every British person knew about Chanel. Clothes, perfume, gardens – a marriage made, if not in heaven, then in Coco Chanel's old headquarters at rue Cambon.

I was intrigued to see how Lagerfeld would play it. Fashion, for all its swish and chic, is always played with the tongue somewhere near its cheek and should be witty and playful and sexy. Now you may

1 In fact it was designed by Tom Stuart-Smith, who has become acknowledged as one of the best garden designers of the age. I wonder how it would have gone down if Tom had 'designed' a range of frocks with Karl Lagerfeld putting them together behind the scenes.

love flower shows, you may be a diehard member of the RHS and you may regard the Press Day at Chelsea Flower Show as one of the highlights of the social calendar, but witty, ironic and sexy are not the first words one would reach for to describe any part of it.

If you want to speak to the best-known gardeners in Britain you find their number and ring them up. To speak to Karl involves an audience at his court and weeks of negotiations with his 'people'. Eventually I was told that I only had fifteen minutes with him, eleven fifteen to eleven thirty, and I must be there at eleven sharp. And that he would be late. I was warned that he could be difficult and that if I didn't know my stuff he *definitely* would be very difficult. I was not sure if this was gardening or fashion stuff, but was intrigued how the difference between difficult and very difficult might express itself.

The night before Press Day I was still at the showground late, waiting for a friend. The foot soldiers slogged slowly back to their billets, horribly anxious and exhausted, no time left to do any more before the next day's judging. Walking past the Chanel garden I noticed three men in immaculate designer jackets, white shirts with those sticky-up collars that don't turn down, and huge shoulders and necks. Designer bodyguards. Inside the garden was a man with a grey ponytail, white jacket and stubby legs, photographing Tom Stuart-Smith nestling up to the golden statue of Venus de Medici that was the garden's focal point. Tom is a tall, serious man with an academic's gravitas and he posed with all the ease of a man embracing a rabid dog.

Next day – judging day, press day and royal day – gardeners turn out in their best bib and tuckers, which rarely encompasses anything much beyond hats and sensible shoes on women and awkward suits and ties on men.

The Chanel garden is called 'Le Bosquet de Chanel'. ('What does Boskay mean?' 'It's another word for Baroque, darling – you know, twiddly bits.') The rumour is that it cost £1 million. This is reckoned to be in its favour. Huge beeches had been selected to be grown into arching frames surrounding the garden and trained in pots for over eighteen months, prepared for Chelsea long before Chelsea knew that they were coming. The planting – exquisite, all in white, as honed as a supermodel's cheekbones – was chosen at and before birth, bred for exhibition and performance like a Chinese gymnast. The parterre and surrounding hedges were grown in boxes and pots in polytunnels in segments and clipped for months whilst still in their pots so that on arrival at Chelsea they only had to be fitted together like a jigsaw. Such precision and attention to detail is everything at Chelsea. Nothing, but absolutely nothing is left to chance. Even the real stroke of genius of the Chanel garden – the fact that the beech hedges were left unclipped and slightly shaggy – was as accurately measured as the déshabillé of the catwalk.

I turn up at the Chanel garden, film crew in tow. It has – unsurprisingly – won a Gold medal. A crowd of photographers and crew are already there, queuing for their slot with Karl, who is sitting hidden in a leafy alcove. Every other second I see a black fan flicker out of the shade like a snake's tongue. His press dominatrix is in a fluster. Mr Lagerfeld will see you in just one minute, she tells us, without the faintest attempt at conviction. The interior of the bosquet is almost filled with a complex parterre in box and there is only room to stand in single file around its outside. Karl is still hiding round the corner. We wait politely. I notice two girls standing, waiting rather shyly in the corner. They are both transfixingly beautiful and dressed in what looks like a very loosely woven check of raw silk or perhaps the finest wool. Cockatiels amongst the hedge sparrows. Their jackets flop to reveal naked breasts, which they seem wholly unconcerned about. More and more women of a certain age step into the garden and walk straight across the box parterre, oblivious to the plants they crush beneath their expensive shoes. One of the landscapers follows them with a trowel, smoothing the gravel behind each footstep.

Half an hour goes by. After forty-five minutes of standing in the boiling sun, only able to move from foot to foot, a mass of photographers are suddenly spilt into the garden from a side entrance. Perhaps twenty squeeze in, taking shots of the models against the statue, gilded as shiny as a chocolate wrapper, with Karl looking proudly on. Tom Stuart-Smith watches from the back, unnoticed.

Finally my turn comes. We now have only five minutes and the interview must be done in the shade. I sit on the little seat next to Karl, slightly too close for comfort. His skin has the pallor of a man living under artificial light. The black fan swooshes past my nose. I ask if he likes to garden. Oh, I love gardening, only cannot stand getting my hands dirty, so I get other people to do it for me, he says. This is not the normal kind of answer one hears at Chelsea. But, he adds, gardens I love. The words flap from his full lips, fast as they will spill, eyes hidden behind dark glasses.

I ask about Coco Chanel's love for camellias, because the garden features white camellias, impossibly flowering in the heat of late May (courtesy of a cold store). His reply is fluent and articulate. Chanel was French so I made a French garden – I am not a Frenchman you know – [I do] and she loved the eighteenth century, so I make a bosquet, you know? He is really asking. A bosquet is a kind of room in the wood where ladies can sit perhaps in the shade. Perhaps they can take a little tea. And Chanel loved the white camellias so we must have camellias and everything in white too. Simple and formal because I do not want to bring an English-style garden to England. This is French, you know. He is not asking.

I thought of the formality of French seventeenth- and eighteenth-century gardens, with their rigid lines and manicured formality pierced with high kitsch. It was Chelsea to a T. Clever Karl had not just paid homage to Chanel but also exactly worked out what was required for this particular collection to be a success. He had Chelsea sussed.

How was gardening like fashion? Fashion is about new things and change, Karl said. Change is always interesting. Gardens change all the time. I am always trying out new ideas in my various gardens.

So why had he done such a formal, retrospective garden? He faltered for a moment, then said that the past was an inspiration and it was a homage to Chanel.

Of course.

As I walked down rue du Faubourg Saint-Honoré, past the Élysée Palace and the British Embassy building and the discreetly flamboyant shops selling bags and clothes at eye-watering prices, I noticed something about the tight self-consciousness of slim black figures, male and female, walking briskly to work, and which you would almost certainly see every day in the exclusive fashion districts of London, Milan and New York. I had completely forgotten about them, having lived in the depths of the countryside for the past twenty-five years but I realised now that their self-consciousness was based on an acute awareness of being constantly judged by every detail of their appearance. To carry this off, everyone has the same slightly detached haughtiness, an insouciance based upon minding very much indeed what people are thinking of you and suppressing an undercurrent – quite often seething – of hysteria.

The garden I was visiting is perched ten metres above the corner of rue du Faubourg Saint-Honoré and rue Boissy d'Anglas, on the roof of the Hermès shop. To get to it I was escorted by a PR minder, talking in extra-polite, hushed tones. Men and women in white lab coats settled to work in a leather workshop, a couple of saddles on the wall. Despite the almost swabbed cleanliness there was a slight aroma of the tack room. Although now better known for its scarves and bags, Hermès was founded on harnessery and superb leatherworking craftsmanship. The thing I liked most about the fashion business in all its manifestations was that it was centred around people who really made things. All the absurdity and front and marketing nonsense is based upon stitching and cutting and skills that take time and dedication to master.[2]

2 Apparently all Hermès bags are still made by a craftsman handstitching each one in its entirety.

The garden is as un-roof-like as a roof garden could conceivably be. This, of course, is quite deliberate. It has French windows opening on to it from a showroom and the idea is to create an impression of a discreet, charming garden hinting at the country and more than hinting at good taste and money. It looks and is substantial and, unlike almost every other roof garden I have visited, nothing is grown in containers. There is a deep layer of soil into which everything, including the large trees, is rooted. The garden was made between 1924 and 1926 and in the war it was used to grow potatoes and – a beautifully Gallic touch – tobacco. Now its fifty square metres (seven of my paces each way) contain two apple trees, a pear, a hawthorn (expertly pruned), clipped box and lavender and a rosemary bush, half sprawling on to the grass. There is a lilac and *Magnolia grandiflora*, white 'Iceberg' roses, white irises and white pansies, with the last remains of white tulips. In the centre is a little lawn, beautifully mown and maintained, and a patch of nettles under an apple tree.

It felt full, fresh and, until you climbed the steps to the parapet or walkway above the two streets, as though it was on the ground behind a nice house in a nice part of town. The raised parapet not only enables you to have a fabulous view over the roofs of Paris (completely unspoilt in the centre by ugly buildings) and to look down on to the garden, but also gives the garden a 1.5-metre wall around it with another metre of balustrade above that, so that it appears as a walled garden surrounded only by sky. This is clever, good design – which is what you might expect from a clever, hugely successful design company.

No one from the company touches it, of course. Like Karl Lagerfeld, they all love gardening as long as they don't have to get their hands dirty, so they have a woman from Aix en Provence who has been coming in to look after it for years. I talked to her and she, who lives in a tower block in one of the *banlieues*, loved her job. But the garden's purpose is not to please those that care for it, any more than the purpose of fashionable frocks is to give satisfaction for those that launder them. It exists up there above the most fashionable shopping street in the world to make potential customers feel that they are part of the most tasteful club in the world, which is what a great deal of high-end fashion is all about. You want people to clock your Hermès, Prada or Gucci bag. You want those that know about these things to be impressed by how much the clothes you are wearing cost, although no one would ever, ever say as much. That would be breaking the rules of the club. So you want to look out on to your garden and know that it accessorises your look.

One of the fascinations of seeing places like this is that I would normally be a barbarian at the gate and never get as close to the inner sanctum. It is a window into the world of a small group of the super-rich, and one of the most surprising things is how anodyne and predictable it is. Because a successful company needs a wide range of customers, its appeal must traverse a wide spectrum of tastes. That inevitably means a lingua franca that is easy to recognise and understand and will span nationalities. It is interesting that the style is based upon an English country garden rather than French formality. Perhaps that is too specific to have a broad enough appeal whereas the white, trim informality, like a beautifully cut jacket with slightly faded elbows, is recognisable everywhere as a deep vein of style.

33

LA DÉFENSE AND PATRICK BLANC

I remember queuing to go up the Arc de Triomphe in 1970 and climbing the dark winding stairs with an echoing clatter from my shoes bought especially for the trip (no laces, brogue, slightly higher heel than anything I had owned hitherto and, most exotic of all, polished with cream and a cloth rather than brushes from the shoe-cleaning box. I loved them), but I remember nothing of what I saw from the top. This time there was a band playing on a sunny Sunday evening, old soldiers in berets standing sharply to attention despite the years, shaming the slack recruits with bright red cravats, and I went up all but the last section in a crammed glass lift.

Paris seen from the roof of the Arc de Triomphe is a revelation. For a start is deceptively high, at fifty metres,[1] and stands at the centre of twelve radiating avenues, so the city wheels about it. The first thing to notice is that from this viewpoint the Louvre appears a coherent palace, whereas on the ground it merges into the streets around it. From fifty metres up, the trees of the Champs Élysées run down into the foreshortened rectangle of the garden of the

---

1 For over 150 years after its construction in 1806, it was the largest triumphal arch in the world.

Tuileries to arrive at the Louvre. Of course, until it was torn down by the Communards in 1871, it arrived at the Tuileries Palace itself and you would not have been able to see the Louvre at all.

The second revelation is how exceptional – and wonderful – it is that Paris has resisted the indiscriminate spread of skyscrapers. There is nothing wrong with these per se, after all, Manhattan is stunningly beautiful precisely because of them, but they diminish any otherwise magnificent buildings they adjoin. They destroy the scale. Look south-east and the city is flat-topped, the individual roofs of buildings smoothed to one harmonious plateau. The Eiffel Tower completely dominates the sky looking directly south, the arch of its legs higher than any of the roofs around it, but look north-west, directly along the same axis as the Champs Élysées and the towers of La Défense are massed like an army encamped at the gates. They are sharp, angular, threatening. It is a leaden irony that a quarter of France's entire wealth is now concentrated in these glass towers.

Look closer and you see a square-topped arch ten kilometres away, built in 1989 as part of the bicentennial celebrations of the Revolution and aligned exactly with the Arc de Triomphe and the Champs Élysées, taking Le Nôtre's vista and opening it out through the guts of the city to the suburbs beyond. Most of the patient, shuffling queue of tourists going up to pay their dues on top of the Arc de Triomphe will never visit La Défense but if you are interested in gardens, new as well as old, then it is well worth the trouble.

The area is called La Défense because of a statue erected there in 1883, commemorating the defence of the city against the Prussian invaders in 1870. Work on La Défense began in the 1950s as a celebration of all that was new and modern and by putting it on the site of an area that had previously been a gallimaufry of factories and poor housing[2] was a symbolic statement of the new

2 And also the university of Paris X campus at Nanterre, which is the district encompassing the northern section of La Défense. The student revolts of May 1968 began here.

post-war France and also meant that the roofline of Paris was not changed.[3]

This new vertical city at the edge of the city has over a hundred skyscrapers with nearly 200,000 people commuting to work there daily. Over 20,000 live there. Driving into it is a maze of under-passes, flyovers and concrete canyons whose sides rise up beyond sight, with more sky reflected in the glassy sides of buildings than is revealed in the square-edged gaps between them. Far easier to take the train. There are shopping malls and plazas and all the barnacles of modern cities that – thankfully – have not yet spoilt Paris. However, given the astonishing energy of the skyscrapers, anything that aped or parodied the old Paris would have been absurd. A new, modern city needs and deserves whatever modern life has to offer.

By the 1970s the area had evolved and shaped itself and it was decided that it should include gardens. A competition was held to design the gardens on the huge kilometre-long central pedestrian concourse, Esplanade du Général de Gaulle, that is set above the road and rail access. This was won by the American garden designer Dan Kiley.

Kiley had come over to France with the US army during the war, had seen the work of Le Nôtre and been hugely influenced by him. Nevertheless, despite this influence, it was a big step for the French to choose an American to design such an important part of the city. But they saw that he got not just the way that gardens can complement this kind of brutalist but exciting building, but also the very French need for order and symmetry and connection to the past.

3 After the construction of Tour GAN (Groupe des Assurances Nationales) in La Défense in the early 1970s, which caused an outrage because it was considered, at 190 metres, too tall and dominant on the Paris skyline, President Valéry Giscard d'Estaing set a height limit of twenty-five metres for buildings inside the city and thirty-seven metres on the periphery. However, this was too late for the cluster of much taller towers that were already built or being built on Paris's horizon. This limit stood for thirty years but was recently revoked and several towers that exceed 300 metres are now under construction.

I have visited La Défense on a grim winter's day, wandering its glass and concrete canyons with a stiletto wind and drenching rain, and also seen it in high blossoming spring, and know that in all weathers and seasons the marriage of gardens, land art and architecture works supremely well. All of it is good and parts of it are triumphant. Because he was steeped in Le Nôtre, Kiley got the tone exactly right without in any way betraying the modernity of the site.

His Esplanade du Général de Gaulle is focused on the Arc de Triomphe, raised up on the horizon, the eye of the needle that the whole of Paris threads through, returning the gaze back towards the unseen Tuileries where 300 years earlier Le Nôtre had first cut a sight line to the horizon and expanded the idea of the enclosed, protected garden. All along the broad concourse are four rows of pollarded planes,[4] their branches knuckled and knobbly with regular pruning, the new growth latticed against the backdrop of steel and glass. These are planted in blocks that are starkly modern yet deliberately and successfully echoing the bosquets of Versailles and Vaux le Vicomte. Underneath the planes there are variously open, sandy areas for pétanque, a bobbly sea of cotoneaster clipped into loose mounds, and tightly levelled box forming a solid green mass, anchoring the trees against every other soaring structure around them. Stretches have flanking slopes of box and yew, angled and cut into terraces, all on a scale that is both fitting and also, in gardening terms at least, breathtaking. God knows how they keep it cut.

Kiley also believed that geometric shapes arranged in grids created the best environment for humans to harmonise with their surroundings, so the planting for La Défense is deliberately geared at counterbalancing the chaotic rush of modern urban moneymaking while still being true to the spirit of the place. Of course, Parisians instantly get these allusions and love the intellectual layers that it is wrapped up in.

All this is planted, rather like the Hermès roof garden, on a man-made layer or roof over the roads and trains below and it rises into different levels and layers of its own, so you have the illusion of solidity and being earthbound until you arrive at a subway which cuts a section through the planting and you see that the whole thing, hundreds of huge trees, bosquets, hedges, pétanque pitches and all, are held in a vast tray.

---

4 Le Nôtre used a mixture of elm, chestnut, hornbeam, beech and oak for his planting in avenues and bosquets, but very few survived the pollution that swamped all western cities after the Industrial Revolution, when coal was burnt in every grate in every room in every house. However, the London plane (*Platanus* x *acerifolia*) proved to be an ideal urban survivor: it can cope with heavily compacted soil and it sheds and renews its bark annually, so the soot deposits that clogged the older bark are not allowed to build up to damaging levels.

La Défense is full of other gardens by a range of designers, some beautiful and exciting, some little patches of floral calm tucked away in a square, some pretentious nonsense and some thought-provoking. But Kiley's central walk ties it all together and is a masterpiece of modern urban design.

However open the French are to conceptual ideas in horticulture as in all art forms, my guess is that few of the hundreds of thousands of people daily flooding in and out of La Défense have heard of Dan Kiley. But Patrick Blanc is extremely well known and currently fêted as the grooviest French garden designer.

You can see why headline writers have latched on to him. His work is always done in a single vertical dimension, cladding the walls of buildings with plants to make Living Walls, and he has made huge ones all over the world. When I was last at La Défense I saw a dismal example (for all I know it might have since become superb), but the one at Musée du quai Branly, just next door to the Eiffel Tower, is dramatic and very well looked after.

Their appeal is obvious. They are always in cities, are immediately visible, lend themselves to huge and fairly quick installations and are new and different. What is not to like? Well, in my own case, almost everything. At best they seemed to me to be overdressed and at worst like particularly bad taste flock wallpaper. Despite this I had the offer to go to his house in Ivry-sur-Seine in the south of the city to see his own 'mur vegetal' (his own preferred description) that he has made inside his home.

He greeted me at the door with bright green hair and as we shook hands I noticed his fingernails were claws several centimetres long.[5] He led me through into a large living space, open to two stories, with the far wall entirely coated in tropical plants. Patrick's desk was in front of this, the floor raised up on a large dais which turned out to be a huge fish tank as big as many a room, the floor made from glass fifteen centimetres thick. Brilliantly coloured little birds flitted about, hopping from bookcase to plants. The light falls on to the leaves, highlighting every shade of green, and then is reflected back up from the water underneath the floor, dashed with flecks and darts of orange from the fishes.

The effect was extraordinary and, for all their exhibitionist drama on the side of huge city buildings, I realised that these living walls were not gardens at all but a combination of decoration and filing cabinet. Inside a room they worked superbly well because you have the immediacy and intimacy of the plants rather than the massed effect, when all the things that make them interesting is lost. In fact

5 After a glass or two of wine I asked him why he grew them so long, slightly worried at the answer I might get. He said that his mother had always told him to keep them cut. Now that his mother was dead he could grow them as long as he liked ...

I think the best living walls I have seen are made from moss and ferns so that the individual plants blend and simply become anonymous green vegetation. However, that is anathema to Patrick. Despite the green hair and the dodgy fingernails he is a dyed-in-the-wool plant geek who has struck upon a way of promoting the plants that obsess him and trying, slightly embarrassingly, to be cool, although the awkwardness of it is endearing. The net effect is to make something that might otherwise be forbiddingly cold and academic warm, accessible and fun.

It is all the opposite of earthy. In many ways it is anti-gardening. The plants never see soil at all, never need tending, never have a season. All that has to be done is to stop the most rampant swamping the slower growers. Patrick essentially fits two layers of thick felt to the wall with water pipes that keep them saturated, the water draining down into a tank (hence the fish tank) and recycled up to the top, and then plants by cutting slits into the outer layer of felt and stuffing the roots in.

Does it do anything that a climbing rose, jasmine or stephanotis would not achieve clambering up a wall? Not a lot, although within doors it seems doubly exotic and can actually work, whereas these other plants need more light than Patrick's selection, all chosen from tropical rainforests where the light levels are no better than the average room and the plants have adapted to growing with very low nutrients – most getting all that they need from the minerals in rainwater.

For Patrick the attraction is all in the botany of the plants. Gardens hold little interest for him. Putting these vast installations out into city streets has the great virtue of getting his beloved plants to a wider audience, but my guess is that he would be as happy here in his house at Ivry with regular plant-hunting trips to add to his collection.

But the nails are weird.

34

GIVERNY

Claude Monet found the farmhouse at Giverny whilst staying at Vernon, a few kilometres down the river. He wanted his children to go to school there, so needed to be near by but preferably not in the town itself. I stayed in Vernon at the Hôtel Normandy, hard on a roundabout and with simple but perfectly comfortable rooms decorated exclusively with reproductions of Monet's paintings.[1] Wandering around the town first thing in the morning, past the Norman church of Notre Dame[2] with its flying buttresses and awkward gaggle of mourners gathering for a funeral, the street cleaner who mysteriously manages to do the job without wearing a hard hat and talks to the shopkeepers and shoppers with neighbourly familiarity because he is their neighbour, the timber-framed buildings that could be in Herefordshire or Suffolk save for the less-finished face of the oak beams, the sandy beach on to the Seine, just minutes

1 Knowing how the locals considered Cézanne in Aix en Provence, I wonder if the residents of Vernon were so proud and supportive of this odd-bod painter with his ultra-modern splashes and daubs? I suspect most of the artistic admiration comes in the wake of the huge tourist trade.
2 It is made from Vernon stone, which was prized as being the best limestone in France and used for the most prominent or most finely carved parts of Chartres, Rouen and Évreux cathedrals and the rose window of Sainte-Chapelle in Paris.

from the centre of town, where children swim, I could not help but wonder, as I had done in so many small French towns, why and how they managed to maintain the sense of community, ownership and identity that is being stripped away in Britain.

Vernon is not particularly old because a lot of it did not survive successive Luftwaffe and Allied bombing in the last war. In Britain we take (some) care over our historic buildings but not so much about our historic ways and customs. There is a self-possession amongst the French people that protects and sustains the small intercourse of daily life that stems from the willingness to accept agreed codes of behaviour. This in turn brings with it a formality about which most people feel very relaxed. I always find this incredibly attractive, although I can see how restrictive and socially conservative it might be.

Monet might have appeared to the citizens of Vernon to be a bohemian but he was an orderly man. He woke every day between four and five, to be up and ready for the light. He took a cold bath, then at five thirty breakfasted 'heartily'. (What was a hearty Norman breakfast in the late nineteenth century? Coffee and not one but two croissants? Beefsteak and cider?) Then he painted – outdoors if possible, otherwise in one of the studios he had built at Giverny – until eleven, when he returned for lunch which was served punctually at eleven thirty. His children were given a special dispensation to leave classes early to walk back along the river from Vernon so as not to be late for the meal. After lunch he was painting again. He would walk round his garden at least twice every day. Dinner was served at seven and he went to bed at nine thirty. The rhythm of the day was made rigid so as best to serve his art. He hated this routine to be broken. Guests came and the household was busy and complicated. But his own patterns did not change.

His working pattern was just as controlled and carefully subdivided. He mapped out light in half-hour segments, focussing furiously on each one. When the half-hour had passed he accepted that the light had changed irrevocably for that day and often himself moved on to another canvas, returning to the former for the same segment of light on the next suitable day. His paintings are pictures of a moment in time that tread the same path as photography. Sometimes majestically better. Sometimes curiously, pointlessly, worse.

Light was his subject. Light was what he tried to represent in splashes of coloured pigment on canvas. It was bound to end in heroic failure and so he endlessly tried to fail better. He once said that the subject was secondary for him. 'What I want to reproduce is that which is in between me and the subject.' Feeling, atmosphere, light.

It is strange that so many of his paintings are cold and objective, clever sketches. Many more are candy-coated. It is as though the valve was unstopped and all the endless disciplined fury recording the effect of light resulted in the absence of any kind of aesthetic. There is genius all right and there are masterpieces. But it all went down on to canvas and the quality – and of course millions will profoundly disagree – is an accident of light.

The garden at Giverny is much like this. I have never seen a garden so stuffed, so crammed and crowded with plants. It is like a catalogue or a plant showroom. At times this is stunning. I recall visiting at six o'clock on a May morning a few years ago when the irises were at their astonishing best, accompanied by sweet rocket, roses, eremurus, clematis and pansies to make washing waves of colour that I floated in deliriously. It was one of the great garden experiences of my life. In August the nasturtiums lapping out over the central gravel path are thrilling. A stroke of horticultural genius.

Yet I have been three other times to Giverny and been frankly bored by it. The excess feels less like abundance than conspicuous waste. Plants, stuffed like socks into a drawer, pushed into the beds to make them fit. The lack of design is also curiously enervating. The garden is a strange mixture of narrow physic garden beds carefully planted by colour like a painter's palette, and loose, island planting that is perfectly true to the style and age of the 1890s to 1920s – my grandparents had a garden planted in a very similar way – but which feels formless and charmless to my twentieth-century eye. In fact the whole garden is remarkably undesigned. There is not a single hedge and, other than the great central *allée*, little coherence in the layout. The reason, of course, is that Monet designed it entirely around light and colour rather than structure. It suited him well. But it is not a particularly good way to organise a garden. There are no spaces, no volumes, no human places at all.

It is unfair to criticise it for being itself – no private garden has to answer to anyone other than its maker – but spending more than an hour or so there can be a curiously unsatisfying experience. Giverny bounces the visitor off its surface. It is so full – of plants, colour and more Monet than anyone needs – that it is impossible to penetrate beneath its glittering surface. This means that it takes nothing from you. There is no sense of intimacy or reciprocation. I once worked with a very well-known comedian who was like this. He endlessly gave out to the audience, and delighted and entertained them with real sparkle. But he resisted anything back from them at all. It was a way of nurturing his deep and inconsolable isolation.

Then there is the water-lily pond. Over 600,000 people a year visit Giverny and every one of them wants to see the paintings of this pond made flesh. The real water, the real bridge, the real flowers floating on the pond. This would, I can only assume, make the pictures fully real to them. My hunch is that nearly all the visitors have never seen a 'real' painting by Monet and will not be going to the Orangerie at the Tuileries to see the *Nymphéas*.

It is a good thing to do. I have said how the Jeu de Paume, with its unique collection of Impressionist paintings, was the biggest draw for me when I first went to Paris. These were all moved to the Musée d'Orsay in 1986, but the Orangerie, which is the mirror building on the south side of the Tuileries, has housed Monet's huge water-lily series since 1927. In fact they cannot go anywhere else because they are fixed to the wall of the building.

I have very mixed feelings about them. I like the fact that they are there and so big and so brave an idea – for essentially they are six paintings, each one of the surface of a pond as large as a pond itself and through its size made completely abstract. But they are kitsch and decorative and have none of the tentative spontaneity of some of Monet's work, where you feel he has held a moment that was so fleeting that a camera shutter could hardly have caught it and yet is deep and rich with humanity. Perhaps we are too influenced by the knowledge that he painted them after the death of his wife and in the shadow of the First World War, when he was slowly going blind and desperately trying to capture all the light left to him. Who can fail to be moved by the artistic greatness of fighting against the dying of the light of civilisation itself and one's failing lonely old age by producing a monumental shout of colour and luminescence? But these vast panoramas are too self-consciously attempting to be great to be great art. They would be perfect for a department store tea room.

And yet. The grateful nation and the whole 'Monay' industry

holds them in the highest regard. It hardly matters at all if I, or anyone else, likes them or not. The building and the galleries and the legend have all assumed mythic status and are therefore part of the history of art and gardens in the twentieth century. To walk around those cool, grey, oval rooms with their curved walls is to enter a shrine to the great man.

People carry that reverence with them when they visit Giverny and see before them the actual pond that he painted from, pose for a picture on the bridge and walk reverentially around the perimeter taking thousands[3] of pictures, secretly hoping that they too will capture that seductive spangle of light.

I wonder if they are secretly as disappointed as I – and everyone else that I have been with – when visiting Giverny. The water itself is fine, as ponds tend to be. Willows dip charmingly into the surface and there is a really good collection of water lilies that do their water-lily thing when the sun shines between June and September. Lovely, but utterly unexceptional were it not for the fact that Monet made from this some of the best-known (and most expensive) paintings ever created.

Around the edge of the pond is a belt of absurdly municipal and plain odd planting designed, so I was told, primarily to stop the endless streams of visitors walking into the water. It is a belted *cordon sanitaire*, with none of the marginal sprawl that any pond of this type must have. I wrote a list of the planting immediately in front of me on 24 April 2012: tiarella, alchemilla, wallflowers, tulips, rose, iris, primrose, spiraea, euonymus and pansy. There is no pond in the world for which these plants, pushed in awkwardly together, make any kind of aesthetic sense. A tarmacked path protects the planting that protects the water with the inevitable plastic chain painted in Monet green and steers the crowds around the garden.

3 If 600,000 visitors each year, each carrying a camera, take a conservative ten pictures each, then they have taken, say, 6 million pictures a year and perhaps 60 million photographs of the pond at Giverny in the last ten years. The odds of one or two being quite good are high. Not my own though.

The path does more than anything to make the garden seem like a busy garden centre. In Monet's day it was mostly grass and would be so much the better for it. But American money and American visitors by the planeload – a visit to see 'Monay' is as much part of the French experience as a photo in front of the Eiffel Tower – have ossified the garden into a kind of Disneyfied stasis. It cannot move forwards or backwards because then it would not be in the exact spot that all these visitors need it to be. The only problem with this is that, like light, the only constant in any garden is change.

The head gardener, an Englishman (albeit one who has lived and gardened in France for his entire adult life) called James Priest, knows all this. He is relatively new to the post, having taken over from the legendary figure of Gilbert Vahé, who helped restore the garden and was head gardener for thirty years. James is a new broom but his room for manoeuvre is very limited. It is a challenge. How do you return to the essence of Giverny without frightening the horses that finance it? He is very, very good at his job. He needs to be.

35

CHAMP DE BATAILLE

When I was visiting Courances, Philippine de Ganay told me a story about the owner of Champ de Bataille. Twenty years ago she was invited to a grand party to celebrate the completion of the magnificent new house of the hugely successful interior designer and collector Jacques Garcia. Everyone who was anyone in the world of French fashion, interiors and high society was there, and quite a few who weren't. Everyone was beautifully dressed and they all sat down to a superb meal. When this was finished Jacques Garcia appeared on a balcony above them and thanked them for coming, hoping that they liked the house and the party and that they would continue to enjoy the evening because – and he paused – this was to be the last party that he would ever hold there.

Then Jacques Garcia told the guests a story. When he was a child in Normandy, the only son of a widow who struggled to make ends meet, on his way to school he would pass a vast old château that was used as a hospital. He would look over the walls and tell his mother that one day he would live there. Time passed. He grew up, left school and became rich and famous as an interior designer to the even richer and more famous. Then that childhood château in Normandy came up for sale and yesterday, he told the guests below, he bought it. So tomorrow morning this house was to be placed on the market to help pay for it.

Philippine said that the château was amazing and the garden even more extraordinary. I must go and see it. It was, she said, quite, quite extraordinary. So I did.

The name, Champ de Bataille, refers to a battle fought on the site of or near to the château in 935 by Guillaume Longue-Épée, William Longsword,[1] the Count of Rouen, as part of his family's control of Normandy that lasted until the Duchy of Normandy ceased to be a separate kingdom and was absorbed into French crown lands in 1204.[2]

The present building was built by Marquis Alexandre de Créquy-Bernieulle, after he was exiled to Normandy in 1650 by Cardinal Mazarin, who was regent for the then eleven-year-old Louis XIV. Having accepted banishment from the Court, the Marquis elected to build himself as courtly and splendid a house as he could as compensation and it was completed by 1665. This was exactly the period that Vaux le Vicomte was made and Versailles begun. There exists a sketch of the garden showing a grand terrace with parterres, broderies and bosquets. Jacques Garcia is convinced that the sketch was done by Le Nôtre and therefore the garden was designed by him, although the evidence seems too scant to support any serious attribution. However, it is not fanciful to suppose that this garden would have been made along the lines of Le Nôtre's contemporaneous masterpieces. Jacques Garcia certainly believed so and has made a garden, based upon that sketch, which is as magnificently elaborate in content, structure and scale as Le Nôtre's Baroque creations. It is a thirty-eight-hectare, glorious, monstrous folly, as tasteless and excessive as a Las Vegas hotel and yet in every detail

1 The name hints at the Viking ancestry of the dukes of Normandy. William was born a pagan Viking to Rollo, the titular first Duke of Normandy (the title was awarded retrospectively), and was great-great-grandfather to William the Conqueror, Duke of Normandy, who became William I of England.
2 The dukedom also ceased to exist, although in 1660 the twenty-one-year-old Louis XIV proclaimed Charles II's brother James, later James II, nominal Duke of Normandy.

accurate and true to the spirit of the seventeenth century. If you want to see what Versailles was like in the 1680s or Vaux le Vicomte on the evening of 17 August 1661, then a visit to Champ de Bataille is the nearest that you will ever get.

I met Jacques Garcia at the garden. His appearance belies the extreme flamboyance of the house and garden. He is of medium height with white hair, spectacles and the well-preserved tan of someone who takes the time and trouble to appear tanned and well preserved. You might think him an advertising executive or the head of a fashion house.

He spoke frankly about the madness of the project, saying that had he known how much it was going to cost and how much work it would involve, he would never have begun. Everyone, he said, laughed at him. They said that he had execrable taste and that he was completely mad, especially the people who now say that it is mar-vellous. He says this without rancour, but I have heard that he has had opprobrium heaped upon him for the presumption of the garden. It is criticism with an envious, sour edge to it. But he stuck with it and even changed his job[3] so that he could make as much money as possible to pay for it.

One of the ironies of the garden, he told me, is that he never intended to make it when he bought the château. It was the building that he wanted, not the land, and he restored it, at great expense, to house his collection of Empire furniture. But a huge storm in 1993 flattened many of the mature trees in the parkland surrounding the house and the job of clearing and repairing the damage was so great that he thought he would use the opportunity to recreate the sketch of the formal garden immediately outside the château.

That was the beginning, nearly twenty years ago, and the work still continues. As we spoke at least fifty men were working on a side

3 As far as I can gather, this did not mean that he gave up design and became a banker but he stopped working for so many private clients and took on designing the interiors of chains of large expensive hotels. In other words, he did what most of us have to do, and sold some of his soul to pay for the stuff he liked.

garden that incorporated an entire temple he had bought in India.[4] It is clear that M. Garcia never does anything by halves.

Until you have to physically go round one, it is hard to conceive how big a thirty-eight-hectare garden is. Fortunately Jacques Garcia provides golf buggies for visitors, to speed the process up, but the enormity is made greater by the intensity and ambition. It is not thirty hectares of paddock and wood with eight hectares of lawns and borders but hectare after hectare of walls, hedges, lawns, buildings, canals, fountains, ponds, temples, grottoes and follies of every kind. It goes on and on. The landscaping alone involved shifting 4 million cubic metres of soil, enough, he told me, for a berm one metre high running from the north of Scotland to the south of England. That calculation must have whiled away an empty hour. Everything, from the yew and hornbeam hedges to the pots, the landscaping fabric put down to mulch the weeds, the gravel paths, the drainage system, the vineyard, everything is installed with the massed energy and equipment of a new town or an army establishing a bridgehead. The garden has not so much accrued as descended rather like a Chelsea Show garden. That it has taken twenty years gives an indication of the scale of the project.

I like this. I like the outrageous energy of it. I like the ambition and the way that it is all done properly. God knows how much it has cost but he said it was a figure in excess of 20 million euros. It is a lot for a garden but then he has got a lot of garden.

There is an enormous long view leading directly from the back of the house, with gardens going off to the side of them, but, like Versailles, it is too much to take in on one visit. I went twice in six months and actually tried to see less on my return and consequentially got more from it. The body can only digest so much garden in one sitting.

---

4 He explained that the Indian garden was to be filled with plants that would represent minerals whereas other parts of the garden represented earth, and so on. This kind of conceptualising, of adding to the physical and aesthetic elements of the garden, is so very French.

Stick to the central vista but walk rather than ride a buggy. Make a slow but stately progress down the flanking gravel path, past statues and urns and high hornbeam hedges and the ornate *parterre de broderie* in box that leads to the central round pool with its gold dolphins and then past the vast gravel square that leads off to other gardens – but resist the temptation to visit them. Not yet at least. Keep straight on across a football pitch-sized lawn, the flanking hornbeam hedges now replaced by yew buttresses the size of buildings with sculpted box infill. The garden is a triumphant example of the power of hedging material as large-scale topiary – and also how small-scale hedging and topiary will happily scale up.

Look back and the château is getting smaller. You arrive at the main water feature, with jets arching across two square side pools, spouting out of a whole succession of marble baths sitting on gold pedestals, pouring from the mouths of gold frogs, fish and a golden fringe on the cascade in the centre – all of which came from the garden of Philippe, Duc d'Orléans, the brother of Louis XIV, at Saint-Cloud,[5] which was

5 His other garden was the Palais Royal.

destroyed in 1870 in the Franco–Prussian war. This gives credence to the gleaming vulgarity of the garden. There is no doubt that, to the modern eye that likes its history to be faded and worn and weathered, the gardens of the Baroque period would have been screamingly camp and over the top. This is what makes restoration so terribly difficult, because to do it faithfully means restoring something to an unfingered, bright, garish state. That is how they liked it.

So you rise up the gravelled slopes above the cascade and there, on this higher level, stretches out a broad canal running as far as the eye can see, lawns and an avenue of limes on each side. For such a coup de théâtre it is hard to restrain applause.

I don't think it matters if anyone likes Jacques Garcia's garden or if they think it good taste. As it happens I do like it a lot, because the world is a richer, jollier place for its existence. But I do think it matters that through it we can see what the great Baroque gardens looked like. This is not a faithful recreation of an existing seventeenth-century garden. But it is a faithful recreation of the spirit of Baroque that illuminates the gardens that Le Nôtre made – as he made them. It is also coming into being. I have visited twice and seen real changes. Even though such an extraordinary amount of work has been completed, it still feels like work in progress. History does not get closer to the bone.

I chatted to Patrick, the head gardener, about the French relationship to formal gardens and garden history and he made the point that after the Revolution gardens were associated with aristocratic power. It was not until well into the nineteenth century that gardens re-entered the popular imagination through the informal parkscapes of the *jardin anglais*. This is what happened at Villandry and here at Champ de Bataille, the informal sweep of the eighteenth-century English garden that Capability Brown did so much to foster a hundred years earlier layering over the oppression of aristocratic formality. There was, said Patrick, a rupture with gardens as with so much else in 1789, and across the Channel we never had that. Our British gardening sensibility has been one long evolving flow.

Patrick made another remark that explains much. We were talking about Courances and how it is the exception that proves the rule, managing to evolve and adapt without losing any of the important essence of either its formal structure or its informal, romantic soul. That is why it is so British, Patrick said. The French do not feel comfortable with dualism. The Cartesian influence is such that the French cannot enjoy the pleasures of the flesh without intellectualising them. Any analysis of gardens will always inevitably lead to an intellectual debate in France – and probably a political and moral one too. This intellectualisation of things that we British consider in entirely practical or sensual terms – and that is almost always true about gardening in general – simply cannot have real authority or validation to the French unless it becomes intellectual.[6]

However, you do not have to think at all at Champ de Bataille in order to take from the garden what you will. Give it some time and energy – you will need both just to see enough to come to any kind of opinion – and it repays and enriches just by being so excessively itself.

---

6 I remember the pernicious influence of structuralist thinking, based upon very French concepts, which dominated literary criticism in Cambridge in the 1970s. It gutted the emotion and vitality of much work whilst adding a superficial veneer of intellectual respectability.

36

LE JARDIN PLUME

In Rouen I stayed in one of the modern, ugly hotel chains that I dipped in and out of around France and whilst my instincts are to bemoan their lack of any hint of style or character, the tireder I feel and the less time I spend in a hotel the more I value the way that the basics work, the rather prissy cleanliness, relative comfort and predictability. Modern travel eventually crushes us all into the submissive cringe of middle management. But stepping out at dawn into the incredible streets around the cathedral in Rouen it did seem sacrilegious to be staying in a late-twentieth-century tribute to bad taste.

Although much of the centre of Rouen was damaged in the Second World War, the half-timbered streets that do remain around the cathedral appear astonishingly unspoilt and charming, not least for the absence of any street furniture or markings. I wanted a day or more just to walk and watch. But time was, as ever, horribly limited and it was the streets of Rouen or a particular garden near by, and the garden won. I had visited it briefly in mid-winter and seen enough to know it would turn into something quite out of the ordinary in high summer.

Le Jardin Plume is about twenty-five kilometres east of Rouen in the middle of open, hedgeless countryside dotted with tiny villages and orchards,[1] sitting in an uneasy cohabitation with an agriculture dominated by huge machines and monoculture. It is a landscape undergoing an identity crisis.

Despite the garden being signposted generously from about ten kilometres out, it is tricky to find. But it is worth any amount of doubling backs, cursing at satnav, feeling car sick as you try to make sense of the map or that feeling of life draining out of a hole in the bucket as you get steadily later and later for the agreed appointment. When you do find it, there is a little farm track, no parking other than the grassy verge, a tiny little gate in the hedge – all as informal and unpretentious as it possibly could be. Yet once through the gate one look will confirm that this is an astonishing garden.

When Sylvie and Patrick Quibel began making it in 1997 their raw material was just the scant remnants of an old orchard and a field with a few dilapidated barns. From the first they have worked with these seemingly unpromising elements, both to be true to the spirit of the area and also as part of the general philosophy of the place, which is minimum interference and maximum design. It is a clever garden, very knowing in how it goes about its business – not least in the way that it seamlessly combines a loose artlesssness with strictly imposed design. It is as though the approach of Gilles Clément at La Vallée has been married to the formality of Vaux le Vicomte,[2] and Le Jardin Plume is their brighter, more vigorous offspring.

It is called Le Jardin Plume (the feather garden) because of the extensive use of grasses, both in the borders and in the large meadow that runs down the centre of the garden. Meadow does not really describe it well. It is also a functioning orchard and a formal grid of *allées* and blocks (the grassy ghosts of bosquets). The *allées* are made

---

1 This is the landscape in which Flaubert set *Madame Bovary*, with his fictitious town of Yonville-l'Abbaye based upon Ry, which is just a few kilometres from Le Jardin Plume.
2 Again and again I find myself coming back to Vaux as the touchstone that all French gardens either return to or depart from.

from mown grass, with four parallel strips running the full length of the 1.6-hectare plot, gridded into forty rectangles,[3] roughly ten metres square, with long grass and an apple tree filling each of the plots. This means that they are big, averaging about a hundred square metres each.[4] They are substantial meadows in their own right and each one is planted slightly differently with bulbs and perennials, all planted directly into the turf. The natural grasses and wild flowers are encouraged and allowed to flourish amongst them. The blocks are left uncut all summer and then in October mown and raked into ricks, which are carted off to make compost. This reduces the nutrients and stops the grasses swamping the bulbs and perennials. The soil is quite heavy, which is traditionally trickier for this kind of thing than a light, well-drained soil, but the evidence is there. It works and it works well.

The central block nearest to the house is filled with a square of dark water, with closely mown grass tight to its edge, an old apple tree reflected with a flare of orange from the tiles on the roofs of the barns. It could not be more different to the pond at Giverny and it is much, much more beautiful.

3 An aerial photograph shows this to be a medley of straight-sided shapes that accommodate the asymmetry of the plot, but you are not aware of anything other than square blocks on the ground.
4 Each plot is twice the size of the Hermès roof garden.

Some of the squares, along either edge, are planted as solid blocks of American perennial grasses, such as *Panicum virgatum* 'Squaw' and *Sporobolus heterolepis*, both of which have a haze of pinky seed heads, that, by late summer, are well over a metre tall and heavy with flower. Grasses used like this, planted by the hundred if not the thousand, have immense effect just by the sheer scale and confidence of the planting which, because they are constantly growing and changing colour and because they move and are sibilant and sinuous, never feels like an unimaginative monoculture. By late summer the uncut meadow grass is sere and tawny whereas the mown grid between them is still a vibrant green, so you have a chequerboard of colour as well as design. The clever thing is that this planting combines the virtues of the wild flower meadow, and all the associations of looseness and natural freedom that come with that, with the precise, carefully maintained formality of the traditional French garden, with all the rhythms and balance that this brings. It is witty, clever, experimental, interesting and very beautiful.

To one side of the house is a spring garden, all green and white, with euphorbias and hellebores lapping in between a grid of immaculately clipped box balls, then a circular lawn surrounded by a waist-high box hedge, and then the jardin plume itself, the original part that has eventually given its name to the whole, made in the old farmyard in the angle of two lovely barns. It consists of just two huge beds, dominated by grasses intermingled with herbaceous perennials in pale blues, mauves and pinks such as asters, eupatorium, verbena and heleniums that make a feathery, shifting crowd, the whole thing planted in long drifts with the narrowest of walkways between them that are almost completely hidden in summer. In winter the entire area is strimmed to the ground and left lying like windrows of cut corn. Although the choice of plants is precise and skilful, it is the most unintrusive, least labour-intensive form of gardening possible.

This old farmyard is closed off by a yew hedge cut into licks

and shark's-fin waves, which is a piece of pure theatre, trans-
forming the conventional idea of a hedge and making it into
performance.

Directly in front of the house is a formal layout of geometric box
hedges – effectively a parterre – with brick paths between the beds
which are filled with blazing colours. Kniphofias, sunflowers,
dahlias, heleniums, nasturtiums – all shades of yellow, orange and
red. The box hedges are extra tall and the paths narrow so you just
fit through them, hemmed in by violent colour. Then round the
other side of the house is the autumn garden, with another breathtaking piece of design in box. It is a vine-covered seating area
surrounded by wings of box hedging fully four metres deep, cut
with a top as flat and green as a huge billiard table. This garden
constantly stops you in your tracks with the extent and boldness of
its simplicity. Sitting under the vine, within the walls of box, you
look out on to the autumn garden, another enclosed area that
repeats the planting of the farmyard, making a dense willowy,
ephemeral, tall jungle of flower and grass contrasting against the
perfection of the clipped hedges.

That contrast is the secret and core of this garden and the loose
planting and tight, sharp edges and hedges works so, so well. The
rhythm of blocks and rectangles, crisp right-angles and straight
lines, coupled with the most open, loose, generous planting devisa-
ble is strangely much more natural than the made-up curves and

swirls that people often use to try and make a garden look softer or more natural. You need rhythm in a garden, the beat and pattern of repeated shapes that then supports and enhances the energy of loose planting.

There is more. A potager that is deliberately informal and slightly wonky with bobbly hedges and earth paths and the remnants of walls and sheds and more wit in a square metre of it than all of Villandry. There is another pool entirely hedged in by miscanthus and, importantly, a nursery where you can buy all and any of the plants that you see in the garden.

Le Jardin Plume is a stage set. Despite the informality and looseness of the planting and the drifting sensuousness of the grasses that set the tone for the garden, it is highly mannered. But that is not a fault. As Patrick puts it, Gardening is a game we play with Nature. There are accidents but the gardener is in control of them.

Gardens are never natural. They are always fussed over, designed, detailed, and planned to within an inch of their lives. Every keen gardener is an obsessive, dreaming their gardens in the middle of the night and straining after a perfection that nothing else can provide and which mostly eludes them. The trick is to make it all seem effortless and one of the most apparent skills at Le Jardin Plume is that Sylvie and Patrick know when to stop. They know the most important thing of all in any design which is what not to do.

37

SÉRICOURT

The restaurant I had been recommended in Amiens turned out not to exist. It had been replaced by a pizza joint and no one had informed their website. But, as is often the case, the funny little place down the road that looked a bit dodgy from outside turned out to be wonderful, serving only the meaty, mostly porky, Norman food that was not available in any of the tourist eateries strung along the edge of the Somme. For once the food was good, local, cheap and the service friendly. Parts of pig made up almost the entire menu but I sidestepped it and ate bone marrow – served as four large columns of bone – followed by tripe à la mode de Caen. Both superb. The fact that my alarm was set for four fifteen the next morning to drive to Charles de Gaulle airport and get the eight-thirty flight home, and that we didn't start to eat until ten at night, didn't spoil a delicious meal.

As I walked back along the cobbles past the vast Gothic cathedral and university buildings, thinking about the First World War and the nailed boots of British, German and French troops that marched the same streets, the playful, absurd and yet underlying seriousness of Séricourt fitted into the beaten-up, bruised pattern of this part of France.

Séricourt is in the Pas de Calais, fifty-odd kilometres north of Amiens in the north-eastern horn of land that buffers France and Belgium. Troops have swept in and scrambled out of this area for centuries. The worst of the First World War was enacted here but it was just another stage in man's violent inhumanity to man played out in this corner of France. The battle grounds of Agincourt is a few kilometres to the north-west of the garden and Crécy[1] a few kilometres to the south-west. The ground is mulched in military history.

So Yves Gosse de Gorre has made a garden both celebrating the inescapable history of the landscape it is set in and as a symbol of peace. It is charming and eccentric – by British standards at least, where British gardens are either rigidly tied to current concepts of what a garden should be or gloriously, wildly off the wall. The space in between, where a garden is unself-consciously a statement and concept, is where the French feel very comfortable but we, the British, horticulturally shuffle and feel awkward.

Yves is a professional nurseryman and landscape designer who came to Séricourt in 1979 and started to lay out the garden in 1983, so it now has that maturity that makes a garden ageless.

Before walking round and whilst rain hammered on the glass roof of the conservatory, Yves gave me lunch – a delicious cold beetroot soup, terrine, bread he had baked, one loaf with salmon and another with bacon, cheese and grapes cut from the vine above our head, washed down with a pale Lubéron rosé.

I asked him why he had made the garden. He laughed. What a

1 When I was a schoolboy the dates of Crécy and Agincourt – 1346 and 1415 – were learnt by rote along with about fifty other 'special' historical dates, all relating to British military or political triumphs. The superiority of the longbow over the French crossbow was the key to these two battles. The very best longbows came from yews grown along the Welsh borders where I have lived for the past twenty-five years, and some years ago I made a longbow following fourteenth-century methods from a Welsh yew that would have been growing at the time of Agincourt. It takes all my strength to pull it and has ferocious power and yet would have been considered a boy's bow and too lightweight to have served at Crécy or Agincourt.

question! Why not? And aside from the huge amount of time, money, skill, patience, labour and vision, why not indeed? People make gardens every day, all over the world. But Séricourt is not like any other garden. It is quirky, odd, in places barmy and not always even good, let alone beautiful. But it is unique and in a sea of crushingly uniform taste it is stimulating and thought-provoking. Again, that is very French. Side by side with the overwhelming desire to do the right thing is a much greater tolerance of controversy of thought and ideas in any medium. I suspect that an interesting garden carries much greater currency in France than in Britain, where gardens are much more of a beauty contest.

The garden is over four hectares in size and gives the impression of having been made up as it went along but always on a scale of thought that somehow belies Yves' jovial, low-key, utterly charming presence. There is a kind of steely wildness there, needed to see through something so extravagantly eccentric and unself-conscious.

Yves told me that he loves the symbolism of plants and that the purpose of the garden is to use them to construct stories. You have to buy into this to enjoy Séricourt. I had Yves to guide me round but the truth is that the plants enact or represent the stories in tableaux but do not tell them. However you come at it, it is a funny, scrambled jumble of ideas and plants, some staggeringly grand in scope and execution, cheek by jowl with others that are clumsy and meaningless until the story behind them is explained.

The centre of the garden conceptually is the war garden. You arrive at it through a winding wooded path lined with erythroniums which opens out to a large block of yellow yew, representing gold or money, as big as many a small garden. Beyond this are serried ranks of golden fastigiate Irish yews, their tops cut off to various heights, representing soldiers in formation, inspired, Yves said, by the Chinese terracotta army. Next to this is a wavy, prickly block of pine, meant to represent a fortress. Around the edge of this area are topiarised evergreen trees of every shape and size, from small box balls to large cypresses, all cut and clipped to cones and blocks and columns. One group, Yves told me, were the weeping women at the edge of the battlefield, another represented deserters, slipping through the deciduous trees. Beyond this is an area of long grass filled with poppies, which are the poppy fields of Flanders.

Then, amongst the astonishingly big idea of this, there are clumsy cartoon faces carved into Lawson cypress. Treading softly, I asked Yves what the inspiration was for these. *Braveheart*, he said. He saw the film *Braveheart* and wanted to reproduce the mask-like face paintings that the Scottish warriors adopted before battle. These are his Braveheart warriors. We have leapt from Goya to Asterix. Perhaps that is a sign of cultural wit, perhaps crassly jarring. I remain genuinely unsure.

A little further on there are a couple of deep cone-shaped holes blocking the grass track through the false cypresses. Bomb craters. A little puddle of water lies in one. The skirts of the trees have grown over and partially obscured the other. The spoil lies neatly coned between the trees, representing the positive to the craters' negative. They are shocking and moving, a piece of land art that works as horticulture.

Looking on, I peer down a long avenue of cypresses to a glimmer of daylight at the end. Hope at the end of the Avenue of Infinity, explains Yves. Inside a seemingly impenetrable and dark stand of *Chaemaeocyparius* the trunks are painted white, and stand ghostly in the little light that comes through a gap cut in the skirting branches. The children love this, said Yves.

The concepts jumble and jostle into each other in a manner which is both chaotic and playful, in a mad, creative splurge. The planting exactly mirrors this. It seems, to this very British eye, curiously eclectic and random. And yet Yves is a plantsman with great knowledge and love of plants and they are all grown with great skill. It is nothing to do with correct or good horticulture and everything to do with how the French view and use their gardens. The plants serve the idea and if, in the eye of the maker, the idea is good, then the planting is made good too.

The humanity garden is, in principle, exactly the sort of thing I love. Box and yew topiary clipped into formal shapes but arranged in a seemingly haphazard manner. There is nothing original in this. I have seen it done the world over, but it rarely fails to please and sometimes – thinking in particular of Jacques Wirtz's garden near Antwerp – it becomes great art. At Séricourt the name redeems it. This piece of garden, which is essentially a path flanked by hundreds of items of topiary all hugger-mugger and higgledy-piggledy, is like the barge and bustle of humanity. It reminds me of the Rock Garden at Chandigarh in India, where there are thousands of figures made from shards of building rubble. It is an example of all that is really good about Séricourt and all that is really bad about it.

The good is in the energy and lack of inhibition. Yves has an idea so, with huge enthusiasm and skill, just does it. Hardly anyone gardens like that and to see it enacted on this scale is uplifting and inspiring. It is filled to bursting point with humanity, warm, welcoming and celebratory. The bad is that it is filled to bursting point with plants without selection or restriction. It is a noisy, jostling crowd of plants. Everyone, including you the visitor, is welcomed in and embraced. Nothing and no one is excluded. And this lack of discrimination stops it being the good art that it intends to be.

But I like it. I like the fact that it does not succumb to good taste. I like the open, frank indulgence in a private, unself-conscious vision. I like the sense of play that runs parallel to the deeply serious theme of the garden and I like the fact that a garden sets out to contain unabashed intellectual seriousness. I like Yves and the warmth of his hospitality. Perhaps that is the garden's greatest attribute. You do not leave it having learnt much about plants or horticulture but it leaves you thinking better of the world.

38

HIGH WOOD

The field poppy (*Papaver rhoeas*) has two sure-fire methods of ensuring propagation and therefore survival. The first is that it produces a lot of seed – around 1,300 per seed capsule – of which only one has to produce its own seed to ensure the plant's evolutionary survival. If this was not enough, the seeds have evolved to lie dormant until disturbed and exposed to light. So plants in a cornfield that is subsequently laid to grass or is even abandoned and becomes thick woodland, can remain viable, waiting underground, undisturbed for generations before reacting to the ground being tilled and bursting into suppressed flowering. This is a rare sight nowadays because modern farmers, armed with herbicides, class anything other than the crop as a weed to be destroyed, but I remember after the 2001 foot and mouth epidemic that wiped out over a million animals and left miles of grassland empty and hollowed out, fields being ploughed that had lain to pasture since the Second World War, and a consequent blaze of poppies that had been biding beneath the turf.

This was the case right across the Western Front between 1914 and 1918, when millions of munitions reduced woods, meadows, cornfields, villages and lanes to cratered mud and dust. The poppies, indifferent to the morality or means of tillage, be it by share or shell, responded by germinating and in due course, as the firing allowed, flowering in great drifts and swathes of crimson petals. It was as though the blood that was so wantonly spilled took root and flowered in that ravished earth.

It is no surprise that their blood red petals were taken as the emblem of the British Legion,[1] although the poem 'In Flanders Fields', published in 1915, was hugely popular[2] and influenced the Legion:

In Flanders fields the poppies blow
Between the crosses, row on row,
That mark our place; and in the sky
The larks, still bravely singing, fly
Scarce heard amid the guns below.

We are the Dead. Short days ago
We lived, felt dawn, saw sunset glow,
Loved and were loved, and now we lie
In Flanders fields.

I remember my father turning a shift selling poppies[3] in Odiham High Street in November, conflating the poppies, made by the 'war

1 Poppies are not the only annual flower stimulated into growth by disturbance. For example, bright blue cornflowers (*Centaurea cyanus*), are just as prevalent, but the poppy has a long literary tradition associated with sleep and oblivion and, by the end of the nineteenth century, with homoerotic love. This homoerotic love, not necessarily sexual but fiercely intense, crops up again and again in First World War poetry and literature.

2 Paul Fussell's 1975 masterpiece *The Great War and Modern Memory* covers this in more detail and very much better on pages 311–327 (Sterling, illustrated edition, 2009).

3 As a career soldier who fought right through the Second World War, my father was passionately attached to the British Legion (it did not gain its Royal prefix until 1971), attended every meeting and event and attended every Remembrance Day parade, dressed in suit, bowler hat and his medals, with a religious solemnity.

wounded' with the grave of the unknown soldier that was such a part of my upbringing and a clear icon of the terrible sense of communal grief and regret that ran through the generation that fought in the war from 1914 to 1918. It was not just about remembering others, the dead, the terrible sacrifice made so that we might live, but also about themselves. A strand of irreparable loss ran through their lives, a wound that would not heal, and the only people who understood or could share this were their fellow old soldiers. Everything was lost and out of those ruins came the pieces of lives and another war, this time entered and engaged with a kind of fierce relief that it was the Right Thing.

My grandfather, George Don, was born and brought up in Wimbledon. Round the corner from him was the home of the Graves family. One of their sons, Robert, went for a while to the same school as him and then later to the same school, Charterhouse, as my other grandfather, Montagu Wyatt.[4] We all go to school with lots of people we never notice much and never meet again. Paths briefly cross, lives briefly touch.

About ten minutes' walk from the Don and Graves households, just past the All England Lawn Tennis Club, was a large villa lived in by the Scottish marmalade baron, William Keiller, and the young family of his second marriage. His youngest daughter, Leila, was my granny. She had a brother, two years older than her, called Eric.

I only discovered the existence of Eric Keiller a couple of years ago. My grandmother and my father, an only child, never mentioned him. In a sense he had not existed since 3 September 1916, because that was the day he was killed in France.

After leaving Mill Hill School he took a commission in the

---

4 I was to be named as an amalgam of these two men. My birth certificate has my name as George Montagu Don. But my father's father, George Don, said that Montagu was a damn fool name to call a child. My mother's father, Montagu Wyatt, had died six months earlier and, uncharacteristically, my father, Denis Don, stood up to his own father and changed my name to Montagu Denis Don. The birth certificate was altered, in handwritten ink, accordingly. Having been George for a week or so, I became Montagu.

Devonshire Regiment, but resigned it at the outbreak of war in August 1914 when he discovered that they were not to be sent to France and joined the Black Watch as a private. That was an astonishing thing to do. Admittedly the overwhelming attitude of the army – which was entirely made up of volunteers until spring 1916 – was that this was a terrific opportunity to engage in the most manly of pursuits and there was a rush to join up, with three-quarters of a million men signing up within two months of war being declared. But to go from being an officer of at least five years' standing – a rich boy, third-generation trade, firmly established in Edwardian monied life – in an old regiment to a private in another one is extraordinary social as well as military behaviour.

In any event the 1st Battalion Black Watch (Royal Highland Regiment) were sent to France at the outbreak of war and Private E. Keiller fought in the trenches there for the next two years.[5] There must have been letters. He would have had at least one opportunity to return home to Wimbledon on leave. Perhaps he felt the alienation that Robert Graves describes in *Goodbye to All That*, with polite middle-class society now stranger and more disturbing to him than a filthy rat-infested trench yards from the enemy.

The facts are few but stark. They centre on High Wood, between Bazentin-le-Petit and Martinpuich on the Somme, a few kilometres east of Albert. High Wood was fought over with particular intensity in the most horrific of all battles in the most intense of all wars.

The Battle of the Somme began at seven thirty on the morning of 1 July 1916. By nightfall British forces had suffered 60,000 casualties of which over 19,000 were killed. Most were volunteers.[6] Many were from 'Pals' brigades which were groups of friends from the same villages and towns that had joined up in the same act of bravado, all living, fighting and dying side by side. Visit any church in Britain and see the memorials to those who died in the First World War. Inevitably there will be just a few names in a long list. Brothers, cousins, pals, all crossing the Channel to France to be blown to bits for King and Country in filth and terror and agony.

It continued for weeks. By 14 July the assault had advanced nearly five kilometres to High Wood. It was just a scrap of woodland, one of the square bosquets that still mark the open plains of northern France, a few hectares broken by rides and glades that had quietly supplied firewood and pannage for pigs for centuries. The Germans had occupied the wood, which was set, in that flat landscape, on a slight elevation. After weeks of shelling that reduced the trees to

5 Part of his rations would have been Keiller's marmalade, as the family firm had secured the incredibly lucrative contract to supply the British army with confectionery.
6 Conscription was not introduced until March 1916.

smashed stumps, the first-ever deployment of tanks in combat and daily hand-to-hand combat that slaughtered and maimed thousands on both sides, the little wood remained held by the German army.

On 20 July, three weeks after the battle started, the 2nd Battalion Royal Welsh Fusiliers were set up in Bazentin graveyard, ready to support an attack on the wood, when they came under shellfire. Captain Robert Graves was badly wounded and reported dead. He survived of course, until 1985, but had a fragment of marble gravestone lodged in his brow for the rest of his life.

On 3 September 1916, sappers tunnelled nearly eight metres deep to excavate a gallery some ninety metres long beneath the German lines on the eastern corner of the wood and filled it with 1,300 kilograms of ammonal.[7] This was detonated to create a huge crater which the 1st Battalion Black Watch, including Private Eric Keiller, then stormed. The history of the battle recounts that the Black Watch were 'bombed from the crater'.[8]

The citation from the Mill Hill 1914–18 Roll of Honour says that Eric Keiller 'was mortally wounded after having successfully rescued a wounded comrade from No Man's Land, under terrific shell and rifle fire. The German trenches were roughly only 30 yards distant from our own.' Perhaps that happened. Perhaps he did die bravely having successfully saved the life of a pal. We all want heroism by association, although it does not square with the evidence of his burial.

There is a War Graves cemetery, the London Cemetery on the western edge of High Wood, but Eric Keiller is commemorated in the cemetery of Dantzig Alley at Mametz, eight kilometres further west. Like all the War Graves cemeteries, it is beautifully tended and all the headstones are paraded simply, all alike. Eric does not

---

7 Ammonal was tested in warfare for the first time at the Battle of the Somme. It is a cheap substitute for TNT, made from ammonium nitrate and aluminium powder with a little charcoal and TNT.

8 *The Hell They Called High Wood*, Terry Norman (Leo Cooper, 1984).

have one. His name is inscribed on a memorial stone. This is because his body was never found, blown, presumably, to uncollectable bits. They reckon that there are still at least 8,000 ungathered bodies in the ground of High Wood, covered now by trees that have grown in the last hundred years. He is almost certainly still there, is tree, is French soil.

I cannot pretend to grieve for him because I did not know of his existence until very recently. But like tens of thousands of other dreadfully similar stories, it is desperately sad and, as anyone with a grain of sensibility must, I grieve deeply for the terrible loss of innocence and the shattered families. Never the same again.[9]

His death explains two things. The first is the deep and long depression that my granny apparently went into a year after my father was born, at the end of June 1915, which he casually told me about, adding, as if barely worth mentioning, that she never touched him again.

The second is the rage that my grandfather flew into when my father announced that he was joining the army in 1938. He told him that he would cut him off without a penny if he did. My father went ahead and joined anyway, finishing his officer training a week before the Second World War was declared. Within days he was in France, fighting the Germans and eventually retreating in May 1940 with the rest of the army to Dunkirk. My grandfather told me that he would go out at night in Surrey to listen to the German guns on the French coast, knowing that his son was one of those being shelled on that exposed shore.

Nevertheless, he still disinherited him. When he died in 1981, he did not leave my father, his only child, a penny. My two brothers and

_____

9 In 1978 I wrote a dissertation on Edward Thomas, whose poetry I loved, then as now. Through him I grew obsessed with the First World War and when I met a man, then aged ninety, who had joined up in August 1914 and spent the entire war in the trenches, I asked if I could talk to him about his experiences. He smiled gently. Young man, he said, I have never spoken to anyone about my experiences and I do not intend to start to do so now.

I were left all his material possessions[10] – scores of paintings, furniture, and an extensive wardrobe in which everything, from silk vests to dozens of suits, was made to measure. I still have full white-tie evening dress with, as had all his suits, the date of completion hand-written in laundry ink inside the inside pocket. In this case it is 1902. My brothers and I asked our father to take anything and all he wanted. He chose a little wooden carving of a Scottie dog that he had given to his father when he was a boy.

My grandmother, Eric's sister, died just a few months later and my father eighteen months after that. We buried the entire family inside two years. That was thirty years ago now, longer than the time I lived with him alive, but his death, for complicated reasons, still haunts me. I think of Robert Graves's reaction when he heard of the Armistice on 11 November 1918: 'The news sent me out walking alone ... cursing and sobbing and thinking of the dead.'

10 This was assuming that my two brothers reached the age of twenty-one, although there was a special clause specifically delaying my inheritance until I was thirty-five unless the trustees deemed I was fit to receive all or part of it. Grandpa did not have a very high regard for my financial probity. This was – is – not entirely unreasonable. Had he known that I was living in sin with a married woman and had a whopping overdraft for the last few years of his life I think he would have cut me out altogether.

39

WAR GRAVES

The songs I had are withered
Or vanished clean,
Yet there are bright tracks
Where I have been,

And there grow flowers
For others' delight.
Think well, O singer,
Soon comes night.[1]

The countryside around Séricourt is sprinkled with over 300
cemeteries which are all run by the Commonwealth War Graves
Commission. I had somehow thought that the First World War
cemeteries were all enormous, with rank upon rank of unmarked
graves symbolising the scale of the killing. But they are not like that
at all. Most are small, even intimate. Every grave is identical in status
but all personalised by name and choice of memorial. There are flowers, for others' delight, chosen carefully to evoke British gardens so
that the dead, although far from home, lie with some sense of home-

1 Ivor Gurney, composer, poet, madcap and lover of Gloucestershire, was enlisted into
the Gloucestershire Regiment, wounded, gassed, and his gentle, odd personality driven
mad. Of a hundred thousand sad stories, his is as tragic as any.

coming. The grass is mown and the edges beautifully neat. There is not so much a sense of orderliness as care. They are looked after because it would be an act of deep disrespect not to do so.

It was not always so. Right up until the Falklands War of 1982 the dead were rarely shipped home and until the First World War non-commissioned soldiers were buried unceremoniously and anonymously in lime-slaked mass graves. The decision to treat all the dead with equal status and almost limitless trouble was a reflection of how different the First World War was. Everything had changed for ever. War was no longer a glorious adventure in some far-flung corner of the empire. Every parish, almost every family, mourned its dead. The war cemeteries exemplify a kind of basic decency that had been tested beyond all imagining and yet survived.

Three of Britain's best architects[2] were commissioned to design the cemeteries and memorials and they had various trials before coming up with the format of a walled enclosure with uniform headstones set in grass, accompanied by garden plants chosen for both their suitability for the place and situation they were growing in – just as one would choose plants for any particular garden – and also to reflect the homes that were left behind. The Imperial War Graves Commission (as it was originally named) decided that the dead would all lie equal,[3] without favour offered to regiment, rank or

2 Sir Edwin Lutyens, designer of New Delhi and, in my opinion, one of the best British garden designers of the twentieth century, designed the Cenotaph in Whitehall and came up with the completely new concept of a monument that was to be a focus for grief rather than triumph. Sir Herbert Baker also worked on New Delhi and was responsible for Tyn Cot, the largest of all the war cemeteries. Sir Reginald Blomfield, who amongst many establishment late-Victorian and Edwardian buildings, designed Moundsmere in Hampshire, just near my childhood home. Gertrude Jekyll, doyenne of British gardening, was also consulted from the outset as to the nature of the accompanying planting.

3 This is a metaphor. The vast majority of the graves do not contain a body, the headstone marking the fact of their death rather than their resting place. Hundreds of thousands of bodies were never recovered. At Passchendaele alone, 90,000 British bodies were too mutilated to be identified and a further 42,000 simply vanished, blown apart without leaving a trace. The dignified headstones mark a horror that mercifully defies imagination at every approach.

creed, with their companions, and although slaughtered far from home, would be surrounded by the flowers they had grown up with. This is nakedly poignant, almost tender.

The nearest cemetery to Séricourt is Ligny St Flochel, set by the side of the road, backed by giant wind turbines idling against the stormy purple sky. It is small, a little walled garden in that undulating, open landscape, but there are over 680 graves, all gathered from a few days' fighting in August and September 1918, during the final hundred-day offensive to regain the territory the Germans had gained that spring. There were three casualty clearing stations based at various times at Ligny St Flochel, which means that the dead are principally those that were brought here alive but did not survive their wounds.

The central grassy path down the middle of the rows of graves leads like a nave to an altar-like central memorial stone: Their Names Liveth Forever. It is too well kept, too clean, too orderly to be anyone's notion of a garden. It is a solemn, upsetting place. Pride crumbles beneath the weight of waste. As ever, it is the detail that breaks hearts. The inarticulate, stutteringly proud and sad epitaphs, the flowers blooming in season like little borders ribboned along the headstones. There are too many eighteen-year-olds, too many proud but broken-hearted mothers and sisters, too many only sons much missed. Too many empty places at the table back home.

A whole generation of very British young men, torn hideously apart, torn away from their homes barely 250 kilometres away, torn from a culture that would and could never understand, remain here in France. In four years nearly a million were killed and more than twice that number wounded. That is over 2,000 killed and mutilated every single day from the declaration of war until the armistice on 11 November 1918. The French casualties were almost twice that. Nearly every family in Britain has a relative who has become part of this French earth. From every town and village, from remote Scottish lochs and city slums, shepherds, ploughboys, poets, public school prefects, colliers, clerks, blacksmiths, coopers, students, men with families far too old to fight and boys far, far too young all came to France and never went home.

There is nothing that one can make from this. Nowhere to take these figures and translate them into anything comprehensible. Words stumble and fall.

The trees of Picardy have all regrown, making woods that are fresh and green,[4] the patches of bosquet quilting the open landscape, and the farmers on their huge machines reap a rich harvest from the fields. All the history, all the stories of our fathers and grandfathers, all that sorrow and horror, is now hidden under earth.

I leave to go back home, dazed and very sorry, the evening light splitting the darkening sky with a deep streak of orange, unable to make sense of anything other than the need to hold this fragile moment dear.

4 'And O the Somme – the valley of the Somme round Amiens! A delight of rolling country, of a lovely river, and trees, trees, trees.' Ivor Gurney, letter to Marion Scott, 5 July 1916. Although experiencing action in the front line, Gurney had not yet taken part in the Somme offensive. He and the Gloucestershire Regiment were to do so in November. By then all the 'trees, trees, trees' had been reduced to broken stumps.

SELECT BIBLIOGRAPHY

William Howard Adams, *The French Garden 1500–1800* (George Braziller, 1979)

John Ardagh, *France Today* (Penguin, 1987)

Jean-Pierre Babelon, Mic Chamblas-Ploton, Jean Baptiste Leroux, *Classic Gardens – The French Style* (Thames & Hudson, 2000)

Kathryn Bardley-Hole, *Villa Gardens of the Mediterranean* (Aurum Press, 2006)

Robert Cole, *A Traveller's History of France* (Bookhaus, 1988)

Alex Danchev, *Cézanne – A Life* (Profile Books, 2012)

John Ellis, *Eye-Deep in Hell* (Fontana/Collins, 1976)

Derek Fell, *Cézanne's Garden* (Simon & Schuster, 2003)

Derek Fell, *The Impressionist Garden* (Frances Lincoln, 1994)

Paul Fussell, *The Great War and Modern Memory* (OUP, 1977)

Martin Gayford, *The Yellow House –Van Gogh, Gaugin and Nine Turbulent Weeks in Arles* (Penguin, 2006)

Françoise Gilot and Carlton Lake, *Life with Picasso* (Nelson, 1964)

Yves Gosse de Gorre, *Sagesse et Déraison au jardin* (Ulmer, 2006)

Robert Graves, *Goodbye to All That* (Jonathan Cape, 1929)

Penelope Hobhouse, *In Search of Paradise* (Frances Lincoln, 2006)

Caroline Holmes, *Monet at Giverny* (Casell, 2001)

Michael Hurd, *The Ordeal of Ivor Gurney* (OUP, 1984)

Leo Jansen, Hans Luitjen and Nienke Bakker (eds.), *Vincent Van Gogh – The Letters* (Thames & Hudson, 2009)

Geoffrey Jellicoe, Susan Jellicoe, Patrick Goode and Michael Lancaster, *The Oxford Companion to Gardens* (OUP, 1986)

Louisa Jones, *The French Country Garden* (Thames & Hudson, 2000)

P. J. Kavanagh (ed.), *Collected Poems of Ivor Gurney* (OUP, 1984)

John Keegan, *The Face of Battle* (Penguin, 1978)

Denise Le Dantec and Jean-Pierre Le Dantec, *Reading the French Garden* (MIT Press, 1993)

Jean-Baptiste Leroux, *The Gardens of Versailles* (Thames & Hudson, 2002)

Sonia Lesot, *Chenonceau – Des jardins de la Renaissance* (Éditions Gaud, 2006)

Monique Mosser and Georges Teyssot (eds.), *The History of Garden Design* (Thames & Hudson, 1991)

Adam Nicolson, *Long Walks in France* (Weidenfeld & Nicolson, 1983)

Terry Norman, *The Hell They Called High Wood, The Somme 1916* (Leo Cooper, 1984)

Stéphane Pincas, *Versailles, The History of the Gardens and Their Sculpture* (Thames & Hudson, 1996)

Fredédéric Richaud, *Gardener to the King* (The Harvill Press, 2000)

Graham Robb, *The Discovery of France* (Picador, 2007)

Graham Robb, *Parisians – An Adventure History of Paris* (Picador, 2010)

Vivian Russell, *Monet's Garden* (Frances Lincoln, 1995)

Vivian Russell, *Monet's Water Lilies* (Frances Lincoln, 1998)

Vivian Russell, *Planting Schemes from Monet's Garden* (Frances Lincoln, 2003)

Ian Thompson, *The Sun King's Garden* (Bloomsbury, 2006)

Georges Truffaut, *L'Art de tailler* (Larousse, 2004)

Marie-Françoise Valéry, *Gardens in France* (Taschen, 2008)

Marie-Françoise Valéry, *Gardens in Normandy* (Flammarion, 1995)

Marie-Françoise Valéry and Georges Lévêque, *French Garden Style* (Frances Lincoln, 1990)

Lucy Wadham, *The Secret Life of France* (Faber & Faber, 2009)

ACKNOWLEDGEMENTS

Caroline Michel encouraged me to write this book in the first place and supported me throughout it. Thank you.

Mike Jones and Jo Whitford at Simon & Schuster have been calmly heroic despite the impositions and limitations of time. It has been a pleasure.

I would like to thank to all those in France who allowed me to enjoy their homes and gardens and unfailingly gave me their time and hospitality. They include Patrick Blanc, Carlo Tailleux at La Bertranne, Patrice Taravella at Prieuré d'Orsan, Gilles Clément at La Vallée, Nicholas and Agnes Bruckin at Les Sambucs, Eliane Daviaud at the Aubervilliers allotments, Antoine Jacobsen at The Potager du Roi in Versailles, Claude Pernix at La Chassagnette, Jacques Garcia at Champs de Bataille, Alexandre de Vogüé at Vaux le Vicomte, Henri Carvallo at Villandry, Philippine de Ganay at Courances, Patrick and Sylvie Quibel at Le Jardin Plume, Yves Gosse de Gorre at Séricourt, James Priest at Giverny, Judith Pilsbury at La Louve and The Sisters of La Monastère de Solan. I would also like to thank Audrey Jacquet, who organised, translated, drove and fixed everything whilst remaining ever calm and elegant.

I was accompanied to many of the gardens I visited by Derry Moore, Alexandra Henderson, Michael Robinson, Peter Eason and Rachel Bell, and they made the best and most stimulating companions possible.

As well as providing much research material both in England and France, Alexandra Henderson has guided, encouraged, bolstered and inspired me throughout and I owe her a particular debt of thanks.

But my greatest gratitude is for the tolerance and support of my family without whom none of this would be possible.

INDEX

Page numbers in *italic* refer to pictures